S0-AYE-465

3 4028 07094 8022
HARRIS COUNTY PUBLIC LIBRARY

741.595 Pow
Power, Natsu Onoda
God of comics : Osamu
Tezuka and the creation
of post-World War II
$25.00
ocn265738388
06/01/2009

DISCARD

GOD OF COMICS

GREAT COMICS ARTISTS SERIES
M. Thomas Inge, General Editor

GOD OF COMICS

Osamu Tezuka and the Creation of
Post–World War II Manga

Natsu Onoda Power

UNIVERSITY PRESS OF MISSISSIPPI
JACKSON

www.upress.state.ms.us

The University Press of Mississippi is a member of the Association of
American University Presses.

Copyright © 2009 by University Press of Mississippi
All rights reserved
Manufactured in the United States of America

Frontis: © Tezuka Productions. Reproduced with permission.

First printing 2009

∞

Library of Congress Cataloging-in-Publication Data

Power, Natsu Onoda.
    God of comics : Osamu Tezuka and the creation of post World War II manga /
Natsu Onoda Power.
        p. cm. — (Great comics artists series)
    Includes bibliographical references and index.
    ISBN 978-1-60473-220-7 (cloth : alk. paper) — ISBN 978-1-60473-221-4 (pbk. :
alk. paper) 1. Tezuka, Osamu, 1928–1989—Criticism and interpretation. 2. Comic
books, strips, etc.—Japan—History and criticism. I. Title.

    NC1709.T48P69 2009
    741.5'952—dc22
    [B]   2008046691

British Library Cataloging-in-Publication Data available

To Tom Onoda Power

CONTENTS

ILLUSTRATIONS

NOTES ON JAPANESE NAMES, TITLES, AND READING ORDER

Some choices have been made to keep the translations of Japanese texts representative of the original language, while also allowing them to be approachable and coherent for non-Japanese speakers.

All Japanese names in the book, including names of cartoonists as well as names of characters, appear in the order of (Family Name), (Given Name), to reflect the original order in the Japanese language, *except* when the names appear in quotes, where the English-language author had already reversed the order. Another exception is the title of this book, which lists Tezuka's name as "Osamu Tezuka." This decision was made in consultation with the University Press of Mississippi, to reflect the fact that Tezuka is widely known in the United States as Osamu Tezuka. We have decided that listing his name in this manner (Osamu Tezuka) would enable readers and researchers to easily find this book through search engines, library catalogues, and databases. Likewise, my name is listed as Natsu Onoda Power, with my given name first. In the body of the book, however, his surname will be listed first, as Tezuka Osamu. I have divided my bibliography into two parts, one listing English and other European language sources, and the other listing Japanese sources. In the latter part of the bibliography, I have listed the names in the order of (Family Name) (Given Name) without a comma in between.

I have used the Hepburn Romanization system to spell Japanese names and other words. In this system, long vowels are spelled using a macron (ō, ū) except when the words have been appropriated into the English language (Tokyo, Kyoto, and so forth). I have applied this rule to terms that may not be parts of everyday English speech, but are commonly used in the existing scholarship on manga or Japanese culture at large, including *shonen* and *shojo* (as opposed to *shōnen* and *shōjo*). When names of people or important words have already been transliterated in older publications using other systems, I have tried to indicate other common spelling options. I followed the MLA format for capitalizing book and essay titles in the Japanese (or other non-European) language, and capitalized only the first letter of the first word in the title, as well as the first letter of all personal pronouns.

When the Japanese-language authors provide English titles of books and essays (as was the case in a number of recent scholarly articles on manga), I have indicated them after the original (transliterated) titles, in the body of the text as well as in my bibliography. When no English title was available for a book or essay title, I have provided a rough translation. When works of manga or anime have already been given English titles, I have used them, even when they are not direct translations of the original titles. This may cause some confusion when multiple versions of the title exist: the direct English translation of *Tetsuwan Atom* would be *Iron-Armed Atom*, though the work is also often called *Mighty Atom*; it was also called *Astro Boy* when it was broadcast in the United States. In such cases, I have chosen the titles that I perceive to be the best known, in this case *Astro Boy*. Though not many of Tezuka's works have been translated into English, his early *akahon* volumes were often accompanied by English titles, translated by the author. Also, each volume of *The Tezuka Osamu manga zenshū* provides an English-language synopsis as well as a translated title. Though some of the English titles are grammatically awkward, I have used them as "official" translations in most cases.

There are a number of words in the Japanese language that were imported from English and other languages. These "loan words," commonly used in titles of books, plays, essays, and magazines, should be spelled according to *romaji* conventions. For instance, the word "comics" would be spelled "komikkusu." I have made exceptions to this rule in this book, and spelled loan words as if they were English-language words for readability. That is, instead of listing magazine titles as *Biggu Komikku, Shonen Kurabu*, and *Shonen Janpu*, I have listed them as *Big Comic, Shonen Club*, and *Shonen Jump*. Similarly, for titles of Tezuka's works that consist of foreign or loan words, I have used the English spelling (*Black Jack*) instead of the *romaji* spelling (*Brakku Jakku*). Other examples include *Metropolis, The Lost World*, and *Captain Ken*. I have spelled the "foreign" sounding names of comic book characters with their approximate "foreign" spelling, to avoid confusion—particularly when the characters are based on historical figures, or when the names are based on existing words in foreign languages. I have used, for instance, Fryderyk Chopin, Peter Kürten, Sapphire, and Rock Home, instead of Furedorikku Shopan, Pētā Kyuruten, Safaia, and Rokku Hōmu. In the bibliography, I have spelled all the loan words according to the Hepburn Romanization system, as they would be spelled in a library catalogue in Japan.

Another cultural issue that arises in writing a book on Japanese comics is the reading order. Japanese comics are bound on the right side, as are most other publications in the Japanese language. Each page generally consists of three or four rows of panels, and readers follow the panels from right to left, starting from the top row. When translating Japanese comics into English (or other European languages), publishers have commonly "flipped" the images (to create mirror images) or rearranged the panels in a page to make it more accessible to readers who are used to the left-to-right reading order. Most often, publishers have "flipped" and "rearranged" the images selectively, so that some of the panels preserve the original orientation. They have also replaced the Japanese sound effects with their English equivalents. While this translation process allows the readers to enjoy the work without having to constantly struggle with cultural differences, it compromises the artists' original works.

Recent translations of Tezuka's works into the English language present an important exception to this rule, and perhaps signifies a shift in the way Tezuka's works—or graphic novels at large—are perceived in the United States. Books such as *Buddha* and *Apollo's Song* are printed in the original Japanese order, bound on the right side. This is significant in multiple ways. By prioritizing the integrity of the composition and the artwork over readability, publishers are recognizing the importance of authorship. In this way, Tezuka's works are treated as "serious" art and literature rather than disposable entertainment, as comic books traditionally have been.

An important outcome of printing comics in the original reading order is the preservation of visual symbolism that comes with it. As in many other cultures, the Japanese culture has assigned a set of symbolic meanings to horizontal directions (left and right). In classical Japanese paintings (particularly narrative paintings), left generally symbolizes future and progress, and right implies past, regression, and reflection (Sakakibara). Similar rules can be applied to manga, and manga artists past and present have extensively used the direction of images and eye movement to control the narrative and the reading speed and to enhance symbolism. For example, in the legendary opening scene of Tezuka's first long story comic *Shin Takarajima* (*New Treasure Island*), the protagonist Pete speeds through the town in his sports car for eight pages, going from right to left. The direction of the car helps readers' eyes to move speedily from right to left (the direction of reading), prompting them to turn the pages and move quickly through the scenes, evoking the sense of speed. A more symbolic use of the directions is seen in a scene from *Ribon no Kishi* (*Princess Knight*). In the scene, Princess Sapphire (dressed as "Prince" Sapphire) and Frantz sit at a table, looking away from each other. In the previous scene, they had fallen in love while Sapphire was disguised in a dress and a flaxen-haired wig. Frantz, unaware that the girl and Sapphire are the same person, looks to the right, reflecting on the fond memory of the lovely girl. Sapphire, however, looks to the left, facing the tormented future in store for her love. In this book, I have cited images in the original Japanese form, even when the comics were available in translation. All the multi-panel comics, therefore, are to be read from right to left within a page, and right-hand page to left-hand page sequentially on facing pages.

I have quoted comic books without flipping the images or the order of panels in this book, but have indicated the reading order when it might be confusing to English-language readers who are unfamiliar to Japanese comics.

ACKNOWLEDGMENTS

The research for *God of Comics: Osamu Tezuka and the Creation of Post–World War II Manga* was conducted at the following archives, libraries, and institutions: National Diet Library (Tokyo), Tezuka Osamu Manga Museum, Ikeda Bunko, Contemporary Manga Museum, Kyoto National Museum, Northwestern University Medical School Library, and the Cartoon Research Library at Ohio State University. The work was partially funded through the Swann Foundation for Research in Comics and Cartoons, the Library of Congress.

I am grateful for my mentors at Northwestern University, who have inspired, encouraged, and shared expertise with me. Tracy Davis's rigor and sense of humor carried me through the process. I am indebted to her acute suggestions and critiques, particularly in the chapter of theatrical cross-dressing. Paul Edwards mentored me since my undergraduate years as I grew as a scholar, an artist, and a person, for over ten years. Much of the theoretical ideas presented here were first developed in Margaret Drewal's class, Modes of Representation, which I took during my coursework. Scott Curtis was extremely generous not only with his expertise in film but also with his time. Mary Zimmerman held my hand through it all, I am truly thankful for being able to call her not only a mentor but also a friend.

I owe special gratitude to Seetha Srinivasan and Walter Biggins at the University Press of Mississippi for giving me this opportunity and for their patience and encouragement. I am honored to have had the opportunity to work with Seetha, with her extraordinary expertise in comics scholarship publication. I am also thankful for Tezuka Productions and Fujiko Studio for their assistance and use of the images.

There are some key institutions and organizations that enabled my research. I am very fortunate to be a part of the supportive, energetic community at Georgetown University Theater and Performance Studies Program, where I currently teach. I am particularly thankful for my closest colleagues, Maya Roth, Derek Goldman, and Karen Berman. The talented and intelligent students in our program have been my constant source of inspiration. I thank Maureen Donovan and Lucy Caswell at the Cartoon Research Library for their insight and hospitality. Dr. John Lent and International Journal of Comic Art provided me with opportunities to publish my first articles on this topic. Ana Hortillosa at San Francisco Asian Art Museum was instrumental in hosting me as an artist-in-residence at the museum during the Tezuka: The Marvel of Manga exhibit in summer 2007. Members of my theater company, Live Action Cartoonists—Gary Ashwal, Andy Brommel, Alex Thomas—have been invaluable collaborators in my investigation of the relationship between comics and live theater.

I would not have been able to complete this book without the support of family and friends, too many to mention in this space. My parents, Noriko and Masaharu Onoda, indulged my obsession with Tezuka's work for as long as I can remember. My aunt Eiko and uncle Michihisa Hotate still send me occasional comic books from Tokyo. I also thank my brother Jun and my close friends, particularly Melissa Sandfort, Daniel Peltz, and Karima Robinson, whose unfailing faith in me and in the project kept me on track, even during the most difficult times.

The timing of the final draft of this manuscript coincided with my wedding ceremony to my partner, Tom Power, in summer 2008. Since the day we moved my several hundred volumes of comic books into his house, Tom has witnessed the transformations of this project as a constant consultant and unfailing supporter. With much love and gratitude, I dedicate this book to my husband.

GOD OF COMICS

Chapter 1

INTRODUCTION AND SOME DEFINITIONS

A certain generation of North Americans may remember the TV animation series *Astro Boy*. The series' superhero, Astro Boy, was an adorable and somewhat androgynous robot boy, with red boots and a shiny black head that had two spikes that never overlapped no matter from what angle you were looking at him. He had an IQ of three hundred and strength equal to one hundred thousand horsepower. His legs turned into jets so he could fly through the sky, and his eyes turned into searchlights so he could see in the dark. He made a very characteristic squeaking sound when he walked. The series was broadcast by NBC starting September 1963, and American children quickly became familiar not only with Astro Boy but also with the series' fun and colorful supporting characters, like his sister Astro Girl or scientist Dr. Elephan. What most children did not know at the time was that *Astro Boy* was adapted from a Japanese comic book series *Tetsuwan Atom* (*Iron-Armed Atom*, 1951–1958), and Astro Boy was called Atom in the original series. Its author, Tezuka Osamu, was already revered as the "God of Manga." *Tetsuwan Atom* was Japan's first TV animation series, with an extremely low budget of about $5,000 per episode. Its theme song, sang by Tokyo Children's Chorus, is somewhat reminiscent of Japan's rapid economic growth era; today, most Japanese people would recognize the song, even if they were born long after the series' end:

So ra wo koete (Through the sky)
La la la ho shi no kanata (Beyond the stars)
Yuku zo Atomu (Go, Atom)
Jetto no kagiri (As far as your jet takes you)
Kokoro yasashi (Gentle hearted)

La la la kagaku no ko (Child of science)
Juman bariki da (One hundred thousand horsepower)
Tetsuwan Atomu (Iron-Armed Atom).

This is a book about Tezuka Osamu (1928–1989), the creator of *Astro Boy*, Japan's most celebrated cartoonist, winner of numerous awards at international animation festivals, a medical doctor, and so much more. His work, which has become available in the English language in the past few years, include (but are not limited to) *Buddha*, a fictionalized biography of Gautama Buddha; *Phoenix*, a mix of science fiction, historical epic, and spiritual tale, dealing with reincarnation and human civilization; *Black Jack*, a story of an unlicensed surgeon; *Metropolis*, an early science fiction that was adapted into an animation film in 2001; and most recently, *Apollo's Song*, a tale of human sexuality and reproduction, which revolves around an emotionally scarred teenager named Chikaishi Shōgo. What is currently available in the English language, however, only represents a very small portion of his body of work. Tezuka started his professional career in 1946, the year after Japan's surrender in World War II. As a first-year student of medicine in Osaka University, Tezuka began a weekly comic strip, *Mā-chan no nikkichō* (*The Diary of Mā-chan*), in a children's newspaper, *Mainichi Shōgakusei Shinbun*. In 1947, Tezuka published his first book-length work, *Shin Takarajima* (*New Treasure Island*). This legendary two-hundred-page volume not only mesmerized the child readers of the time but also influenced a number of younger artists and became a model for others to emulate.

"Prolific" does not even start to describe the sheer volume or breadth of Tezuka's work. During his lifetime, Tezuka published approximately 150,000 pages of comics in virtually every genre imaginable. As an animator, he produced TV animation series, feature films, and experimental shorts. He wrote essays on topics of comics, film, theater, education, music, and much more. Other projects include novellas, children's books, character and mascot design, and manuals on comics and cartooning. He acted in a couple of films, got a Ph.D. in medicine, and played music in his spare time. Today, his influences—however indirectly—are apparent in works of most Japanese manga artists.

Tezuka's first visit to the United States in 1963, when NBC was broadcasting *Astro Boy*, is dramatized in his autobiographical short comic, *Gachaboi ichidaiki* (*Gachaboi's Record of One Generation*, 1970). On the streets of New York, he approaches a group of little boys: "I will give you a dime each if you answer my question . . . do you know *Astro Boy*?" One of them answers, "Of course I do, you don't know it?" Elated, Tezuka jumps up and down, exclaiming, "Whoo hoo! How happy I am! Here, take all the money I have!" and throwing the

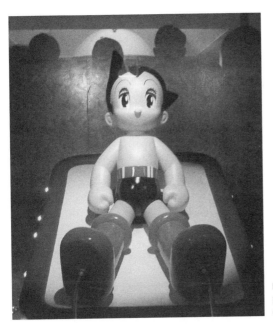

Figure 1.1. The life-size Astroboy puppet on display at the Tezuka Osamu Manga Museum.

contents of his pockets in the air. For Tezuka, who had idolized Walt Disney since a young age, this was a pivotal moment: his Astro Boy now occupied a place in the minds of American children, just like Mickey Mouse and Donald Duck. Rereading this passage today, I often wonder what Tezuka would say to the popularity of manga and anime in the United States, if he had lived to see it. Animation films by Japanese directors compete with Disney films in the box office. Graphic novel sections of major national bookstore chains are stocked with translated manga titles; amateur cartoonists can easily pick up one of the ubiquitous "how to" books on drawing "manga style." Manga conventions in the United States are well attended by fans, collectors, and impersonators who dress up as popular characters. According to a 2003 *New York Times* article, "American television is now broadcasting almost 20 shows of anime" and "sales of anime videocassettes and DVD's are expected to reach about $500 million this year" (Brooke). On August 5, 2004, the *Wall Street Journal* printed an article on how the motivations of Japanese-language students in U.S. universities are changing: "Back in the late 1980s and early 1990s, Japan's economy was booming, Japanese management terms like kaizen (continuous improvement) were all the rage, and the country seemed poised to dominate international commerce. Studying Japanese was considered a smart choice for ambitious, business-minded college students. [. . .] Now, the typical Japanese-language student is a Japan-culture fanatic like 19-year-old Rachel Maurer, a

UGA undergrad with maroon hair and skull earrings who also goes by the Japanese name Reiko" (Parker A.1). Of one hundred students surveyed at the University of Georgia, Athens, "about half [. . .] cite Japanese pop culture—including animation, comics, pop songs and video games—as their top reason for studying the language." This was also true of my own students. In 2004, I taught a course at the University of Chicago called Performing Japaneseness. The small class consisted of bright and diligent undergraduates who were also manga readers, video game players, and members of the Anime Club.

As the terms manga and anime started to become a part of the English-language vocabulary, their meanings also departed from the original Japanese definition. This is similar to the way the word *sushi* has become a commonly used word in English, one that is automatically associated with raw fish. The term refers, in Japanese, more broadly to the vinegared rice mixture, regardless of whether it sits in neat bundles beneath cuts of raw tuna and fish roe or in a bowl mixed with cooked carrots and shiitake mushrooms. The term manga, in Japanese, has been used since the seventeenth century. Today it means comics, cartoons, and caricature of any kind or origin. Similarly, the term anime is simply a shortened form of "animation." Terms like *Disney anime, jikken anime* (experimental animation), or *ningyō anime* (puppet animation) may sound oxymoronic in English, but they are perfectly acceptable in Japanese. Because anime is a much newer term than manga, older generations still use manga to refer to animation as well, similarly to how the term cartoon is used in English: terms like *terebi manga* (TV animation) and *manga eiga* (cartoon film) are still common, though somewhat old-fashioned.

In the global context, manga seems to refer more narrowly to certain genres of comics that originate from post–World War II Japan—or, more precisely, certain genres of Japanese comics that the U.S. publishers have chosen to translate and publish, characterized by particular pictorial styles and character design. The aforementioned *Wall Street Journal* article defines anime as "the highly stylized cartoons featuring idealized, doe-eyed characters." Manga and anime has also become heavily associated with violent and/or sexual content. In a scene from the 2000 film *Unbreakable* directed by M. Night Shyamalan, a comic book store attendant yells to a character (played by Samuel L. Jackson) who has been spending too much time in the store: "You'd better not be jerking off to the *Japanese* comics!" I hesitate to call these stereotypes "misperceptions," because North American readers are not exactly responsible for having "misperceived" manga. While these perceptions do not represent accurate views of the Japanese comic industry or the definition of the Japanese term manga, they are logical consequences of the ways in which Japanese comics are imported and marketed in the United States. What may strike me (or others who grew up in Japan reading manga) as strange misperceptions are also perfectly reasonable and accurate perceptions of "manga," not a word for "comics" in Japanese but a term that refers to a new genre of comics in the global context.

This new definition of manga may have to do with, at least partly, the stereotypes associated with "comic readers" in North America, who represent a much narrower and far more specific demographic. While Japan produces comics for virtually every gender and age group in a variety of genres and styles, comics remains a subculture in North America. It is true that the popularity of critically acclaimed graphic novels and ubiquitous "mainstream" film adaptations of otherwise lesser-known works have drawn a wider audience to comic book stores in recent years. Still, comics and comic book culture is strongly associated with readers with certain age, gender, and personality traits. In the fall of 2004, when I was starting a comics "book club" at a comic book store in Evanston, Illinois, the shop owner expressed a concern that "comic readers are so anti-social and socially awkward, nobody will show up." The concern turned out to be true—no one showed up at any of the sessions, despite our efforts at advertising. The enrollment for my undergraduate course, "The Graphic Novel," at Georgetown University (2006) drew 80 percent male students, which was highly unusual in an English department elective. Some of them were die-hard graphic novel fans who could discuss, in detail, the subtle differences between different editions of Alan Moore's *Watchmen*. Given such differences, it is perhaps natural that the American publishers have selected the kinds of manga that would cater to the existing stereotypes of comics readers. It is important to note, however, that the image of "Japanese comics" in North America reflects more about the state of the American comic book industry than about the Japanese comic book culture.

As more of Tezuka's works become available in English, more studies that deal closely with Tezuka have emerged. At the time of my writing, two important new books on Tezuka have just come out in print: one is Fredrik Schodt's *Astro Boy Essays*. Schodt, who was a friend of Tezuka's and perhaps the single most important figure in introducing Tezuka to the English-language readers, offers an affectionate and detailed discussion of *Astro Boy* from multiple perspectives: as a graphic novel, cultural phenomenon, and the first TV animation series to be imported from Japan to America. Another is *Tezuka: The Marvel of Manga*, which is a companion book to the exhibit of the same title at the National Gallery of Victoria, Australia (November 3, 2006–January 28, 2007). The exhibit subsequently traveled internationally, and in the United States it was installed at the San Francisco Asian Art Museum. The book includes pictorial reproductions, several essays both by Japanese and English-language authors, and snippets of Tezuka's writings on his own work. Other books available in English include Paul Gravett's *Sixty Years of Manga* (2004), which has a chapter on Tezuka, discussing his life, works, and influences. Two of Schodt's older books, *Manga! Manga! The World of Japanese Comics* (1983) and *Dreamland Japan: Writings on Modern Manga* (1994), also dealt closely with Tezuka (as well as other artists and manga in general), offering a much-needed overview to English-language readers. Other notable works that deal with Tezuka include Sharon Kinsella's *Adult Manga* (2000), a socioeconomic study on Japan's comic book industry with a section on manga's history; *Shojo Manga!: Girl Power!*, a catalogue of an exhibit, edited by Masami Toku. These works mark a clear departure from earlier scholarship on manga, which tended to treat manga as mirrors that subconsciously "reflect" larger issues in studies about Japanese motherhood, sexuality, or social codes.

This is an exciting moment in the English-language scholarship of manga in building a fuller relationship with Japanese-language scholarship and criticism. Previously, cultural and linguistic differences have made translations of Japanese scholarship on manga inaccessible for publishers and readers outside Japan. While there are countless sources on manga (or on Tezuka) in Japanese, most assume the readers' familiarity with manga, its history, and its place in Japanese popular culture. They also take significantly different approaches to the study of manga: while Japanese scholars tend to perceive the history of manga as an evolutionary process, scholars outside Japan have been interested in manga's cultural specificity. For those who encountered manga for the first time after it reached the global market, manga's "transformation" did not happen: manga was already different from American or European comics, and its uniqueness was most often explained as "cultural." The default question is, "Why are Japanese comics so different from ours?" rather than "How did Japanese comics come to take their current form?" The chronology of manga publication in North America has also thrown off the sense of its history; readers became familiar with "contemporary" works from the 1990s ten years before they had access to the "classics." This is not to say that Japanese studies of manga is "better," though there is clearly more of it and perhaps in greater depth. While I struggle to write a somewhat "comprehensive" book on Tezuka for my English-language readers, Japanese scholars have long "agreed to diagree," approaching Tezuka's works from various perspectives and disciplinary orientations, constantly coming up with new arguments and theories, all of which perfectly coexist and make for a rich discourse.

Perhaps the first step in integrating the Japanese- and English-language studies on manga is to address the differences in how the term "manga" is defined in those two separate spheres. As I have mentioned, manga simply means comics, but there are various connotations and subtleties associated with the term. Such nuances are often communicated through the written form. The

漫画

まんが

マンガ

Figure 1.2. Three transcriptions of the word "manga" in Japanese.

word "manga" has three different iterations in its written form: *kanji, hiragana,* and *katakana* (fig. 1.2). *Kanji* is the pictographic system of writing that was adapted from the Chinese language. It is unclear just how many *kanji* exist; a commonly used *kanji* dictionary, *Kanjigen,* contains 12,600 *kanji* characters; in public media, they normally use 1,945 *jōyō kanji.*[1] Each *kanji* contains a set of meanings and has a few pronunciation options. *Hiragana* was invented during the fifth century by simplifying *kanji* characters to represent a syllable, rather than a meaning set, in the Japanese language. The fifty *hiragana* characters function similarly to the English alphabet, representing sounds (and not meanings) that can be combined to form words. *Hiragana* allowed the Japanese to write in their native language. Since the Japanese had no "native" form of written language, all recordkeeping and correspondences had been conducted in Chinese prior to the invention of *hiragana. Katakana,* the newest form of writing, developed during the late eighth century. Buddhist monk-scholars invented them by isolating parts of *kanji* and giving them specific sounds. The simple characters allowed them to insert notes in the margins of their scripture texts. Today, the use of *katakana* is commonly reserved for onomatopoeia, "loan words" (foreign words that are commonly used in Japanese everyday speech), as well as foreign words and names that have no Japanese equivalents. In modern Japanese writing, a single sentence usually contains some combination of *kanji, hiragana,* and *katakana.*

What we generally know as manga, or the story comic genre that has become mainstream since the postwar era, is usually written in *katakana.* The

---

1. The list of *jōyō kanji* ("commonly used kanji") was announced by the Japanese Ministry of Education in 1981. The list contains 1,006 *kanji* taught in primary school and 939 more *kanji* taught in secondary school.

literary critic Ishiko Junzō (Junzou) prefers the *katakana* term, as the most inclusive: "What is called manga (*kanji*) today has a very narrow range of meanings [. . .] constrained by its history. My theory of manga (*katakana*) includes, and goes beyond, the study of manga (*kanji*) or *giga*" (*Manga geijutsu ron* 27–28). According to Ishiko, manga is "a *coherent* and *representational* form of pictorial art that are mass-reproduced for a variety of purposes such as satire, nonsense, or documentation [. . .] modern paintings have moved towards greater abstraction, while manga has become increasingly easier to understand" (51–52). Such "coherence" of manga owes much to the mode of abstraction that manga artists call *deforume*, commonly understood to be taken from the French term *déformer*. The verb *deforume suru* means to abstract, exaggerate, and simplify the images to the point of unlikeness to life, without losing its representational quality. A comic book character's face does not resemble a human face in its proportions and/or dimensionality, but it still clearly represents a "face" with all of its expressive and communicative functions.

The historian Shimizu Isao distinguishes manga (*katakana*) and manga (*kanji*) by the historical periods, defining manga (*katakana*) as "manga that has developed in the modern society" (*Koramu mangakan* 8). The *kanji* term, according to Shimizu, refers to older forms of comics, dating back to *Hokusai manga*, the Edo-period serial ink-drawing monographs by artist Katsushika Hokusai (1760–1849). Hokusai's works started out as loose sketches of humans, animals, and plants, and later transformed into satiric arts that parodied and criticized the feudal government. Because of this historical association, the *kanji* term manga emphasizes the satirical function and is preferred by manga scholars with art history background. Shimizu defines manga as "pictures drawn with the spirit of satire and play" (*Koramu* 12).

According to *Kanjigen, man,* the first of the two characters that make up the word "manga," denotes (1) to proliferate or to cover a large surface; (2) long and continuing; (3) rambling, loose, idle, or lax; (4) wonderingly or unconsciously (907). The second character, *ga,* is a pictograph that depicts the borders of a rice field, signifying borders, divisions, to create a border, or to divide an area into smaller areas. From these definitions, the character *ga* subsequently came to denote picture, painting, drawing, and film, as well as the act of drawing and painting. The word "manga," which combines the two characters *man* and *ga,* was invented in Japan, and was later appropriated in the Chinese language during the early twentieth century. The Chinese artist Lu Hsun's use of the term "manga" in 1918 reveals the term's association with journalism and rebellion: "Manga is [a form of representation] that pierces through the societal disease. It draws on methods of exaggeration but in an organized manner. It does not distort the object of criticism or exposure for no reason, but does so through seriousness and diligence" (Shimizu, *Nihon no shinryaku* 8).

The *hiragana* term manga emphasizes the humor, not necessarily with political or subversive overtones. Ozaki Hideki uses the *hiragana* in his 1972 book *Gendai manga no genten: warai gengo no atakku* (*The Origins of Modern Manga: Investigating the Language of Laughter*), defining manga as "interpretations of the universe [. . .] through humor" (Ozaki 80). As *hiragana* is the first form of writing that children learn in school, the *hiragana* term manga is also associated with children's comics. The Japanese term for "cartoonists," *manga ka*, was coined by cartoonist Okamoto Ippei (1886–1948) during the Taishō period (1912–1925). Today, its usage in the Japanese language is identical to the term "cartoonist": Tezuka Osamu, Walt Disney, and William Hogarth can all equally be called *manga ka* in the Japanese language. The term can be written in any of the three forms of writing, though the *kanji* is most common. Tezuka often used the combination of *katakana* (manga) and *kanji* (ka) within one word, which is also a common variation.

It is impossible—and unnecessary—to "correct" the usage of the term "manga" outside Japan to refer to all things comics, as it does in the Japanese language. Perhaps we should accept the term MANGA, written in Roman alphabets (here I am using all capital letters to distinguish it from the Japanese term), as a new word that carries a set of meanings specific to our historical and cultural contexts. When I show Tezuka's older works to my students, they often respond by saying, "this doesn't look much like MANGA." This puzzled me at first, but now I have come to understand the term MANGA as a word in the English language, appropriated from the Japanese language, but is more narrowly defined. As *katakana*, *hiragana*, and *kanji* iterations of the term manga carry different connotations, the term MANGA has now entered this set, bringing new meanings. This is only another step in the history of manga as an evolutionary and ever-changing art form. Cultural origin ("Japanese"), historical period ("post–World War II"), pictorial traits ("highly idealized, doe-eyed characters"), and typical contents ("you'd better not be jerking off to the *Japanese* comics!") are, after all, not misconceptions of manga but definitions of MANGA, a new genre of story comics—only as "Japanese" as, say, California Rolls and saketini—that emerged as a result of the global circulation of comics in the late twentieth century.

In this book, I am using the term "manga" primarily when I refer to the larger idea of MANGA ("Japanese comics of the post–World War II period"). When discussing a specific work, I will simply use the term "comic book" or "comics." There are several reasons for this. One is simply that "comics" is similar to the way "manga" has been used in the Japanese language, particularly during Tezuka's lifetime, before manga's international popularity. Another is that I wanted the focus of the book to remain on Tezuka as a cartoonist of great international caliber, not as an artist of an exotic art form called MANGA. Of course, the terms comics and cartoonists are just as (if not more) elusive as manga, but this term also allows me to discuss American and European cartoonists' influences on Tezuka's work, perceiving them as artists working in the same genre, as opposed to one working in "comics" and another working in "MANGA." This is also the reason why I used the phrase "God of Comics" in the title of the book. When the Japanese call Tezuka *"manga no kamisama,"* they are not referring to Tezuka as the god of MANGA, the specific genre of (Japanese) comics that is associated with a specific pictorial or narrative style. They are calling him the god of all "comics."[2]

As I have already mentioned, critical writings on Tezuka's work in the Japanese language have been unavailable to the English-language readers, with few exceptions. The National Museum of Modern Art in Tokyo published a bilingual catalogue to accompany the exhibit Osamu Tezuka in 1990, including a few essays on Tezuka's work. Other studies on Tezuka, most of which have never been translated into English, can be loosely categorized in four genres, though they are not mutually exclusive: biographies, analytical/critical essays, contextual studies, and anecdotes/trivia/fan literature.

The oldest and best-known book on Tezuka is his autobiography, *Boku wa manga ka* (*I Am a Cartoonist*). I make frequent references to this autobiography throughout this book, for it is not only a compelling autobiography but also a uniquely told history of manga, from a cartoonist's perspective. It is important, however, to note that the "accuracy" of this autobiography is often questioned. Tezuka is first and foremost an entertainer, and the anecdotes in his autobiography are said to be somewhat embellished, as they are in his autobiographical comics. Still, the book gives an important glimpse into Tezuka's views on the trends of prewar manga, or *gekiga*.

Many biographies or biographic essays were published after Tezuka's death in 1989. *Tezuka Osamu: Jidai to kirimusubu kyogensha* (*Tezuka Osamu: An Artist Who Confronted His Times*, 1990) by Sakurai Tetsuo includes lesser-known anecdotes that may not have been published while the artist was alive, mixed with the author's critical analysis. Another important biography is *Otto Tezuka Osamu to tomoni* (*With My Husband Tezuka Osamu*, 1995) by his wife, Tezuka Etsuko. The book paints an affectionate portrayal of the cartoonist as a father and a husband—quite literally, since the cover of the book is an oil portrait of Tezuka by the author. The image of Tezuka that emerges, ironically, is not un-

2. It is also important to note that the word "god" here does not automatically denote the sole almighty creator, which Western readers may associate with the term. Since Japan is a mostly secular country with numerous religious traditions coexisting (even in one family), it refers, more likely, to an abstract idea of a "higher being" or a polytheistic deity that is characteristic of the Japanese Shinto tradition.

like a caricature of a Japanese workaholic father—absent, unreliable, and sometimes inconsiderate. At the same time, the book also reveals an image of Tezuka as a strict and opinionated father who is emotionally devoted to his family—and is deeply loved and respected in return. Published six years after Tezuka's death, it also documents Tezuka's battle with cancer in moving detail. Tezuka Osamu Production's *Tezuka Osamu Monogatari* (*Tezuka Osamu Story*, 1992) is a biography written in the form of comics. Other popular books include Ōshita Eiji's *Tezuka Osamu: Roman daiuchu* (*Tezuka Osamu: Romantic Galaxy*, 1995) and Shimotsuki Takanaka's *Tanjo! Tezuka Osamu: Manga no kamisama sodateta background* (*Birth! Tezuka Osamu: Background That Brought up the God of Comics*, 1998), which focuses on Tezuka's early years. Among those biographical studies, Kojima Hideaki's essays are unusual in that they focus on Tezuka as a doctor and medical researcher.

There are multitudes of analytical works on Tezuka, with new works constantly added to the scholarship. While there is no single definitive study, there have been some key publications and scholars in this area. Ishigami Mitsutoshi's *Tezuka Osamu no kimyō na sekai* (*Tezuka Osamu's Strange World*, 1977) is said to be the only study Tezuka himself "approved" in his lifetime. It introduces Tezuka's works through the lens of film (Ishigami is primarily a film critic), though, of course, it only covers works published before 1977. *Gendai Manga Theater Volume 1: Tezuka Osamu* (1979) features a series of essays by cultural and literary critics, including Iwatani Kokushi, who have written on Tezuka extensively in journals and magazines. After Tezuka's death, a large number of analytical studies quickly inundated the market, including Takeuchi Osamu's *Tezuka Osamu ron* (*On Tezuka Osamu*, 1990). Natsume Fusanosuke (1950–) became a popular and prolific critic during the 1990s. An experienced cartoonist himself, Natsume takes a decidedly formalist approach focusing on pictorial details. This was a clear departure from earlier, more thematically based studies. His *Tezuka Osamu no boken* (*Adventures of Tezuka Osamu*, 1998) is a collection of his lecture transcripts, while *Tezuka Osamu wa doko ni iru* (*Where Is Tezuka Osamu?*, 1995) is a collection of essays written for publication. Nakano Haruyuki combined biographical information and close analysis in his work, such as *Tezuka Osamu to rojiura no manga ka tachi* (*Tezuka Osamu and Manga Artists in the Alley*, 1993) and *Tezuka Osamu no Takarazuka* (*Tezuka Osamu's Takarazuka*, 1994). Nimiya Kazuko's *Tezuka manga no kokochi yosa: Zuka fan ryū Tezuka ron* (*The Comfort of Tezuka Manga: Takarazuka Fan on Tezuka*, 1996) juxtaposes Tezuka's works with theatrical productions by Takarazuka Kagekidan, focusing on gender representations in Tezuka's work. Most of these works deal with selective comics, some focusing on single work.

"Contextual" studies include works that do not exclusively deal with Tezuka or that may not deal with Tezuka at all—but rather with the contexts of his work, such as the history of manga, children's literature, or postwar popular culture. These works have been very resourceful to my research. I have extensively consulted works of Shimizu Isao, a prolific historian/critic. Shimizu's works cover periods starting in the seventeenth century, giving a sense of manga as a continuously evolving art form. Another important figure in this category is the literary theorist Ishiko Junzō (1929–1977). Ishiko used manga as a site of investigation for issues such as humor, high and low arts, and kitsch since the early 1960s, locating manga within larger discourses of literature and cultural studies. His writings are informative not only because of their analysis, but also because of his unique status as Tezuka's contemporary, born only a year apart. Also important are works by Ishiko Jun (1935–), a literary and film critic (with no relation to Ishiko Junzō despite the name resemblance). Ishiko Jun perceives manga as children's literature and conducts a comparative analysis focusing on authorship. He was concerned particularly with manga's role in elementary education. As an educator, he advocated for a system to "censor" children's comics, distinguishing the "good (appropriate, of educational value)" manga from the "bad (violent, sexually explicit, etc.)" (Ishiko Jun 1976). Though the value of Ishiko Jun's work as "scholarship" has been questioned in recent years, his writings during the early 1970s function as valuable primary texts: they give a glimpse into the moment in history when manga transcended its status as a unanimously "low" entertainment.

"Anecdotes/trivia" include a wide range of work that target fans and popular readership, discussing some aspect of Tezuka's work with little theoretical or critical framework. There are books that catalogue appearance of various animals in Tezuka's works in an encyclopedia style (Kobayashi J 1997, 1998). Another book debunks some of the anecdotal "myths" that surround Tezuka's life and works (Hasegawa 1990). There are numerous pseudo-academic books: Yamamoto Atsushi's book playfully conducts psychoanalysis on some of the popular characters in manga, including some of Tezuka's (1998). Similarly, there are books and essays that deal specifically with *Astro Boy* and robot science, evaluating today's technological advancement against what was depicted in the *Astro Boy* series, or providing scientific explanations of Astro Boy's superpowers. While these books have little value or credibility as scholarship, I have used some of them as terrific "concordances" in order to navigate through Tezuka's massive body of work.

It is also important to note here that artistic practice of manga is closely interdependent with its scholarship. Scholarly and popular writings on manga have profoundly influenced, and continue to influence, the trends of manga since the 1960s. Even a most densely written research project finds popular readership and may have an impact on consumption and distribution. It is common for cartoonists to also function as critics. Takemiya Keiko, a *shojo* manga artist particularly active during the early 1970s, now teaches at Kyoto Seika University, the first university in Japan to introduce Manga Studies as an undergraduate major. Tezuka was a prime example of this, writing extensively on his and others' works throughout his life. His writings on his own work are both playful and eloquent. Upon publication of *Tezuka Osamu manga zenshū* (*Complete Works of Tezuka Osamu*), Tezuka wrote postscripts for each of his work in this series. These short essays contain anecdotes, backgrounds, and commentary, looking back at the work from a new perspective. Having a prose "postscript" by the author in a comic book was unusual at the time of its publication.

The goal of this book, at its core, is to situate Tezuka's achievements in their historical, cultural, and political contexts for an English-language audience. It is partly missionary work, partly cultural history, and partly a suggestion of a new framework in studying manga or comics at large. It is important to me that this book introduces the great wealth of work that Tezuka has produced that remain largely untapped in the English language. At the same time, I am interested in investigating the historical, cultural, and geopolitical forces that contributed to Tezuka's success. The central question is, "What did Tezuka do that others didn't?" How was Tezuka able to achieve his fame so quickly? What made his work so appealing, and how did he maintain his popularity? Tezuka stayed on the forefront of the manga industry mostly throughout his forty-five-year career, constantly taking on multiple projects and reaching out to different genres. How was he able to appeal to so many groups of audience, old and young, men and women? What enabled him to create such a strong fan culture, one that still lives on today?

I have no doubt that Tezuka was an artist of unusual talent, drive, and inspiration. Few would disagree that he was someone we would call a "genius." But then again, is it also true that a genius needs to be born at the right time in the right place to leave his mark in history? If Tezuka had been born elsewhere in the world, would that nation have replaced Japan as the contemporary mecca of comics? Would manga be just a subculture? There is no way of answering these questions, but they inspire a series of more feasible questions that link this artist's talent to the very unusual historical and cultural moment in which he worked. How did the timing of his debut (immediately after, not before, Japan's surrender in World War II) influence his work and his popularity? How were comics perceived and consumed before and after Tezuka's debut? Who were his readers during the time of his major "break"? What were their needs and interests?

My observations are based, first and foremost, on examining nearly 150,000 pages of comics, animation films, prose writings, interviews, documentaries, and illustrations that Tezuka produced in his lifetime. I do not claim to have studied everything Tezuka has ever created; despite my efforts at archives and my long history as a fan, there are some sources that I have not read or seen, though I know they exist. While I still find myself—even as I write this—obsessing about "lost episodes" and "alternate endings," I have decided that it is unnecessary for me to include them in this book. My guess is that we will have increasingly easier access to some of those "unseen" works as the interest keeps growing. For example, in 2007, Tezuka's early draft for his unfinished work, *Neo Faust* (1989), was included in a new anthology. The draft, in a playscript format, contains a significantly different storyline than the published comic book. For the readers of my particular book, however, I have decided that discussions of more popularly read or widely influential works would be more useful. Similarly, I omitted discussions of different versions of the same work for most part. Tezuka was known to rework his manuscript when he reprinted his magazine comics as books. *Shin Takarajima* (*New Treasure Island*), originally published in 1947, is a quintessential example of this—Tezuka rewrote the entire book when he included it in *Complete Works*. In *Ayako* (1973), Tezuka completely changed the ending, killing four additional characters and making the story's heroine, Ayako, mysteriously disappear. Tezuka wrote that he was not satisfied with the way the series ended and that he intended to continue the story beyond these three volumes. Tezuka was often forced to make compromises when serializing in magazines because of the publication schedule and page restrictions. Tezuka often spoke that he intended the *Complete Works* to be the definitive versions of his works. Most of the works I discuss in this book refer to the *Complete Works* version, with a few exceptions. Comparing different versions of Tezuka's work would make a compelling study, but it is out of scope for this book in most cases.

Critics have commonly described Tezuka's works using terms such as "heroism," "lyricism," "epic," "righteousness," and "peace," but any attempt to define Tezuka's "style" is potentially dangerous. Tezuka wrote in 1966:

Recently, I started a series called *The Vampires* in a magazine, and received so much criticism.

"Unparalleled failure! Stop it! Tezuka's career is over."

"Stupid Tezuka! Unsophisticated drawings, trite storyline. No trace of creativity. Do you want to earn money this badly?"

Outraged, I jump up, scratch my throat, pull out five hairs from each of my nostrils, scrape my calluses with a knife. Most often, these readers tend to be old fans above high school age. I feel defeated, grateful, sad, helpless, hateful, happy, demoralized. [. . .] I understand that my readers are attached to their ideas of my "style," and are happy with it [. . .] I do not want to betray them, but I am afraid of stalling. [. . .] Children change through time. [. . .] I need to keep transforming in order for my young readers to be able to relate to me. So, while I feel badly for the old fans, I have to betray them. I identify with Hamlet, pushing away Ophelia, saying "Go to the nunnery!" (Tezuka, "Tezuka Osamu e no tōji" 18)

While there are clearly repeated themes and motifs, Tezuka's "style" is not defined by themes, storylines, or genres. Similarly, Tezuka also changed drawing styles to cater to different age and gender groups: the simple, two-dimensional, deadpan drawings in his adult comics have little resemblance to the round, cute, and expressive characters in his children's comics. Tezuka's "signature style" should be characterized not by a thematic or pictorial characteristic but by the lack of it—by intertextuality and constant transformation.

Tezuka was an interdisciplinary artist in the truest sense of the term. Any one of Tezuka's works is filled with references not only to other comics, but also to live theater (traditional and contemporary), dance, music, literature, *rakugo* (comic storytelling performance), music, and, most prominent, film. Tezuka, throughout his life, actively incorporated techniques and conventions of these other art forms into his comic books. Tezuka's experiments resulted in unconventionally long comic books with substantial plots and multiple subplots (often adaptations of literary classics, such as *Faust* [1949] or *Crime and Punishment* [1953]), innovative premises, characters with complex personalities, and a sense of speed and cinematic flow. A master of quotations, Tezuka's style can be compared to that of the novelist Umberto Eco—he constantly borrowed images, phrases, and sequences from other media, filling his work with rich intertexts that may or may not be recognizable to his readers. He often quoted himself as well, giving his readers a "bonus" chance to enjoy the work in relation to another, even when there was no apparent plot connections between the two works.

Because of this, intertextuality serves as an important framework in this book in two different ways. First, I discuss Tezuka's work, using his myriad of references, quotations, borrowed images, and adapted techniques as points of entry. An appearance of a child pianist character in *Shiro kujaku no uta* (*The Song of a White Peacock*, 1959) prompts my discussion on popularity of young child-stars in the Japanese media during the 1950s, and the discussion of Tezuka's

Ph.D. dissertation, a study on spermatozoa in Japanese pond snails, provides a context for the themes of human sexuality in *Apollo's Song*. Of course, these references are more associative than exhaustive, limited to what I can recognize, or more important, what I choose to discuss in this small space. I also do not claim that important influences or quotations are always legible in the finished work—some of Tezuka's quotations may be so obscured to the point of being unrecognizable from the original. Still, this way of discussing Tezuka's works mimics the way in which the first readers of these comics, living in the moment of Tezuka's writing, experienced the work as he or she moved through it.

Second, the book focuses on Tezuka's strategic use of intertextuality within the body of his work. Tezuka planted recurring visual jokes and recognizable characters in his works, creating an illusion that all of his works belonged to one coherent world. By recognizing the same character playing different "roles" in different comic books, a reader starts to develop a relationship with the character, imagining the character's "offstage identity." Likewise, a recurrent visual joke functions as an intimate exchange between the author and a reader, like a familiar nod, or a wink, fraught with meanings and recognizable only to those who belong to the community. The community is both inclusive and exclusive: entering it is as easy as picking up any two books by Tezuka; navigating perfectly through its complex web of references is almost impossible.

The God of Manga did not create the world out of nothingness, but from a wide range of cultural resources. Such references, intertexts, and quotations resonated with his readers and created a complex universe within his work. This is a study of how an artist's role as a "reader of various texts" (Worton and Still 1) affects his or her role as a generator of texts, navigating between different forms of art, borrowing and adapting vocabularies. It is also a study on the relationships between an artist's craft and the conditions of his production. This is not the definitive approach in studying Tezuka's work, but one that situates him in his historical and cultural context, as well as us, the readers, in ours. My hope is that this book becomes a start of a dialogue, an inspiration for a forum where we can create a rich discourse by "agreeing to disagree."

Chapter 2

TEZUKA IN HISTORY / HISTORY IN TEZUKA

While Tezuka's responsibility in the boom of story comics in post–World War II Japan is undeniable, it would be a mistake to say that comic books, or comic book culture, did not exist in Japan prior to Tezuka. Comics and visual storytelling have always been important elements of Japanese visual culture, and Tezuka often made references to older forms of comics in his work. Many characteristics of modern comics, such as animal anthropomorphism, movement lines, and graphically represented sound were already well established before World War II. References to film, self-conscious humor, crowd scenes, and other techniques strongly associated Tezuka can also be located in prewar comics before Tezuka's debut. Similarly, the global readership of comics is not particularly a new phenomenon; the Japanese public enjoyed works by American and European cartoonists since the late nineteenth century, becoming familiar with some of the key techniques such as speech balloons. Tezuka studied "foreign" comics and animation as a child, actively absorbing their techniques and vocabularies.

Tezuka is an "evolutionary" as well as a "revolutionary": his innovations are based on and derived from his knowledge of existing comics, old and new, domestic and foreign. This view of Tezuka does not discount Tezuka's accomplishment, but rather, characterizes him as a master of traditional techniques as well as an innovator. Recognizing references to prewar comics in Tezuka's work also help us see where conventions end and innovations start.

The twelfth-century scroll painting *Chōjū giga* (*The Animal Scrolls*) is attributed to Kakuyū (1053–1140), also called Toba Sōjō, an artist-monk who served as the forty-seventh head priest of the Tendai sect of Buddhism.[1] This play-ful picture scroll is often considered the oldest surviving example of Japanese comic art, though some scholars contest this perception (Nihon Mangakai 21). Tanaka Yūko argues that historians have relied on "textbook knowledge" of art history, overlooking the importance of less mainstream works in favor of this massively popular work (Tanaka 32–33). Tanaka is right in pointing out that "Chōjū giga" has become unabashedly "mainstream": images from this scroll are ubiquitously reproduced not only in textbooks and art books, but also on stationeries, mugs, or mouse pads, in a manner similarly to Van Gogh's self-portrait or Munch's screaming face.

Regardless of the historical accuracy of such perception, it is safe to say that *Chōjū giga* is the oldest surviving work that is frequently discussed through the lens of comics. *Chōjū giga* uses the system of simplification and abstraction that is common to modern comics, in which the characters' emotions are commu-nicated through simple pictorial signs instead of likeness to reality. In the first volume of the scroll, the rabbit's eyes are depicted as a set of curved lines to indicate the expression of "laughter," though it is not physiologically possible for the eyes of a "real" rabbit to assume this shape (Fig. 2.1). Since laughter is a uniquely human expression, symbolic gestures associated with laughter are extracted and abstracted, then imposed onto an animal. *Chōjū giga* consists of four volumes that vary in themes and styles, but the first is by far the best known. Fredrik Schodt includes it in his *Manga! Manga! The World of Japanese Comics*, describing it as "Walt-Disney style anthropomorphized animals in an-tics that mock Toba's own calling . . . the Buddhist clergy" (Schodt 28). R. H. Blyth describes it in his book *Oriental Humour*: "It is a scene of humour, hu-manity, religion, and innocence. Bishop Toba seems to be telling us his idea [. . .] of what Buddhism could be, how the sexes should mix, and what the aim of life is" (Blyth 87). The three subsequent scrolls are less known, and less nar-rative. The scrolls have no text or panels, and a viewer follows the narrative from right to left as he or she unrolls the scroll. Toba Sōjō used the term *giga* to refer to the genre of his painting. The word stem *"gi"* in *giga*, means "to play, to joke or to laugh" (*Kanjigen* 582).

Tezuka displays his familiarity with *Chōjū giga* in *Hi no tori Ransei hen* (*Phoenix: Chapter of Turbulent Times*), depicting the artist finishing the scroll. Tezuka's comic book attributes the scroll not to Kakuyū but to a younger

---

1. Alternate spellings of "Chōjū" include Choujyu, Chouju, and Choju; alternate spellings of "Sōjō" include Soujyou, Soujou, and Sojo; alternate spellings of "Kakuyū" include Kakuyuu and Kakuyu.

Figure 2.1. Toba Sōjō, *Chōjū giga.*

priest, Myōun (1115–1184), who served as the head priest during the fifty-fifth
and fifty-seventh terms. Myōun (Myoun, Myouun), one of the central characters in *Chapter of Turbulent Times*, is portrayed as a multitalented and compassionate man who is also deeply involved in the politics. In figure 2.2, Tezuka depicts Myōun as he finishes the first volume of the scroll. Myōun then shows it
to his colleague, Kakuyū. Tezuka depicts Myōun and Kakuyū as two contem-
poraries, two older men around the same age—though, according to records,
Kakuyū should be sixty-two years older than Myōun:

Myōun: Kakuyū, this is done.
Kakuyū: Hmmm, this is spectacular. Truly exquisite.
Myōun: You should help me with *beta.*[2]
Kakuyū: What is this? Animals are dancing like humans.
Myōun: This? This is my rendition of the world, animals and birds stand-
ing in for people. (61)

In the page immediately following, Tezuka "reveals" why the scroll is attributed to Kakuyū:

---

2. *Beta* is a technical term in modern comics, referring to the solid black areas of the manuscript,
or the action of painting the areas with ink. This work is generally assigned to assistants.

Kakuyū: Ah, like comics, isn't it? The monkey looks like he is reading a scripture . . .

Myōun: That's making fun of priests. Priests these days collect lots of money but are praying to frogs!

Kakuyū: Ha ha ha, I get it!

Myōun: I wanted to convey that the world is rotten. We humans are acting no different from animals or birds. Why do we still call ourselves the greatest creature on earth? That's really presumptuous.

Kakuyū: I see.

Myōun: Kakuyū, you should sign this.

Kakuyū: You are joking! It's your work, not mine!

Myōun: I really don't want to attach my name to paintings or novels of this sort, so I always get other people to sign them. The government might take them away from me any minute. The officials will burn them.

Kakuyū: That would be terrible. Ok, I will sign it.

Myōun: I want this work to survive for a long time, as *Chōjū giga* by Toba Kakuyū Sōjō. (62)

Tezuka playfully equates this work to modern comics, as seen in the reference to *beta*, a technical term for painting in the solid black areas of the manuscript (such as hair, shadows, background, and so on). Elsewhere in the work, Tezuka also attributes *Heike monogatari*, an anonymous epic tale of the battle between two families, Heike and Genji, to Myōun. Tezuka's version of the story behind *Chōjū giga*'s creation presents a delightfully unexpected—if purely speculative or largely unlikely—alternative to the common beliefs.

While Tezuka's reference to *beta* should be interpreted as an anachronistic joke, some of the visual conventions of modern comics can be seen in *Chōjū giga* or other picture scrolls of the same period. For example, the use of "movement line" can be seen in an anonymous ink painting dated 1447, called *Hōhi gassen emaki* (*Scroll of Farting Contest*). The comical scroll shows images of men competing to see who could fart the loudest; farts shooting out from the characters' behinds are depicted as straight lines of various lengths and widths, representing the "strengths" of the farts (Sakakibara 16–17). The painting belongs to a genre called *wokoe* (*okoe*), literally "stupid pictures," which became popular during the twelfth century. The art historian Sakakibara Satoru names five stylistic traits of *wokoe* in his book *Nihon kaiga no asobi* (*The Sense of Play in Japanese Paintings*), including emphasis on line, improvisation, sense of surprise, wit, and vulgarity (14). The idea of a "farting contest" itself was not so original to this work, for a number of other artists, including Toba Sōjō, had also au-

Figure 2.2. A sequence from *Hi no Tori* [*Phoenix*,] showing Toba Sōjō as a character. © Tezuka Productions. Reproduced with permission.

thored similar works of *wokoe* titled *Hōhi gassen emaki* during the previous century.

Comics as a mass-produced art form emerged during the Edo period (1600–1868). In the early seventeenth century, the advancement of printing technology allowed the production of small booklets called *ezōshi*, inexpensive books of illustrated erotica or humor. *Ezōshi* also had several alternative terms that referred to the colors of ink and paper used in the printing, such as *akahon* (red books), *kurohon* (black books), *aohon* (blue books), and *kibyōshi* (yellow cover). Some scholars argue that *ezōshi* is the direct precursor to contemporary manga, pointing to its "lowbrow" content, mass reproduction, low price, bound format (as opposed to rolled), and wide circulation (Tanaka). Shimizu Isao points out that the term manga first appeared during this period, in the title *Hokusai manga* (1814–1878), a series of monographs by Katsushika Hokusai (1760–1849). Sometimes known as *Hokusai Sketchbooks*, *Hokusai manga* is a collection of humorous black-and-white prints depicting animals, plants, and human activities. Hokusai used the term manga to refer to "essays through pictures" or "leisurely essays with pictures," based on an existing literary term *manpitsu*, "leisurely essays" (*Manga tanjō* 3). Hokusai's works go through several transformations throughout the series from innocent humor to biting satire, but the most prominent shift occurs in Volume 12. Published in 1834, this issue harshly parodies the lifestyles of the ruling class. One image shows a warrior defecating in a public restroom, with a caption that says "Warrior or commoner, it smells the same." The success of *Hokusai manga* inspired other artists to take on similar projects.

Commodore Perry's visit to Japan in 1853 and the subsequent "opening" of Japan caused major shifts in many aspects of Japanese culture, including comics. For two and a half centuries prior, Japan had been a "closed" country with very limited contact with the rest of the world. The post–Perry Edo and Meiji era "saw Japan in the complete break from the old, and almost indiscriminate embracing of the new" (Morrison 55). Meat and dairy became a part of the diet; wealthy women dressed in Western-style garments; and English-language literature became available in translation. This sudden Western influence caused much panic and confusion among the Japanese; the images of the Japanese trying to adjust to the changes in culture and society are humorously depicted and circulated in a number of popular prints, called *awatee*, literally, "panic pictures." The presence of Western journalists in Japan during this period also resulted in cartoons in American and European publications depicting the Japanese people.

Charles Wirgman (1835–1891), a British cartoonist who was active in Japan during the Meiji period (1868–1911), appears as a minor character in Tezuka's

Hidamari no ki (*Tree in the Sun*) in two scenes. In the first scene, Wirgman sketches the training site for the first European-style army in Edo (present-day Tokyo). In the second scene, he tries to interview Ibuya Manjirō, the captain of the army and one of the two protagonists of the series. Ibuya chases the cartoonist away in both scenes, not understanding Wirgman's friendly intentions. Wirgman's monthly magazine, *The Japan Punch* (1862–1887), was modeled after *Punch, or the London Charivari* (1841–1992), itself a takeoff of *Le Charivari* (1832–1937) a satiric daily paper from Paris. Though the magazine only had two hundred copies per issue, it became popular among foreigners and the Japanese alike, later inspiring publications of Nomura Fumio's *Marumaru Chinbun* (1877–1907) and *Kibi Dango* (1878–1883). *The Japan Punch* also instigated a new term for humorous or satiric artwork, *ponchie* (literally, "punch pictures"). The term soon left behind its original meaning and started to refer to lowbrow humor prints, not necessarily political cartoons. The multipanel, "sequential" art that resembles the format of contemporary comics started to appear in *The Japan Punch* in the late 1860s.

Another important figure during this period is George Bigot (1860–1927) from France. Bigot started as a newspaper illustrator, working for *Marumaru Chinbun* and *Kaishin Shinbun*, and later launched his own magazine, *Tôbaé*. The magazine was named after the common Japanese term for satiric art, *tobae*, derived from Toba Sōjō. While the primary target readers of *The Japan Punch* were English-speaking foreigners in Japan, *Tôbaé* featured both French and Japanese captions.

Japanese cartoonists such as Honda Nishikichirō also started to produce narrative comics in the late 1870s in *Marumaru Chinbun* and *Kibi Dango*. The two magazines featured not only cartoons but also essays and satiric poems (*kyōka* and *senryū*), critiquing the Meiji government and the Imperial system via humor. The comics in these magazines often quote and parody comics in *The Japan Punch*, featuring similar layout and subject matter. In 1896, *Marumaru Chinbun* introduced serial narrative comics by Taguchi Beisaku (1864–1903), titled *Enoshima Kamakura chōtan ryokō* (*The Long and Short Trip to Enoshima and Kamakura*). The readership of comics also expanded to younger generations around this time. Japanese magazines for children, such as *Yōnen Zasshi* (1891–), started introducing American comics translated into Japanese.

Many consider Kitazawa Rakuten (1876–1955), who used the term *manga shi* (manga artisan) to refer to his profession, to be the first professional, full-time cartoonist in Japan. Kitazawa learned cartooning from the Australian-born cartoonist Frank Nankivell (1869–1959), and worked for a newspaper company, *Jiji Shimpō*. Kitazawa integrated the Japanese tradition of humorous art with Western conventions of multipanel comics. His series *Tagosaku to*

Mokubei no Tokyo kenbutsu (*Tagosaku and Mokubei's Trip to Tokyo*) features two country folk, Tagosaku and Mokubei, who travel to Tokyo and experience culture shock upon encountering the city culture. *Chame to Dekobō* is a Japanese takeoff on *The Yellow Kid*,[3] featuring two children named Chame and Dekobō. Kitazawa later published his own comic magazines *Tokyo Puck*, *Rakuten Puck*, and *Katei Puck*. Kitazawa redefined manga as a mass-produced art form "characterized by satire, laughter and exaggeration, consciously examining the world and caricaturizing it" (Ishiko Jun, *Manga no rekishi* 18–19).

After the introduction of the cinematograph in Japan in 1897, Japanese comics rapidly absorbed the influence of film. As a skilled writer and film enthusiast, Okamoto Ippei (1886–1948) introduced the techniques of literature and film into his comics, which later made a strong impact on Tezuka. In *Onna hyakumensō* (*One Hundred Faces of a Woman*, 1917), Okamoto lays out his panels to look like a strip of film with perforation, calling it an *eiga shōsetsu*, literally, "cinema novel." *Onna hyakumensō* featured a series of images interwoven with short prose texts, mimicking the form of silent film that alternates scenes with intertitles (Shimizu, *Manga no rekishi* 123). Okamoto's single-panel cartoons with short, elaborate prose texts, the format he called *manga manbun*, also makes formal and syntactic references to the kind of live storytelling performance that accompanied film screenings during this era.

There is no doubt that Okamoto's self-conscious and inter-media approach created a precedent for Tezuka's more extensive "borrowing" from other art forms. Tezuka's manga manual *Manga no kakikata* (*How to Write Comics*, 1977) contains a number of images and lessons derivative of Okamoto's earlier book *Ippei manga kōza* (*Ippei's Manga Lessons*), such as a chart showing how to depict human emotions with simple lines. In the following passage from a published interview, Tezuka recalls encountering the works of Kitazawa and Okamoto as a young child:

I was looking through my father's bookshelf [. . .] and found *Ippei zenshū* (*The Collected Works of Okamoto Ippei*), *Rakuten zenshū* (*The Collected Works of Kitazawa Rakuten*), and even *Gendai manga taikan* (*The Anthology of Contemporary Manga*, 1928–). [. . .] I remember, when I was in elementary school, I noticed the fundamental differences between the works of Rakuten and Ippei [. . .] Rakuten's images were very close to foreign cartoons, and Ippei's works were somewhat "Buddhist." [. . .] Okamoto Ippei was a much "craftier" artist than Rakuten. He was fluent in pen drawings, ink brush paintings, Japanese

---

3. The serial comics by R. F. Outcault in the *New York World*; widely considered the first example of "story comics" in the United States.

color paintings or *nanga*. He did not take after Wirgman or Bigot, and thereby lacked the international perspective like the British *Punch*. [. . .] Conversely, Rakuten, with his stiff drawing styles, was always interested in expanding his world. (Tezuka, *Manga no shūgi* 16–20)

Compared to Kitazawa, who approached comics as a social action, Okamoto's work is more self-reflexive, or "Buddhist" as Tezuka calls it; his deep involvement in Buddhism had undoubtedly permeated his work. This is apparent even in his definition of the term manga: "Manga is that which depicts the beauty of the universe that emerges when you closely re-examine the conditions and correlations of all things" (Okamoto 9). Okamoto further distinguishes manga from *ponchie*, arguing: "*ponchi* thrives on its funniness, [. . .] it uses humor only to please the readers, both thematically and pictorially. All it needs to accomplish is to make them laugh. Manga, in contrast, thrives on truthfulness. The humor in it must organically emerge from the subject (Okamoto, *Ippei manga kōza* 18–19). Okamoto, however, continued to call children's comics *ponchie* to distinguish them from manga, the term he reserved for comics for adult or "serious" audiences (Tezuka, *Manga no shugi* 30).

Comics for children and teenagers started to enter the mainstream by the time of Tezuka's birth. In 1914, publisher Kōdansha launched a boys' monthly magazine, *Shonen Club*. Girls and younger children waited longer: *Shojo Club* for girls was launched in 1923, followed by *Yōnen Club* for young children in 1926. Some of the most popular children's comics during this period, such as Tagawa Suihō's *Norakuro* and Sakamoto Gajō's *Tanku Tankurō*, were serialized in *Shonen Club* and *Yōnen Club*, respectively. Comics in those magazines featured some of the basic traits of modern *shonen* manga: serial or episodic format, the hero figure (occasionally an animal or other nonhuman character), gender-specific readership, and adventure as a popular genre. In 1933, a smaller publisher Nakamura Shoten launched its *Nakamura Manga Library* series, an eighty-two-volume hardcover anthology containing children's comics by artists such as Ōshiro Noboru (1905–1998), Niizeki Seika (1900–1953), and Shaka Bontarō (dates unknown). Unlike *Shonen Club*, whose primarily focus was prose literature, *Nakamura Manga Library* consisted entirely of comics, often with "educational" overtones. *Akahon*, cheaply made comics sold through toy and candy shops, also began to appear during this period.

Tezuka Osamu was born on November 3, 1928, as the oldest son of Tezuka Yutaka and Fumiko in the city of Toyonaka, Japan. The family moved to the city of Takarazuka three years later, where Tezuka lived until he graduated from college. During this period, Takarazuka was one of the most desirable suburbs in Japan, surrounded by modern conveniences as well as lush nature, and with

easy train access to large cities (Osaka and Kyoto). Tezuka consistently described his childhood as an idyllic period filled with parental affection and material wealth: his hobbyist father "bought anything new and modern" and his
mother spoiled the three children with outings to theaters, books, comics, and
magazines. Tezuka accompanied his mother to theaters and watched movies on
his father's 9.5 mm projector.

While Tezuka was enjoying his childhood, Japan was steadily moving toward militarism. The military started taking control of the Japanese government in the early 1920s; navy and army personnel occupied most of the important offices, including that of the prime minister. The military government
assassinated a number of communist leaders and political enemies and held
control over education and media. Chian Iji Hō (Public Order Maintenance
Act) was established in 1925 to ban socialist and communist movements, as
they were considered threats to the *kokutai*, or "national essence," of Japan. The
tokubetsu keisatsu (literally "special police") and other governmental officials
enforced this act, often through violence. In the early morning of March 15,
1928, the *tokubetsu keisatsu* raided the homes of all known Japan Communist
Party members all over Japan, arresting 1,568. Some of them were subsequently
tortured and/or killed. This event is commonly referred to today as the "3.15
incident." In June of the same year, the government revised the Peace Preservation Act to impose even tighter control on any antigovernment or antimilitary
gestures, proscribing the death penalty for violations of this act. The increased
power of the military also forced Japan into the long period of conflict with
China. Ishiwara Kanji and Itagaki Seishirō of Kantōgun (the Japanese Army in
China) set up a bomb on the Manchurian railroad on September 18, 1931 (the
Mukden Incident). The Japanese Army falsely accused the Chinese Army of
planting the bomb and promptly used "self-defense" as a pretext for invasion.
They conquered the whole of Manchuria in three months, declaring an independent state, Manshūkoku, which was in effect a puppet state controlled by
the Japanese Army. In the same year, the Japanese Air Force bombarded Shanghai, claiming that it was necessary in order to protect Japanese residents from
anti-Japanese movements. The 1943 propaganda brochure *Mohan sangyō senshi
hōmon ki* (*Visits to the Model Citizens*) describes the event in a comic strip, the
text reading as follows: "The Manshū Incident was the first of (Japan's) projects
to cleanse the world. At that time, the world had gotten tremendously messy
and rotten, and the thorough cleaning was much needed for Japan as well as
for the rest of the world" (Kondō Hidezō et al. 25).

Looking at the comics published during the war years gives us a glimpse
into the kind of transformation Tezuka brought to the Japanese audience in
1947. Ishiko Junzō argues: "The history of Japanese comics during the first half

of the twentieth century was also the process through which comics gradually lost its political edge [. . .] this is most apparent in the comics during the Pacific War" (*Manga no shisō* 195). Comics during this period quickly lost the subversive quality that flourished in earlier periods. They increasingly gained nationalist overtones, endorsing the status quo. *Norakuro* by Tagawa Suihō (1899–1989), serialized in *Shonen Club* from 1931 to 1941, is probably the best known among wartime children's comics. Its hero was a black stray dog, Norakuro (literally, "Stray Black"), who engages in war games with other dogs. In 1984, Tezuka created a parody of Norakuro in *Norakuro modoki* (*Pseudo Norakuro*), a series that closely mimicked Tagawa's style.

Norakuro inspired other militarist "animal comics," such as *Chinta nitōhei* and *Shirochibi Suihei* by Ōshiro Noboru, featuring a monkey and a white bear, respectively. The *Bōken Dankichi* (1933–1939) series by Shimada Keizō (1900–1973) depicts the colonialist adventures of a Japanese boy, Dankichi, who eventually becomes the king of the "natives" on an unidentified tropical island. The simple, seemingly innocent narrative is chilling to a contemporary reader—it glorifies Japan's invasion of Asia, depicting the "natives" as good natured but primitive and intellectually inferior to the protagonist Dankichi. Comics of this period also familiarized children with war technologies: in *Speed Tarō* by Shishido Sakō, the hero, Speed Tarō, fights the enemies from a warplane in the fictional land of Gelmania. Tank Tankurō, the hero of Sakamoto Gajō's series *Tank Tankurō*, is an early precursor of a cyborg fighter, a cross between a human and a war tank. Akiyama Masami calls this work the "first Japanese science fiction" (27).

It will do disservice to dismiss these wartime children's comics as blatant "propaganda" and nothing else. They were also innovative and captivating adventure comics, often with mixed messages. Norakuro's adventures in military training consist mostly of humorous failures rather than glorious victories. Tagawa's wife and literary critic Takamizawa Junko later argued: "The numerous failures of the clumsy Norakuro promoted anti-war sentiments through humor" (Takamizawa, quoted in Kajii 66). Still, it is more common to assume that they inspired young readers to dream of participating in battles for their nation's honor. In his book on wartime comics, Ishijko Jun quotes a surviving suicide attack soldier: "Those of us who were born during the early Shōwa era idealized the war. In grade school, *Norakuro* and *Bōken Dankichi* became our bibles [. . .] I believe it was the children's comics that drove us into the war" (Ishiko Jun, *Nihon no shinryaku* 118). But is propaganda always so simple? Do these comics allow for multiple voices or what James C. Scott calls "hidden transcripts," the critique of power that goes on "offstage"? Albeit their nationalistic content, some of the characters in those comics were clearly modeled after characters of "enemy nation" comics. Japanese cinemas had been show-ing American and European animations since 1931, and the popularity of Dis-ney and Fleischer brothers' animations inspired a number of *akahon* artists to produce pirated or imitated comics, featuring Mickey Mouse or Popeye. It was impossible to completely shut out their influences even after the official ban on American comics. *Tokkan Suihei* by Niizeki Seika closely resemble the Bel-gian *Tintin* series, and *Nekoshichi Sensei* (1929–1930) by Shimada Keizō was clearly a Japanese takeoff on *Felix the Cat*. Among these comics, perhaps the most complex example is *Speed Tarō* by Shishido Sakō (1888–1969), who had studied cartooning for over ten years in the United States. After returning to Japan, Shishido produced works that combined nationalist messages and a dis-tinctly "American" style with cosmopolitan settings, "Americanized" character design, and dynamic panel layout. *Speed Tarō* was named the "masterwork of children's comics" by critics for its rhythmical text and artwork (Kaji 90). This work is still distinguished from other wartime comics by its formal sophisti-cation and spirit of experimentation. Critics suggest that *Speed Tarō* managed to constantly "stand outside the war, providing a distanced perspective and parodic readings not only of the war itself but also of other wartime comics," by flying in a warplane rather than participating in the ground battle (Sakuta Keiichi et al., quoted in Kaji 91). Tezuka later named Shishido as one of the first cartoonists who experimented with cinematic techniques.

Sakuramoto Tomio points out: "There is no existing scholarship on Japa-nese wartime comics that discusses the works in detail, drawing on concrete resources" (Sakuramoto 14). The reason for this is complex, involving political, historical, and technical factors: the control over the comics medium by the Japanese military government; the destruction of the wartime propaganda by the GHQ; Japan's infamous "amnesia" for its dark wartime regime, both exter-nal (foreign atrocities) and internal (nationalist propaganda, censorship); the guilt felt by individual cartoonists (which made them reluctant to acknowl-edge the influence of their wartime works on the public mind); the postwar media's willful ignorance of the "imperialist" past of well-respected veteran cartoonists; the poor quality and the scarceness of the paper supply toward the end of World War II; and the destruction of wartime publications kept in urban areas, due to heavy bombing. The government's censorship and con-trol over the media, combined with the shortage of paper, significantly re-duced the production and distribution of comics, particularly toward the end of World War II. In 1938, the Japanese government passed a set of regulations on children's literature, naming comics, particularly *akahon*, as an example of a "poor quality" or "harmful" publication, and ordering the publishers to take all *akahon* off the market.

The newspapers still continued printing daily comic strips, though virtually all comics (even *Norakuro* and other "pro-war" comics) disappeared from children's magazines and bookstores by 1942. *Asahi Shinbun*'s daily strip, the *Fuku-chan* series by Yokoyama Ryūichi (1909–2001), kept its space on the page and continued to be popular. The series consisted of heartwarming episodes from the daily life of five-year-old Fuku-chan. The character Fuku-chan started out as a supporting character in *Edokko Ken-chan* in January 1936, but soon became the protagonist of his own series *Yōshi no Fuku-chan* (*Adopted Child, Fuku-chan*). The series changed its name to the militaristic *Fuku-chan butai* (*Fuku-chan Unit*) in January 1938. The series subsequently went through several other title changes. During Yokoyama's service in the military as a war correspondent, the setting of the series changed to Java (*Jawa no Fuku-chan* [*Fuku-chan in Java*], 1942). Fuku-chan and Yokoyama returned to Japan in September 1942 in *Fuku-chan kaeru* (*Fuku-chan Returns*, September 15–20, 1942).

Even after his return to Japan, *Fuku-chan* was no longer the optimistic, heartwarming series it once was. In the two-part New Year's Day special in 1944, "Fuku-chan dai tōa kodomo kaigi (Fuku-chan's Children's Meeting in the Great East Asia)," Fuku-chan eats the traditional New Year's dish, *ozōni*, with children from Thailand and Burma; in *Fuku-chan rensei no maki* and *Fuku-chan rensei hen* (*Fuku-chan in Training*), Fuku-chan and his friends train for the battle against *kichiku beiei* ("monster-animals of America and Britain"). Fuku-chan even flies a warplane in *Fuku-chan sora no maki* (*Fuku-chan: Chapter of the Sky*). By this time, the size of the comic strip was drastically reduced, as newspapers themselves had shrunk considerably due to the shortage of paper. On March 4, 1944, the *Fuku-chan* series abruptly ended in an episode in which Grandpa decides to go away to the countryside. The retreat from the city to avoid heavy bombing in the city, called *sokai*, was a common practice toward the end of World War II. A few days later, Fuku-chan said goodbye to the readers of *Asahi Shinbun*: "Dear Friends, thank you for supporting me for a long time. I am going away on a *sokai*, from the newspaper pages that have become too busy with the war. [. . .] I will send you the reports when I have an opportunity. Goodbye now." *Fuku-chan* series restarted twelve years later, in 1956 in *Mainichi Shinbun*. Fuku-chan resumed his life in Tokyo with the same neighbors and family members, as if the destruction of the city and his participation in the war never took place.

Still, the view of World War II as the dark, futile period in the history of Japanese comics is worth reexamining. While the imperial government restricted the publication and distribution of children's comics, it also gave generous support to cartoonists who promoted nationalist ideologies and patriotism. This is the only period during which cartoonists worked under, and were paid by, the government. Tracing the rise and fall of cartoonists' associations and collectives during this period also illuminates the history of Japanese cartoonists as war laborers. In August 1940, Shin Nihon Mangaka Kyōkai (New Japanese Cartoonists' Association) was founded, uniting cartoonists who had previously belonged to numerous smaller associations and artistic units (such as Shin Manga ha Shūdan and Manga Kyōdan). This was a response to the Konoe Shintaisei Undo (Konoe New Political Order), Prime Minister Konoe's political reform that involved dismantling all political parties and labor unions, consolidating them under larger, nationwide organizations. Shin Nihon Mangaka Kyōkai had sixty-three members to start with, and its primary activity was the publication of the magazine titled *Manga*, published monthly from October 1940 to June 1951.

The artists in Shin Nihon Mangaka Kyōkai collaboratively designed eleven cartoon characters, a family called *Yokusan ikka* (Yokusan family) and set up a system where anyone could use the characters to produce nationalist comics (*yokusan* manga). Some cartoonists felt that the Shin Nihon Mangaka Kyōkai's policies were "lukewarm," and they founded another group, Kensetsu Manga Kai (Constructive Manga Association), with even more nationalistic views. After Japan's attack on Pearl Harbor, the government requested cartoonists to produce propaganda bills under supervision, and some cartoonists were sent to Japanese colonies in Asia as war correspondents. Yokoyama Ryūichi's memoir contains an anecdote of being locked in a hotel to produce propaganda *kamishibai* for children in Japanese colonies (Yokoyama, *Fuku-chan zuihitsu* 172).[4] Cartoonist-reporters sent in their comics to *Manga*, depicting their new lives in Java, the Philippines, and other faraway locations.

In his interviews with Ishiko Jun, Tezuka spoke in depth about cartoonists' responsibility in World War II. Tezuka identifies the three distinct attitudes toward the war among the Japanese cartoonists of the era. He described the first category as the ones who "actively and voluntarily participated in the war [. . .] it is a part of the Japanese' national character to believe that the good always wins, and that which wins is the good [. . .] conversely, when their side loses, they are easily convinced that the other was actually the 'good.' [. . .] In a way, [propaganda cartoonists] are victims of war as well as being war criminals" (Tezuka, *Manga no shugi* 119–21). Those cartoonists actively produced and published comics in color-printed, large-format magazines while other publications, even newspapers, suffered from a shortage of paper sup-

---

4. Kamishibai is a form of storytelling that uses paper placards with images on the front, and texts on the back. Usually performed spontaneously by a single performer on the street, it was a popular children's entertainment before cinema became affordable.

plies. Ishiko Junzō calls the propaganda-based manga magazine *Manga* "the high point in the history of Japanese comics, when it was most generously funded and highly regarded by the government" (Ishiko 196). Tezuka calls the second category of cartoonists "opportunists": they did not necessarily believe in "Japan's sacred war," but sided with the status quo in order to get their works published. Tezuka's portrayal of those cartoonists is sympathetic, presenting them as those who truly loved the comics medium and found ways to produce and show work. Tezuka names Tagawa Suihō as an example, who "tried hard to fit in [. . .] I have seen a number of critics who criticize *Norakuro* for promoting militarism, but few are aware that Tagawa-san produced comics other than *Norakuro*. Of course I agree that he should be held accountable (for his war participation), but there were plenty of others who did the same in other fields" (126).

Tezuka then describes the third category, ones who refused to produce propaganda or nationalist comics. Some completely stopped producing work during the war. Tezuka is at the same time empathetic and surprisingly critical:

I wonder if we can still call them cartoonists. I believe that cartoonists must produce cartoons. [. . .] If I were told that I could not draw cartoons, I might as well be dead. [. . .] Even if this kind of regime returned and we became subjected to thought control and oppression, I would still draw. If I were handcuffed, I would still draw with my feet. Not only that, but I would find ways to show my work to people. If they killed me for it, that's just too bad. But I bet I could come up with a clever way of surviving, ways of showing my work without being caught. (Tezuka, *Manga no shugi* 128–29)

Though Tezuka does not name cartoonists who actively resisted the war, one such cartoonist is Yanase Masamu (1900–1945). Yanase was a member of the Japan Communist Party and one of the victims of the Public Order Maintenance Act. He was imprisoned in 1932 and suffered brutal torture. He continued to refuse to produce propaganda comics during the war years, and he died in the Tokyo Air Raids of March–May 1945. Yanase's vivid life is detailed in a 1996 biography by Ide Magoroku, *Neji kugi no gotoku* (*Like a Twisted Nail*).

After incessant air raids and two atomic bombs turned many urban areas of Japan into rubble, Japan finally surrendered on August 15, 1945. Cartoonists who had served in the military or had moved to the countryside to escape the air raids returned to the cities, though many others had died in battle, from illness, by torture, or from malnutrition. Still, publishers launched new comic magazines one after another, and the surviving cartoonists suddenly became extremely busy. Major magazines that were launched in 1945 include

Manga Club, Manga Jin, VAN, Manga Times, Manga Hō, Shinsō (Truth), and *Hope.* Among them, *VAN* played a particularly important role in the history of postwar political comics, providing a venue for new artists, such as Yokoyama Taizō, Kato Yoshirō, Taniuchi Rokurō, and Kazama Shinjin. The front section of the magazine featured "photo comics," created by the editor Ito Ippei himself (Tezuka, *Boku wa manga ka* 62–63). Smaller publishers also resumed publication of thin, cheap magazines that featured comics, such as *Liberal, Pin-up, Aka to Kuro (Red and Black), Ryōki, Number One, OK,* and *Madam.* Those cheaply printed, poor-quality magazines were called *kasutori zasshi,* the term *kasutori* referring to the kind of poor-quality, strong alcohol made from rice or potatoes, a popular drink during the postwar era sold primarily through black markets. *Kasutori zasshi* soon became popular, with more than a few hundred titles in print by 1950. American comics were reintroduced to the Japanese readers through both official and unofficial routes. *VAN* had a special section for foreign comics, introducing works by Saul Steinberg and Raymond Peynet. *Shūkan Asahi* began printing a translated version of Dean Young's *Blondie* in June 1946. The Japanese citizens were shocked by the American middle-class lifestyle depicted in *Blondie,* equipped with refrigerators, cars, and telephones. At this time, most Japanese relied on candles to light their homes, due to the unreliable supply of electricity. Some Japanese "unofficially" obtained access to American print media through comic books and pulp magazines brought by American GIs. Children's comics also resumed publication during this era. Magazines *Kodomo Manga, Manga Land, Shonen Manga Chō, Gekkan Kodomo Manga,* and *Kodomo Manga Club* were launched and widely circulated. While *Shonen Club* of the prewar era consisted mostly of prose texts, comics were the main features of these new magazines. Another popular format of children's publications during this period was "children's newspapers," such as *Mainichi Shōgakusei Shinbun.* Those illustrated newspapers featured simplified news articles, short stories, illustrations, and comics.

The end of the war did not mean the end of media censorship, but simply a change of the censor, from the Imperial Government to the General Headquarters (GHQ) of the Allied Occupation Forces. This shift almost reversed the criteria of media censorship, practically overnight. The cover of the September 1945 issue of *Manga* featured a demeaning caricature of the Japanese military leader Tōjō Hideki in a prison cell, a striking change from its wartime issues, which featured caricatures of American and British political leaders. The same abrupt ideological transitions are evident in virtually every form of print media, from newspapers to children's magazines to arts magazines. Comparing the issues of the same magazine from the war and postwar periods reveals a shocking contrast. The June 1942 issue of *Shonen Club* included a lengthy memoir of the Japanese parachute attack on Sumatra by Lieutenant Tokunaga Etsutarō, a photo report on a bomb factory, and "heartwarming" anecdotes of children's self-sacrificial acts, such as a farmer's child giving up his own vegetables and eating grass from the field so that the people in the city could have "one more leaf of spinach." In November 1945, the same magazine printed a long article on the virtues of American democracy: "Democracy means government for every citizen (of Japan). We will discard the old, mistaken belief that one person can just dominate the country however he wants; we will strive for a nation where each person can freely state his own opinions, and everyone can trust each other" (Nakano Goro 40). The article implies, without explicitly naming it, that the imperial system misled the Japanese. What is truly ironic about this article is that the supposedly "free" society of postwar Japan was in fact under extremely tight media control by the Allied Forces.

On September 19, 1945, General McArthur's General Headquarters issued the "Press Code for Japan," detailing the principles for media censorship in postwar Japan. According to the report by the GHQ on September 10, 1945, the censorship code was designed to "eradicate the Japanese militaristic nationalism" and to "encourage democracy." The Civil Censorship Detachment (CCD), an organization belonging to the Civil Intelligence Section (CIS) of the General Headquarters, established a department called the Press, Pictorial and Broadcast Division (PPB) to undertake censorship of all civilian communications: not only of the mass media such as publication, radio, and film, but also of personal mail, telephone, and telegraph. The censorship was conducted discreetly, which left most Japanese oblivious to it. Publishers were required to submit a full proof copy of all publications to GHQ prior to sending them to the printer, including the front and back covers, tables of contents, illustrations, and advertisements, in addition to the main body. The censors went through the documents, marking the documents "delete," "hold," or "suppressed," or, in case of no changes, stamping them with the Censor Pass Stamp (*Senryōki no kodomo bunka* 64–65). The official guidelines for newspapers listed thirty criteria for "inappropriate" content, including critical views of countries such as the United States, Britain, China, or of the Allied Forces; references to the censorship itself; the occupation soldiers' sexual relations with Japanese women; predictions of a "Third World War"; descriptions of the black market; starvation; and favorable depictions of Japanese militarism, nationalism, or war criminals. The GHQ also temporarily banned Japanese history, geography, and *shūshin* (moral and ethics) classes in elementary school, since they were concerned that the curriculum had become too nationalistic during the war period. The censorship also extended to imported media. While GHQ promoted distributions of American films to encourage positive image of the United States, films that depict social problems in American society, such as slavery, poverty, anti-Semitism, or political corruption, were considered inappropriate. Major American films that were prohibited from distribution in Japan during this period include *Gone with the Wind* (1939), *The Grapes of Wrath* (1940), *Crossfire* (1947), *Gentleman's Agreement* (1947), and *All the King's Men* (1949) (Tanikawa 108).

Though comics (along with magazines and children's literature) were censored according to similar standards, the actual occurrences of the censorship were inconsistent. *Jidaigeki* (period drama) still remained the major target of censorship in comics as it was in film. Of approximately two thousand comic books in the Prange collection, fifteen were altered or suppressed. Fourteen out of those fifteen were in the *jidaigeki* genre. Meanwhile, some of the comics that clearly depict sword fights or murder somehow passed the censorship. Such inconsistencies emerged because comics were subject exclusively to *jigo kenetsu*, or postpublication censorship. This meant that the publishers sent the proofs to the GHQ only after the books had been stocked by retail stores. This, combined with the discreet ways in which the censorship was conducted, made it virtually impossible to take comics off the market even if they were considered problematic. Some argue that the techniques cultivated during this period for building a climax without sword fights resulted in the enrichment of storytelling techniques in the *jidaigeki* (*Senryōki* 60, 130). At the same time, genres that were practically dismissed by the CCD as "harmless," such as science fiction, flourished during this period and subsequently became major genres of postwar comics.

World War II and its aftermath became some of the most important themes in Tezuka's work after the 1960s. Tezuka often said that his experiences of the war were his primary motivation for producing work. Many of Tezuka's autobiographical comics take place during the late stages of the war or the immediate postwar era. In *Kami no Toride* (*The Fort of Paper*, 1974), Tezuka's alter ego, Ōsamu Tetsurō, is a young aspiring cartoonist. Though he is a high school student, his days are spent not in the classroom but at the factory, a common practice during the Pacific War called *gakuto dōin* (student labor force). Tetsurō is discouraged from drawing comics, but he finds ways of continuing his creative practice and sharing the product. He draws in secret and puts them up on the wall of the bathroom so people read them while using the toilet; he draws during an air raid, when his supervisors are in the shelters. Another semiautobiographical work, *Sukippara no blues* (*Hungry Blues*, 1975), takes place in the immediate postwar era, when Tetsurō finally makes his debut as a cartoonist for a children's newspaper. In *Dotsuitare* (1979–1980), Takatsuka Osamu, another alter ego, is commissioned to draw a series of female nudes in a postwar *kasutori zasshi.* The image of the young Tezuka that emerges from this series of works is that of a talented boy whose drive to draw and publish comics during the war was suppressed.

In a way, not being able to professionally produce comics during the war was a blessing in disguise for Tezuka. Under the postwar censorship and media reform of the GHQ, former producers of militarist propaganda were subjected to punishment and censure. Cartoonists, artists, and journalists endured social criticism as "war criminals." Some of those artists moved overseas to escape this stigma, and others discontinued their work altogether. Kajii Jun points out: "Tezuka's works are characterized by the humanism and humor that are appealing to most (postwar) readers. The reason why Tezuka was capable of incorporating peace messages in his works in a direct, naive manner was that Tezuka did not have the (traumatic) experience of having produced propaganda comics under constant surveillance" (Kajii 38). Though characterizing Tezuka's works simply as that of "humanism and humor" is much too simplistic, Kajii's point is well taken: not having published "propaganda comics" exempted Tezuka from the sense of guilt and shame that most cartoonists suffered during the postwar period.

In April 1946, as *kasutori* magazines inundated the black market and American GIs threw candies and gums to orphaned children on the streets, Tezuka Osamu entered Osaka University as a student in medicine. Soon he would make an even larger entrance, into the world of *akahon* comics and life as a cartoonist.

Chapter 3

MOVIE IN A BOOK

Tezuka Osamu's professional career started in 1946 with a comic strip, *Mā-chan no nikkichō* (*The Diary of Mā-chan*). This classic four-panel comic strip was serialized in a local children's newspaper, *Mainichi Shōgakusei Shinbun*, depicting humorous incidents in the daily life of a young boy named Mā-chan. The Allied Occupation Forces controlled not only the contents of all print material but also the paper supply in Japan during the postwar years, which meant that the newspapers were thin, with little room for comics. Mā-chan's adventures were restricted to the standard four-panel form. After a long absence of newspaper cartoons in Japan, Japanese children in the area most warmly welcomed Mā-chan.

Artistically speaking, *The Diary of Mā-chan* was a step back for Tezuka, who had already completed a number of long, book-length comics by this time. As a high school student, he had produced several ambitious pieces including the first draft of *The Lost World* (later published in 1948). Still, *Diary of Mā-chan* was important in that it allowed Tezuka to enter the circle of local professional cartoonists. It also earned Tezuka other newspaper commissions, though they were not as successful as his first. For a Kyoto area paper, *Kyoto Nichi Nichi Shinbun*, Tezuka serialized *Chinnen to Kyō-chan* (*Chinnen and Kyō-chan*), featuring a very "Kyoto-like" pair of main characters: a Buddhist apprentice monk, Chinnen, and a *maiko* (an apprentice *geisha*), Kyō-chan. Others include *A-ko chan B-ko chan tanken ki* (*Adventures of A-ko and B-ko*), *Kasei kara kita otoko* (*A Man from Mars*), and *Lost World* (not the same as the earlier version). These were slightly more experimental in that they had continuous plots, though they still took the form of four-panel comics, but were also short-lived. Tezuka also became a regular contributor to *Hello Manga*, a publication put out by Kansai Manga Man Club, a cartoonists' organization founded by a children's book writer, Sakai Shichima. Tezuka also contributed illustrations, essays, and short comics to *Takarazuka Graph* and *Kageki*, both fan magazines for a local theater company Takarazuka Kagekidan.

What earned Tezuka his popularity and fame was his *Shin takarajima* (*New Treasure Island*), a two-hundred-page adventure comic book based on a script by Sakai Shichima. Tezuka had met Sakai through *Hello Manga* and was approached by him for this collaboration. *New Treasure Island* was published from Ikuei Shuppan in January 1947 in the format called *akahon*, cheaply manufactured children's comics sold through toy and candy stores. Publishers were able to put out thick volumes of comics by using inexpensive paper called *senkashi*, which was outside the regulation by the Allied Forces. The term *akahon*, literally "red book," referred to their bright red covers often used to catch the potential buyers' eyes. With little other entertainment sources combined with the long absence of comics in Japanese media, these inexpensive comic books were guaranteed to sell. The success of *New Treasure Island* was unparalleled. The book went through several reprints, selling over 400,000 copies (some sources claim as many as 800,000). The famous opening sequence shows the protagonist, Pete, speeding through the countryside in a sports car. Compared to other *akahon*, *New Treasure Island* also had a classier appearance with a sophisticated cover design.

The scene in Fujiko Fujio A's comic autobiography *Manga michi* (*The Way of Manga*), where the two protagonists Michio and Shigeru encounter Tezuka's *New Treasure Island*, gives a sense of how *New Treasure Island* mesmerized young boys at the time of its publication. The scene has been translated into English by Fredrik Schodt: "(The two boys) opened the first page of the book (they) had borrowed without permission, and reeled in shock!" "*New Treasure Island* began with a flowing scene in which young Pete roared off in his sports car. It was Osamu Tezuka's debut publication—a revolution in post-war comics! [*sic*]" (fig. 3.1; translated by Schodt in *Manga! Manga!* 63). In another autobiography, *Futari de shonen manga bakari kaite ita* (*All We Ever Did Was Draw Boys' Comics*), Fujiko Fujio A describes the experience in prose:

In the upper right hand corner of the opened pages was a chapter title, "Bōken no umi e" (To the Sea of Adventure), and in the frame below, a fashionable boy in a hat drives his sports car from right to left. [. . .]

I have never seen a comic book like this. All you see is a car running for two pages. Then, why does this get me so excited? I feel as if I am driving this car and speeding towards the peer.

This is a static comics printed on paper, but, this car *is* running at full speed! It's just like I am watching a movie! (Fujiko Fujio A, quoted in Aki-yama 71)

Fujiko also claims to have hand-copied *Shin takarajima* in its entirety shortly after reading it, in order to learn and embody Tezuka's process. Similar testaments are given not only by cartoonists (Ishinomori Shōtarō, Matsumoto Reiji) but also among writers (Tanaka Yachiyo) and critics (Ishigami Mitsutoshi). Readers describe *New Treasure Island* as "like a movie in the form of a book" (Fujiko; Ishinomori).

After reading and hearing such vivid descriptions of this work over and over, encountering the actual text of *New Treasure Island* can be a confusing experience. To a contemporary reader of manga (or graphic novels at large), *New Treature Island* may not seem as "mesmerizing," "absorbing," or even particularly "cinematic." The readers' responses to *New Treasure Island* are largely subjective, having just as much to do with the historical and cultural climate of this period as with Tezuka's innovation. The recurring line in readers' memoirs, "I had never seen comics like this before," should not be interpreted as "comics like this did not exist before." Prewar cartoonists such as Shishido Sako were already experimenting with film perspectives and angles, producing fast-moving, highly visual comics.

The readers' reactions to *New Treasure Island* do not so much describe the artistic quality of the work, but rather exemplify an experience of a child who grew up during the late stages of World War II. The ten years' age difference between Tezuka and the target readers of *New Treasure Island* was crucial: while Tezuka grew up reading hardcover story comics by Ōshiro Noboru and Shishido Sakō, younger, less affluent children had little access to comics of any kind. Moreover, *New Treasure Island* was published as cheap *akahon* as opposed to hardcover children's literature (as in prewar *Nakamura Manga Library*); the quality of the work was incongruous to the format. There is also a question of what precisely was "cinematic" to the readers of the time. When young Fujiko Fujio A described *New Treasure Island* as being like a "movie in a book," he was not thinking of a twenty-first century Hollywood action flick, full of car chases and special effects. The restriction on films during the last years of World War II meant that most people's perception of film had stopped at 1941; the Japanese public had not yet seen *Citizen Kane* or *Fantasia*. Their idea of what was "cinematic" was built around their memory of prewar films or *kokusaku eiga* (propaganda films).

Still, it is clear that Tezuka was consciously trying to promote a new kind of comics through this work and was doing so by heavily referencing film.

Figure 3.1. An excerpt from *Manga michi*. Two boys read Tezuka's *Shin takarajima* [*New Treasure Island*]. © Fujiko Fujio A. Reproduced with permission.

The following passage from his autobiography is frequently quoted in writings on Tezuka:

I felt (after the war) that existing comics were limiting . . . Most were drawn . . . as if seated in an audience viewing a stage, where the actors emerge from the wings and interact. This made it impossible to create dramatic or psychological effects, so I began to use cinematic techniques . . . French and German movies that I had seen as a schoolboy became my model. I experimented with close-ups and different angles, and instead of using only one frame for an action scene or the climax (as was customary), I made a point of depicting a movement of facial expression with many frames, even many pages… The result was a super-long comic that ran to 500, 600, even 1,000 pages . . . I also believed that comics were capable of more than just making people laugh. So in my themes I incorporated tears, grief, anger, and hate, and I created stories where the ending was not always "happy." (Translated by Fredrik Schodt in *Manga! Manga! The World of Japanese Comics* 63; *Boku wa manga ka* 76–77; quoted in Hasegawa 74; Natsume, *Tezuka Osamu wa dokoni iru* 27–28; Ōshita 288; Tezuka, *Manga no kaki kata* 185–86)

While this passage is ubiquitously quoted to illustrate the importance of film in Tezuka's work, what is often left out is this: allusion to film was not a new technique, and Tezuka was fully aware of it. In a 1975 interview with literary critic Iwatani Kokushi, Tezuka points out that the use of cinematic techniques were imported from American cartoonists long before Tezuka's debut:

Iwatani: Are there any differences in panel layout between the 3000 page version of *The Lost World* you wrote during the war, and the version you published later?
Tezuka: The fundamental elements are the same. *Eiga teki shuhō* (cinematic techniques), for instance.
Iwatani: You were already using *eiga teki shuhō* in your childhood, then.
Tezuka: Well, yes.
Iwatani: Now we are on to our main topic!
Tezuka: Actually, I was not the first one to use *eiga teki shuhō* (in comics). For example, Shishido Sakō returned from the United States during the prewar period and wrote *Speed Tarō*, adopted the American style of comics. Also, Ōshiro [Noboru] seems to be very conscious of film [. . .]. ("Nijusseiki no inshō" 110–11)

Later in this interview, Iwatani suggests that Tezuka's technique is one that "translates the cinematic techniques onto paper." To this Tezuka responds:

"Many cartoonists before me used cinematic techniques [. . .] I made a big impact because I was so conscious of it" (111).

The version of *New Treasure Island* widely available today does not contain any of the original *akahon* version published by Ikuei Shuppan. Tezuka completely reworked it in the 1980s when he included it in *Tezuka Osamu manga zenshū* (*The Complete Works of Osamu Tezuka*), due to the loss of the original manuscript as well as the circumstances around the conditions of its original publication. Although the process of photographic reproduction for books and prints had been available since the late nineteenth century, in the *akahon* industry of the late 1940s to the early 1950s it was commonplace to reproduce the original through a manual process called *kakiban*. This process involved a technician (*gako*) hand-tracing the original onto a celluloid sheet and then onto a zinc plate for printing. As a result, the original images were often distorted and simplified. Upon inclusion of his earlier works in *Collected Works*, Tezuka retouched some of the poor-quality *kakiban* images, so as to bring the works close to his "intended" style.

Poor printing technology was not the only (or the most important) problem surrounding the publication of *New Treasure Island*. Though the project was framed as "collaboration" between Tezuka and Sakai Shichima, the dynamic between the two was not as equals. Sakai, who was already an established cartoonist with a number of followers, clearly took the lead and held the position of superiority over Tezuka. Nishigami Haruo describes: "Sakai wrote the story, breaking it down to different scenes and making rough panel layout, and passed it on to Tezuka. Then Sakai designed the cover to finish it up" (quoted in *Ichiokunin* 78). Tezuka's draft was cut down from 250 pages to 60 pages by Sakai. Sakai even changed some of the drawings without consulting Tezuka. Tezuka's unresolved feelings about the project are apparent in his autobiography. In the following passage, Tezuka recalls his struggles with the Tarzan character:

Drawing the Tarzan character was a huge challenge. At the time, I was skinny as a burdock, and I just could not visualize a strong man with big muscles. Every drawing I did of Tarzan looked like a burdock. Eventually I gave up and just drew what I could. Sakai then pasted pieces of paper over Tarzan's faces and completely redrew them. But the bodies still looked miserable and burdock-like, a total mismatch to his new Superman-like feature. (*Boku wa manga ka* 73–74)

Ironically, Sakai also claimed that the cinematic techniques in *New Treasure Island* were his own innovation: "I worked in the film medium, and I really loved film. I started thinking about the possibility of *eiga teki shuhō*, and decided to collaborate with Tezuka to create *New Treasure Island*" (Sakai in *Ichiokunin* 79).

In the reworked version of *New Treasure Island* published in 1984, the opening sequence of a speeding car is stretched to eight pages (fig. 3.2). This version also includes a sequence that was not in the original: as Pete speeds down the country road, he almost runs over a puppy. Pete's face, which starts in a close-up, becomes larger than the frame, ending in a close-up of his left eye. As the image gets larger and larger, an image of a puppy, standing in the middle of the road, appears inside the pupil, representing both the reflection of the eye and Pete's point of view. At the same time, readers also hear—read—the squeaking sound of Pete's brake, written vertically across three panels, signifying the duration of the sound. When the car stops, the readers realize that their orientation has been reversed: they are no longer facing Pete, but are facing the puppy on the road, sharing the perspective with Pete. Pete stops the car, gets out of the car and talks to the puppy: "Be careful! I almost hit you!" The readers' eye movement slows down as they read the texts inside the speech balloons— the car is now stagnant, and so are the readers. Pete takes the puppy into the car and starts speeding again. The "sense of movement" in many descriptions of *New Treasure Island* is more present in this short sequence than in the "original."

Few copies of the original *New Treasure Island* have survived until today, due to its poor quality in paper and binding. Most readers' perception of this work is formed through memoirs and descriptions. It has only been reprinted once in 1961, as a part of a journal *Jun Manga*. By the 1970s, the original copies of *New Treasure Island* were being sold at high prices at rare book stores and auctions. Records indicate that a rare books auction in 1975 sold a copy for 400,000 yen (approximately $3,250). Another went for 250,000 yen (approximately $2,000) at a gallery at Odakyū Department Store in Tokyo in 1976 (*Ichiokunin* 363).

The success of *New Treasure Island* brought forth the "*akahon boom*" in Osaka area, and some marked successes comparable to *New Treasure Island*. Yamakawa Sōji's *Shonen Ōja* (*Boy King*) sold 50,000 copies, and Nagamatsu Kaneo's *Ōgon Bat* (*Golden Bat*) sold 30,000. At the height of the *akahon boom*, there were as many as 600 new titles in a month. Other cartoonists started producing long narratives for *akahon* market, and Tezuka's works were constantly pirated or copied by other artists. A large number of *akahon* during this period included the word "takara jima (treasure island)" in their titles to reference Tezuka's earlier hit. Examples include *Takarajima sōdō* (*Treasure Island Incidents*, 1948) by Nakamura Kazuo, *Takajima tanken* (*Treasure Island Adventures*, 1947) by Saitō Hiroyuki, and *Chieko no bōken shin takarajima* (*Chieko's Adventure: New Treasure Island*, 1947) by Wada Yoshizō. *Kinsei tanken* (*Adventures on*

Figure 3.2. The opening sequence from the reworked version of *New Treasure Island.* © Tezuka Productions. Reproduced with permission.

Mars) by Tanaka Masao features an opening sequence identical to *New Treasure Island*, where a boy drives a sports car down a country road.

Tezuka put out seven more *akahon* volumes in 1947, *King Kong, Kasei Hakase* (*Dr. Mars*), *Kaijin koronko hakase* (*Dr. Koronko the Mystery Man*), and *Kaitō Ōgon Bat* (*Great Thief Golden Bat*), *Takarajima* (*Treasure Island*), *Bat hakase to Jim* (*Dr. Bat and Jim*), and *Momōn yama no arashi* (*Storm at Mt. Momōn*). Though none surpassed the success of *New Treasure Island*, Japanese children became familiar with this young prolific cartoonist named Tezuka Osamushi.[1]

---

1. Tezuka pronounced his pen name "Osamushi" during the 1940s. His pen name Osamu is a combination of his given name (Osamu) and a character for insect (mushi). Tezuka continued to use the same characters as his pen name, but pronounced it "Osamu" after the 1950s.

In February 1948, Tezuka published *Chiteikoku no kaijin* (*The Mysterious Underground Man*), which marked a clear departure from other *akahon*. This work featured an unusual character, Mimio, a rabbit that has been genetically altered to possess the intelligence of a human. Mimio accompanies the story's hero, John, on a trip to the center of the earth on an underground train, where they discover that the queen of the insect world is plotting to take over the earth. The story ends with Mimio sacrificing his life to save the earth. In the last panel of the comic book, readers see Mimio on a hospital bed in his final moment. He is surrounded by other characters (including John) who previously treated him cruelly, because of his appearance as a rabbit. His last words are: "John, I am a human, aren't I?" The scene, both moving and demoralizing, had a complexity and seriousness that was unprecedented in *akahon* comics, or in children's comics at large. Tezuka regards this work as his first true story comic.

Seeing that his readers were ready to accept the tragic, somewhat demoralizing ending of *The Mysterious Underground Man*, Tezuka started experimenting even more. His works grew more complex and started to contain clear "messages" or "morals," which often revealed Tezuka's sensibility as a young medical student. *Mahō yashiki* (*Magic House*) depicted a battle between science and magic (in which science triumphs), and *Kyūketsu madan* (*Vampire Devils*) celebrated the advancement of modern medicine in curing tuberculosis. In December 1948, Tezuka finally published *The Lost World*, the ambitious epic that he originally completed as a high school student and that he attempted to rework as a newspaper comic strip in 1946. This new version of the book was divided into two volumes, "Chapter of Earth" and "Chapter of Space." In "Chapter of Earth," the main characters find a mysterious planet approaching the earth. It turns out that the planet, Mamango, was a part of the earth separated from its main body five million years ago. In "Chapter of Space," characters explore the Planet Mamango, inhabited by dinosaurs and other prehistoric creatures. Considered one of Tezuka's finest works, this ambitious work is part space travel, part *Jurassic Park*, part Old Testament, and part cautionary fable about greed. *The Lost World*, *Metropolis* (1949), and *Kitaru beki sekai* (*Next World*, 1951) are referred to as Tezuka's *SF sambu saku*, the three greatest works of his early science fiction.

Tezuka's comics were distinct from other *akahon* at first glance. While most *akahon* covers were filled with vividly colored, eye-catching illustrations, Tezuka's were consistently more understated. His color schemes were subtler, and the composition more sophisticated. In Tezuka's cover design for *The Lost World*, the image—more like a film still than a comic book cover—is encased in a classic-looking picture frame (fig. 3.3). This design had become so iconic that it was later used as an inspiration for the cover design for his four-hundred-volume anthology.

Figure 3.3. The cover of Tezuka's *akahon*, *The Lost World*. © Tezuka Productions. Reproduced with permission.

In addition to the unusual design choices, Tezuka almost always wrote his titles in English (in addition to Japanese), or in *Romaji*,[2] which gave his books a modern and exotic flair, and marked the coming of a new era. The presence of the Allied Forces as well as the aggressive reintroduction of the English language into Japanese culture characterized it as the language of the powerful. Toward the end of World War II, the use of the English language was completely banned in Japan. This meant not only prohibition of English education in classrooms or control of media, but also disappearance of English loan words in everyday speech. Words that were originally imported from English and had become naturalized into the Japanese language, such as "studio" and "soccer," were replaced by newly invented, somewhat awkward Japanese equivalents. Figure 3.4 is a single-panel comic from 1944 that denounces the English language as the "enemy language," titled "Yogoreta mono wa Yogoreta basho de" (Dirty Places for Dirty Things). The image depicts a student reciting from an English textbook. He reads the text into a garbage can, as if he is throwing his own speech into the garbage can. Though the cartoon characterizes the English language as "dirty," it also self-parodically comments on the Japanese public who experience difficulty letting go of their former education.

2. Transliteration of the Japanese language using the Roman alphabet.

英語の勉強

汚れたものは、汚れたところで「すんだら、盥まいてあげるわよ。」

Figure 3.4. Sugiura Yukio, "Eigo no benkyo."

Ii Sadamu points out, "The association that exists in contemporary Japanese culture, that equates 'Foreign language = English = (the only) Universal Language' [. . .] is the result of the Occupation Force's political reform during the post-war period" (92). This reform started almost immediately upon Japan's surrender. English became ubiquitously heard through media as well as on the streets, and the English-speaking characters in American films were perceived as wealthy and glamorous. Though it took until 1947 for the Allied Forces to institute the program of teaching English as an international language in junior high schools, Japanese magazine articles in 1945 and 1946 are already heavily speckled with English loan words such as "star," "director," and "screen." Tezuka's use of English titles on his *akahon* covers both "reflects" this trend and actively reinforces it, even on the pages of cheap, lowbrow children's entertainment.

The strong association of Tezuka's works with film was already present in his first hit, *New Treasure Island*, but it became even more prominent as he continued to churn out more *akahon* volumes. Tezuka's works diverged into genres that corresponded to popular film genres. He quoted images from popular films, and he borrowed titles. This was both a natural outcome of Tezuka's long interest in film and a result of his efforts at incorporating the public's interests into his work. At this particular moment of the history of Japanese film culture, where American films were reintroduced after many years of absence, a strong reference to film was bound to spark people's interests.

Tezuka's success in incorporating film in his comics has much to do with the long history of film culture in Japan, which is worth discussing here in some length. Prior to the censorship by the Imperial Government, movies—both domestic and foreign—were an important part of Japanese popular culture. They also existed in a close relationship with cartoons and comics. The Kinetoscope, the forerunner of projected motion pictures, was imported and shown to the public in 1896 by a showman and a firearms dealer, Takahashi Nobuharu. In February of the following year, an import dealer by the name of Inabata Katsutarō introduced the Lumière Brothers' Cinématographe to the public in Osaka. Inabata and his family appear in a short film *Rapas en famille* (*A Family Dinner*) by Constant Girel (1873–1952). Around the same time, Vitascope, an improved version of the Kinetoscope which employed a projection mechanism, was shown in Tokyo (Richie 17; Yomota, *Nihon eiga shi* 40). George Bigot, a French cartoonist who worked in Japan during the Meiji period, produced drawings and single-frame cartoons dealing with the introduction of the Kinetoscope. Japan's first movie was made in Tokyo by Asano Shirō in 1898, and the first permanent movie theater opened in 1903 (Thompson, *Exporting Entertainment* 44; Yomota 42). After recovering from the Great Kanto Earthquake in 1923, Japan became the most prolific movie-producing nation in the world, putting out six to eight hundred films per year, mostly for domestic distribution. The studios also held tight control over imported films during this era, which prevented them from overshadowing the domestic market. In 1926, 39.2 percent of all theaters showed only domestic films; the number steadily increased to 71.0 percent by 1931 (Thompson 142). Still, the Japanese public became familiar with stars of imported films as well as their own stars. The images of the Hollywood stars permeated Japanese culture not only through actual films but also through movie magazines such as *Star* and *Eiga no tomo*, which featured glamorous color portraits.

By the time of Tezuka's birth, Japanese cinema had reached its golden era. In his autobiography, Tezuka describes his first experiences of going to a movie theater:

I have vivid memories of movies. My first experience of going to the movie was when I was in kindergarden, and it was a movie with young Kataoka Chiezō in it. My parents took me to the theatre, it was dark and there was a benshi. It was a silent film, and the benshi would narrate the film using different voices. There were also a couple of violinists who would play music during the climax.

I remember feeling a little scared [. . .] The prefecture of Tokyo set up "Jidō eiga no hi (Children's Film Day)" in 1928, promoting good films to schoolchildren in Tokyo. Following this, Osaka founded Gakkō Junkai Eiga Renmei (The Association for Film Screenings for Schools). The organization's activity consisted of going around different schools with 16mm and 35mm films, showing movies to children. [. . .] There were fifty schools involved in 1929, but in 1935 the member schools increased to 500. In 1941 it reached 5000. (Tezuka, *Boku no manga jinsei* 14)

Tezuka describes how he enjoyed the five-minute animated film better than the feature presentation, and how the films at school tended to be "educational, dark and preachy" (15). With Japan's participation in World War II, war documentaries became staples at such school screenings. Tezuka remembers seeing titles named *Gonin no sekkō hei*, *Shogun to sanbō to shi*, and *Shanghai*. "They were more interesting than the 'educational' ones, but the school screenings continued to be dull and boring" (15).

Aside from going to the movie theaters and school screenings, Tezuka also had the privilege of seeing movies at home. Tezuka's father, Yutaka, owned a 9.5 film projector with which he often entertained his family:

My father was crazy about film, and, he owned a rare hand-crank movie projector called Pathé Baby. He also bought tons of films. 16mm and 35mm films were common at the time, which have perforations along the sides. But, there was also a variation called 9.5 mm films, which did not have this perforation but had holes between the frames. [. . .] Department stores carried films to show at home. My father bought them one after another. He bought American short comedies, animations, and Chaplin films. There were *Mickey Mouse* and other animations. My father used to project them for us. So, since second grade until middle school, I had the good fortune to watch movies at home. (Tezuka, *Boku no manga jinsei* 18–19)

Yutaka also owned an 8 mm camera, with which he occasionally filmed his family and community events. Young Osamu grew familiar with the process of film shooting and editing through his father's hobby, until Yutaka was drafted in 1941.

As the Pacific War intensified, all American and British cultural products, including film, were banned from Japanese media. Domestic films, too, suffered strict censorship. In October 1939, the Japanese imperial government passed new legislation on production and distribution of films, called Eiga Hō

(Film Law), modeled after the film restriction laws that were in effect in Nazi Germany and Italy. Under this new legislation, "profit motive was utilized as a carrot for studios to use pre-censorship to ensure that its creative staff automatically incorporated politically acceptable sentiments" (Darrel Davis 7). Requirements included submission and approval of all scripts, as well as government registration of all personnel including directors, actors, and technicians. The filmmakers at the time welcomed, rather than resisted, this new law, for it implied that film had a special status among the arts that made it worthy of legal attention and governmental protection (Shimizu Akira 69). Older actors embraced the registration system, particularly because it prevented a new unknown actor from suddenly becoming a star. The only major public figure who actively opposed this law was the film critic Iwasaki Akira (*Asahi Shimbun*, April 11, 1939); he was arrested in January 1940 and spent the following eight months in a holding cell. Iwasaki was subsequently charged for violating the Chian Iji Hō (Public Order Maintenance Act), spending six additional months in prison (Shimizu 71). All Japanese film magazines were discontinued in 1940, and ten of those titles were reissued in 1941, but with drastically different contents. Among the ten magazines was *Shin Eiga* (*New Cinema*), which, after 1941, turned into more of a war report magazine than a film magazine, with articles that had only peripherally to do with films, such as interviews with military personnel on their favorite films. Photographs of men in military uniforms and warplanes replaced the images of foreign film stars on the covers.

Still, the Japanese public did not lose their affection for American and British films and their stars. Iwasaki Akira writes: "Old issues of *Star* and *Eiga no Tomo*, filled with articles and full-color portraits of Hollywood stars, were highly valued like antiques, and were sold through rare book stores—secretly of course—for high prices. The allure of Hollywood films did not disappear so quickly as the imperial government had hoped, even during the long battle" (Iwasaki 28). Figure 3.5 is a single-panel cartoon from this period, which shows two women reading old issues of *Star*, in a room decorated with pictures of foreign stars. The caption reads: "Soredemo kimiwa nihonjun ka" (How do you call yourself a Japanese citizen?). The cartoon criticizes its characters for their laziness, escapism, and consumption of American cultural products: the two women wear dresses (as opposed to the typical *monpe*, the loose-fitting cotton work pants that were common during the war years), lounging around reading old magazines, in a room adorned with photographs of foreign stars. The women are not only lazy but also vain: there is a vanity in one corner of the room and what seems to be a jar of face cream; there is also a basin and a bottle of perfume by the window. This is further contrasted with a line of women

Figure 3.5. Sugiura Yukio, "Soredemo kimiwa nihonjin ka."

in *monpe* outside the window, participating in civilian defense training. The image sends a mixed message: though the caption harshly criticizes the two women in the room, their physical appearances are not evil or even unattractive. Ironically, to a contemporary eye, the cartoon almost reads as a sympathetic portrayal of the Japanese citizens who have been deprived of simple, innocent pleasures.

Reuniting with American and British films after Japan's defeat in 1945 was emotionally charged for many Japanese, including Tezuka. In his autobiographic manga, *Dotsuitare*, Tezuka's alter ego, Takatsuka Osamu, weeps at the movie theater upon seeing an American film. Osamu exclaims: "Why are American films so different from Japanese ones? Why did they make such great films during the war?" The new abundance of American films inspired Tezuka, who watched them obsessively, often repeatedly—he claims to have watched *Bambi* more than thirty times during its first run at the theater. The film director Ozu Yasujiro told that he sensed Japan's impending defeat upon seeing *Citizen Kane* (1941) in an occupied movie theater in Singapore (Yomota 98). The first American films in postwar Japan were shown in February 1946. The films were *Madame Curie* (1943) and *His Butler's Sister* (1943). Iwasaki writes:

There were long lines at the box office on the first day. It was as if there was no courage needed to go and see American films, or perhaps many people already had that sort of courage. [. . .] The three things that the Japanese craved after the war were American cigarettes, American chocolate, and American films [. . .] a nation like Japan, that was so attracted to the films made by the enemy, so enthusiastically and so soon after the war, was probably unheard of elsewhere. (Iwasaki 29)

The box office success of the American films is particularly compelling considering that the admission to American films was far more expensive than that to domestic films, at ten yen as opposed to three yen (Ōshima 62). In his autobiography, the film director Ōshima Nagisa recalls a sense of urgency and fascination:

We watched American films, feverishly—but was it really film that we were watching? They were unmistakably films, but did we really perceive them as films? I somehow doubt it now. I remember (the films) as the equivalent of the gum, the chocolate, the cigarettes and other foods that the GIs threw at us. [. . .] Films were something that satisfied our hunger. They were something that had directly to do with survival. When I remember, they were not films. They were something entirely different. (Oshima 60)

In that moment in history, it is no surprise that readers embraced Tezuka's work with such enthusiasm. Referencing film was like feeding the hungry. Tezuka's works were "filmlike" not only because Tezuka made a conscious effort to make them as such, but also because films were on the minds of Japanese readers. During the years following Japan's defeat, the Japanese movie-going public played a chaotic game of catch-up with wartime American and British films. Magazines reverted their foci to entertainment films. In June 1945, the cover of *Shin Eiga* featured a photograph of a man in military uniform and his wife; the same magazine printed a portrait drawing of Claudette Colbert in October. Publishers also launched new magazines, most notably *Eiga Hyōron* (*The Filmcrit*) and *America eiga* (*Cine-America*). All of these magazines featured articles discussing American and British films that were made during the years of their absence from Japanese movie theaters. Since the Japanese film critics had not seen the films, the articles were often written based on old press releases and advertisements. The film critic Iijima Tadashi writes in the May 1947 issue of *The Filmcrit*: "It is ridiculous to try to make any comments on the trends of American films at the moment. We are commenting on films that were made in 1941! We are seeing all these films that were made during the War in no particular

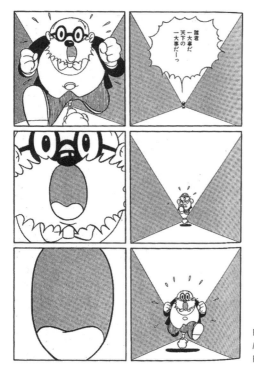

Figure 3.6. The opening scene of *Metropolis.* © Tezuka Productions. Reproduced with permission.

order, and are trying to make sense out of it" (Iijima 17). The films were introduced out of sequence, now under the monitoring and censorship by the Allied Forces, instead of the Imperial Government. The films that presented the "friendly" images of the United States were favored; hostility toward Japan or the Japanese was carefully avoided, as were revenge plots and other "inappropriate" themes, which included depictions of slavery, poverty, anti-Semitism, and political dishonesty.

In *Metropolis* (1948), Tezuka started incorporating a more solid vocabulary of "cinematic techniques," which later became his trademark. He mimicked the visual effect of cinematography in his composition and framing, creating a comic book that looked like the scenes are being "filmed" with an imaginary movie camera. In the opening sequence, a scientist runs toward the reader from the opposite end of the hallway (fig. 3.6). The point of view is stationary, as if the scene were shot with a stationary camera. The scientist's figure becomes larger and larger as he approaches the viewer, and the "shot" eventually ends with an extreme close-up of his mouth.

Another example of cinematic images in *Metropolis* is crowd scenes. The "crowd scene," of hundreds of extras filling the screen, has long been a staple in narrative films, since as early as D. W. Griffith's *Intolerance* (1916). Tezuka, however, names the works of another cartoonist, George McManus (1884–1954), as his main influence for his crowd scenes. McManus's *Bringing up Father* (1913–), originally published as a daily strip in *Journal American*, was translated into Japanese and printed in a daily newspaper, *Asahi Shinbun*, during the prewar period. In one interview, Tezuka talks about how he, as a middle school student, shuffled through old issues of *Asahi Shinbun* that his father kept in their shed, cutting out comics and cartoons and copying them to practice drawing. Tezuka recalls: "What was impressive about *Bringing up Father* was [. . .] the crowd scenes. [. . .] the frame shows so many people [. . .] characters with no relation to the main characters, and each one of them is saying something that has nothing to do with the plot [. . .] I started drawing crowd scenes everywhere—in *Metropolis*, for instance" (*Manga no shugi* 64–65). What sets Tezuka's use of crowd scenes apart from other cartoonists', and gives it a particularly cinematic effect, is the focalization and identification in the frames leading up to, and unfolding from, the large-panel crowd scenes. Natsume Fusanosuke describes a crowd scene in Tezuka's *Crime and Punishment* (1953) as follows: "The close-up panel invites the reader to identify with the protagonist. Then, in the next frame, the identification is immediately unsettled by the crowd scene, in which the protagonist—and the reader who identifies with him—becomes one of the many 'extras.' The protagonist is represented here as a small and insignificant part of the larger society" (Natsume 36). Tezuka's crowd scenes are often used in combination with extreme close-ups, creating not only the sense of panic or crowdedness in large spaces, but also the effect of identification and distancing, allowing the reader to move fluidly in and out of the narrative.

Unlike a crowd that contains an interminable length of time in one panel, Tezuka's crowd often moves through time and space, transforming itself and taking the readers with it. In *Metropolis*, the crowd scene continues for five large panels, during which the crowd moves from the state of "stagnation" to "panic," to use Elias Canetti's terms. The first panel shows a large number of scientists, in a confined space, uttering random lines to one another (fig 3.7). In this panel, Tezuka already inserts signs of transformation by depicting a scientist running in (*bottom left*) with an urgent report. The next panel shows a medium shot of the scientist, in a state of fear and shock, telling other scientists, "It is the end of the world!" (fig. 3.8). The readers are placed within the crowd looking at the panicked scientist, as if through the eyes of one of the other scientists crowded around him. The cause of the scientists' panic is made apparent, presumably by another scientist responding to the first: "What, there is an enormous sun spot?!" Upon receiving this report, the crowd disintegrates

Figure 3.7. A crowd scene in *Metropolis*. © Tezuka Productions. Reproduced with permission.

into another, more panicked crowd within the original crowd. In this frame, Tezuka also returns the readers' view to that of an outside spectator, looking at the crowd from above, but not at a great distance. The panic reaches its peak as the scientists look at the sun through a giant telescope, crammed into a small space, pushing and fighting with one another (fig. 3.9). In the last panel of the sequence, the crowd returns to a somewhat organized state, in a lecture-hall setting discussing possible solutions. This crowd is somewhat similar to the first panel, marking no definite duration and confined in a closed space.

Among numerous references to film technology in *Metropolis*, images inspired by deep-focus cinematography are particularly characteristic of this period. Deep focus, which allows objects in several planes of depth to be in equally sharp focus, was one of the major advances in Hollywood film technology during its absence from Japanese movie theaters. Cinematographers took advantage of this new invention, often strategically placing the foreground objects very close to the camera, capturing two activities simultaneously in a scene (Bordwell, Staiger, and Thompson 344; Cook 51). *Citizen Kane* (1941) was one of the first films to employ this technology, and by the late 1940s deep focus became the signature style of certain filmmakers such as the cinematographer Gregg Toland. The publication of *Metropolis* coincided with the Japanese re-

Figure 3.8. A crowd scene in *Metropolis.* © Tezuka Productions. Reproduced with permission.

lease of William Wyler's 1946 film *The Best Years of Our Lives,* celebrated for its deep-focus cinematography. The climax scene of the film takes place at a pub, where Fred, a former air force captain, has called on his friend and former in-fantry sergeant, Al. Al, a married man, has been having an affair with Fred's daughter, Peggy. Fred, concerned for his daughter, asks Al to end the relation-ship. Al agrees and goes to make a phone call to Peggy. In the frame in fig-ure 3.10, Fred, in the foreground, watches Al; in the background, Al makes the call in a phone booth. Both characters remain in sharp focus, engaged in two different actions in two separate spaces (fig. 3.10).

Metropolis included several frames and sequences that seem to reference deep focus, showing actions happening in multiple planes of depth within one frame. Tezuka had employed drawings with spectacular "depth" in his frames prior to *Metropolis,* even in his childhood cartoons such as *The Lost World* (1941), but the deep focus in *Metropolis* is far more sophisticated. The compo-sition not only is visually compelling, but also interacts with the plot. In fig-ure 3.11, Dr. Lawton watches artificial human cells growing in a glass tank, un-aware of the evil Duke Red approaching from the background. In another example from *Metropolis,* the detective Higeoyaji peeks through a crack of a door to spy on Duke Red's conspiracy (fig. 3.12). The difference between Tezuka's early use of deep focus and that in *Metropolis* is somewhat similar to the evolution of deep-focus shots in film from the earlier period to the late 1940s here described by André Bazin:

All you need to do is compare two frame shots in depth, one from 1910, the other from a film by Wyler or Welles, to understand just by looking at the im-

Figure 3.9. A crowd scene in *Metropolis*. © Tezuka Productions. Reproduced with permission.

Figure 3.10. A scene from *The Best Years of Our Lives* with deep-focus cinematography.

age, even apart from the context of the film, how different their functions are. The framing in the 1910 film is intended, to all intents and purposes, as a substitute for the missing fourth wall of the theatrical stage, or at least in exterior shots, for the best vantage point to view the action, whereas in the second case the setting, the lighting, and the camera angles give an entirely different reading. Between them, director and cameraman have converted the screen into a dramatic checkerboard, planned down to the last detail. (Bazin 51)

It is important to note here that deep-focus imagery is not *inherently* cinematic. That is, it could have been achieved in the comics medium at any time in the history of comics, with no relation to film. What marks Tezuka's use of deep-focus "cinematic" is the surrounding discourse of film culture, or the "buzz" around deep focus, at the time of its publication. In the July 1948 issue of *CINE-AMERICA*, a new magazine specializing in American films, six leading

Figure 3.11. A deep-focus scene in *Metropolis*. © Tezuka Productions. Reproduced with permission.

Japanese film critics discuss *The Best Years of Our Lives* in a "roundtable" format. In the article, Oka Toshio describes two scenes in the film that make innovative use of deep focus, discussing them in relation to Greg Toland's other works (29). Numerous other film magazines discussed this film, familiarizing the viewers with its cinematographic innovation long before its release in Japan. The image of Higeoyaji in close foreground becomes associated with film only in this context.

Similarly, Tezuka borrowed other images and motifs from trends of film. Tezuka depicted a kiss between the hero and his romantic interest in *Kenjū tenshi* (*Gun Angel*, 1949), most likely as a response to the newly popular "kiss scenes" in Japanese film. Around this time, Japanese films started showing scenes of romantic intimacy, which had been prohibited during the war. Filmmakers and actors were initially tentative in this arena, which resulted in a number of creative alternatives to the more straightforward love scenes of American films. Imai Tadashi's *Mata au himade* (*Till We Meet Again*, 1950) featured a poignant scene in which two lovers, destined to part, put their lips to opposite sides of a glass window, without their lips actually touching (Hirano). A kiss automatically made a film more exciting, more talked about, and more liberating. The Japanese public, however, was still too prudish to accept a kiss

Figure 3.12. A deep-focus scene in *Metropolis*. © Tezuka Productions. Reproduced with permission.

in a comic book; Tezuka's brief—one panel, and not even a close-up—kiss scene caused much controversy, with concerned parents protesting against Tezuka's comics as harmful to children.

While embracing the new influences of American media and navigating through censorship, Tezuka's narratives often gained emotional impact from drawing on more traditional Japanese values and sensibilities, such as glorification of self-sacrifice. Tezuka claims to have been the first cartoonist to introduce "the anti-happy-ending" to children's comics, sometimes "killing" his protagonists at the end. However, what made Tezuka's "anti-happy-ending" emotionally charged for the Japanese readers was not simply that they die, but that they die *for others*. In *The Mysterious Underground Man*, Mimio chooses his own death in order to save humans. The theme of self-sacrifice is repeated over and over throughout his career, reenacted by Leo in *Jungle taitei* (*Jungle Emperor*), by Atom (Astro Boy) in *Tetsuwan Atom* (*Astro Boy*), and countless others.

Though it became increasingly difficult for Tezuka to manage his schedule as a popular manga artist and a medical student, he continued to stay in school, finishing his coursework and moving on to a residency at Osaka University Medical School Hospital in 1948. Tezuka's life as a medical student was later comically rendered in his autobiographical comics. In *Gachaboi ichidaiki* (1970), Tezuka is caught working on his manga when he drops his ink jar

Figure 3.13. A scene from *Dotsuitare*. The character Osamu is discovered sketching a nurse. © Tezuka Productions. Reproduced with permission.

on the floor during a lecture. The professor initially scolds Tezuka, but then asks him to draw his caricature. Later, the same professor advises him to become a cartoonist, so as not to end up killing his patients from malpractice. In *Dotsuitare* (1979), the character Takatsuka Osamu, an emerging cartoonist, asks the nurses at Osaka University Medical School Hospital to pose for him as models for his erotic manga. When Osamu is discovered, his professor punishes him by locking him in a room with a life-size anatomical model (fig 3.13). Around the same time, Tezuka started to look toward Tokyo for new venues for publication. Tezuka first visited publishers in Tokyo in the summer of 1947, bringing copies of *New Treasure Island* and asking if they needed new talent. Prompted by the *akahon boom* in Osaka, small publishing houses in Tokyo were showing interest in putting out comics and children's books. The effort of this trip resulted in a four-panel cartoon in a magazine called *Manga to Yomimono* half a year later. After a few more small commissions, Tezuka started his first magazine serial, *Tiger hakase no chin ryokō* (*Dr. Tiger's Strange Trip*, later retitled *Tiger hakase*) in April 1950.

Transitioning from *akahon* to magazine serials raised a new challenge for Tezuka. Unlike *akahon*, where a reader reads the story from beginning to end in one sitting, magazine serials were divided into monthly segments of around ten pages. This called for a radical change in his storytelling style. Tezuka recalls his first magazine project: "Despite my initial enthusiasm, my first magazine serial quickly turned into a tormenting task. Writing eight pages a month required skill sets completely different from writing an entire book. Every segment needs to be full in content; there also needs to be a visual climax every month. Compared to other artists', my work looked plain, in addition to being hard to follow" (Tezuka, postscript to *Shin sekai Rurū*). In a serial format, foreshadowing and subplots got lost, as did elaborate framing devices. Instead of a large number of characters who develop complex relationships, Tezuka needed to invent a single charismatic hero to keep the readers' interest. The plot structure changed from being multilayered and complex to more episodic. At the same time, it gave birth to some of Tezuka's best-known and unique heroes and heroines, such as Leo, Atom, and Princess Sapphire.

One of Tezuka's primary venues for publication in Tokyo was *Manga Shonen*, a magazine launched by a small publishing house, Gakudōsha, in 1947. The magazine featured "all-star" cartoonists due to the editor Kato Ken'ichi's connections and charisma: Kato, who had served as the editor-in-chief of *Shonen Club* at *Kōdansha*, had been dismissed from the editor post because of his "propaganda" work during the war period. *Manga Shonen* not only featured some of the most popular cartoonists, but also became the gateway to success for many young aspiring cartoonists. It included a unique "readers' section," where readers could send in their own works for prizes and feedback from established cartoonists. Publishers often contacted the young cartoonists who were published in *Manga Shonen* to offer commissions. The cartoonists who originally started out as reader-contributors to *Manga Shonen* and eventually became major successes include Ishinomori Shōtarō (1938–1998) and Mizuno Hideko (1939–). Tezuka often "scouted" young cartoonists to become his assistants, in order to manage his tremendous workload. The young cartoonists considered it a great honor to help Tezuka, erasing pencil lines, painting in the solid black (a process called *beta*), or drawing the background and crowd scenes. Ishinomori Shōtarō was a high school student when he received a telegram from Tezuka asking him to come and assist him with his work (Ishinomori 37; Maruyama 71–72).

Tezuka started work on *Jungle taitei* (*Jungle Emperor*) in 1950, his second magazine project that lasted for three years. While the format still required for simpler storytelling, sophisticated readers of *Manga Shonen* were primed for deeper, more challenging thematic exploration. *Jungle Emperor*, which later inspired the Disney animation film *The Lion King*, begins with a scene in which Panja the white lion, the king of the jungle, is killed by humans. Panja's queen and the prince, Leo, are captured by humans and find themselves on a ship. The queen, concerned about Leo's future in captivity, encourages him to escape the ship. Leo ends up in Japan, where he learns the human language, and eventually returns to the jungle to inherit the throne. The plot encompasses three generations of white lions, ending with Leo's death. This work drew on the convention of animal anthropomorphism and infused it with a sense of epic as well as gritty, often disturbing realism. In *Jungle Emperor*, Tezuka was unafraid to show some of the cruelty of nature and wildlife: animals kill and eat each other, and male lions fight over a female. A nursing female becomes violent toward her mate to protect her children. In the meantime, the animals and humans engage in complex relationships that involve friendship, respect, loyalty, jealousy, greed, honor, and self-sacrifice. At the end of the series, Leo and a group of scientists climb Mount Moon and become lost in a snowstorm over many days. Members of the expedition team lose their lives one by one, leaving only Leo and Higeoyaji, Leo's former teacher in Japan. When they find themselves with no food or fire, Leo asks Higeoyaji to kill him, eat his flesh, and use his fur to keep warm. Higeoyaji refuses, and Leo pretends to attack him. Higeoyaji, startled, shoots him with his rifle. Leo dies, saying, "This is the right thing. . ." The ending repeats the self-sacrifice theme introduced earlier with Mimio's death in *The Mysterious Underground Man*, but with a more complex twist. Higeoyaji, after accidentally shooting Leo, immediately does what he was asked: while mourning the death of his friend, he cuts open Leo's body to use the flesh and the fur. The scene does not simply glorify self-sacrifice, but also comments on the cruelty of survival, and portrays the material reality of death.

By the end of 1951, Tezuka had a slot in most major boys' magazines in Tokyo: *Saboten kun* (*Cactus Boy*) in *Shonen Gahō*; *Shin sekai Rurū* (*New World Rurū*) in *Manga to Yomimono*; *Rock bōkenki* (*Adventures of Rock*) in *Shonen Club*, as well as a few others. The most important among them was *Atomu taishi* (*Captain Atom*), serialized in *Shonen*. This series depicted a number of incidents that surround a group of space aliens who try to immigrate to the earth. The aliens look identical to humans, except they have larger ears. The series explores the themes of immigration and xenophobia, but more important, it gave birth to Atom, the robot boy superhero who becomes, and remains, the most popular comic book character in Japan to this day. The premise of *Captain Atom* was carried over to another series, *Tetsuwan Atom* (*Iron-Armed Atom*, also known as *Mighty Atom*), starting in April 1952. By 1953, Tezuka completely transitioned from *akahon* to magazines. *Tsumi to batsu* (*Crime and Punishment*, 1953), an adaptation from Dostevsky, was his very last *akahon* publication. This was also the year Tezuka completed his medical residency at Osaka University Hospital and passed the national exam for a physician's license. Soon after the exam, however, Tezuka moved permanently to Tokyo, to become not a practicing physician but a full-time cartoonist, entering the new era of competition and genre diversification.

Chapter 4

STARS AND JOKES

There is a unique sense, which a reader starts to experience as he or she gets to know more than a few of Tezuka's works, that all Tezuka's works, regardless of genre, topic, or style, are somehow connected. While each work is independent and coherent, there emerges another layer of meaning—a kind of meta-narrative—when one reads it in context of other works. This sense of inclusiveness is far more extensive, far more complete, and far less common to simply call a "style." The two important techniques that Tezuka used in creating this sense of unity were the Star System and recurrent jokes. Tezuka started developing both of these techniques as a young child, establishing them as a part of his signature style by the end of his *akahon* era in Osaka.

The Star System entails producing story comics based on a group of stock characters and "casting" them to play different roles in different comics. "Stars" come with distinct appearances, personalities, habitual gestures, and speech patterns; once they are "cast," Tezuka gave them different costumes and variation on hairstyles as necessary. It differs from the more conventional stock character systems, such as Disney cartoons in which Mickey Mouse appears in various independent plots, in that each of Tezuka's "stars" has a strong "off-stage" identity that is independent of (though closely related to) the character he or she plays in a given episode. Some stars were purely fictional, while others were loosely based on his friends, colleagues, or existing film stars; some were human, others were animals or robots; while some played leading roles, others specialized in supporting "character roles." Ken'ichi, who appeared in the role of Pete in *New Treasure Island*, was the leading boy in virtually all of Tezuka's *akahon*. An honest, brave, and intelligent boy, Ken'ichi was a quintessential "model student," well raised and gentle natured. He went on numerous adventures, fighting against tuberculosis viruses in *Vampire Devils* and becoming the Adam to Ayame's Eve on Planet Mamango in *The Lost World*. Mimi-chan, another early principle star, is a bunny with the intelligence of a human.

Some of Tezuka's stars were created before his professional debut. Tezuka's busiest star, Higeoyaji, aka Ban Shunsaku, first appeared in Tezuka's elementary school drawings. This middle-aged man with a large white mustache often plays detective and teacher roles, such as Astro Boy's homeroom teacher at school (fig. 4.1). Outspoken, athletic, and compassionate, Higeoyaji has a big heart and a strong sense of moral. As he was modeled after a childhood friend's grandfather, he spoke with a *Kansai* dialect from western Japan during his early years; later, Higeoyaji repositioned himself as a man born and raised in Tokyo, speaking with the brisk *Edokko* accent that became his trademark. Higeoyaji appeared in most of Tezuka's *akahon* volumes, playing uncle to the hero, Ken'ichi. Another example of Tezuka's old star is Acetylene Lamp, who often plays a small-time villain in a plaid suit. Lamp has a strange "habit"—whenever he is excited, a candle spontaneously "appears" on his head (and none of the other characters acknowledge or even notice it). Many fans know that Lamp was modeled after Tezuka's childhood friend who had a dent on his head and was often teased that one could use the dent as a candle stand. Lamp's appearance can be puzzling to unfamiliar readers; even in a "serious" graphic novel such as *Adolf*, Acetylene Lamp is seen with an occasional flaming candle on his head, with no explanation (Thorn 9).

The Star System is a meticulously planned and organized system, which characterizes his "stars" as separate from the "characters" they play in the comics. The Tezuka Osamu Manga Museum displays Tezuka's idea notebook from his early period, showing a playful catalogue of his fictional "stars." Figure 4.2 shows one of his leading actresses, Micchii, in various costumes. The accompanying bio gives a list of comics in which she has been featured. The text reads: "Her dedication to the roles is truly admirable. For instance, she maintained a very short haircut for a year to play a male part in *Metropolis*." Another page in this notebook shows a list of stars, their studio affiliation, and their fees (fig. 4.3). Fans and scholars have discussed, studied, and analyzed the Star System: There are books dedicated to certain stars, and the official Tezuka Osamu website allows fans to track their favorite stars' appearances through Tezuka's lifetime. This system, rich in intertextual references, becomes a challenging factor when introducing Tezuka's work outside Japan. For a new reader, encountering Tezuka's stars for the first time may be a confusing experience. Without prior knowledge of the Star System, a reader may simply dismiss the resemblance between two characters in two different works as a coincidence. They may call it a style, thinking "many of Tezuka's characters look the same."

Figure 4.1. Higeoyaji, one of Tezuka's oldest stars. © Tezuka Productions. Reproduced with permission.

Figure 4.2. Micchii, Tezuka's early leading lady. © Tezuka Productions. Reproduced with permission.

It is unlikely that the reader reads the two as the same character, and less likely that they know it is the same "star" playing two different characters.

In some instances, the Star System may induce more active bafflement for unfamiliar readers. A *Black Jack* episode called "Omae ga hannin da (You Are the Murderer)," starring Astro Boy, is a good example (fig. 4.4). In the scene, Astro Boy stabs himself, falls to the ground, and bleeds. The reader's first response may be: "What is Astro Boy doing in *Black Jack*?" The sequence is puzzling, not only because it is taken out of the context, but also because it seems to contradict everything we know about Astro Boy, a robot boy made of metal and plastic parts. Can a robot hurt himself with a knife? Can a robot bleed? Can a robot experience pain? When we examine the image more carefully, we find that Astro Boy looks a little different from his usual self: he has some loose hair around his spikes. His head also lacks the white "squares," indicating shininess, which we are used to seeing. These details seem to suggest that the boy in this image is *not* a robot made of metal and plastic, but a human boy whose

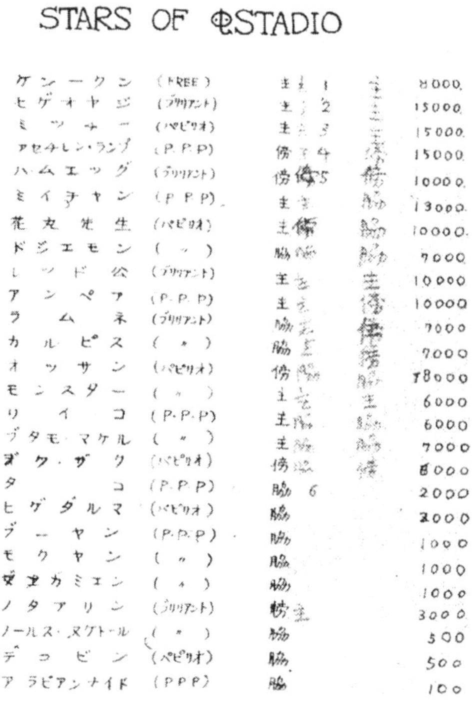

STARS OF φSTADIO

Figure 4.3. A chart showing the stars' affiliation and fees. © Tezuka Productions. Reproduced with permission.

head consists of real hair. Sweat is also visible on his face, though this could be symbolic—a robot cannot or does not need to sweat, but Astro Boy is sometimes seen "sweating" in the original *Astro Boy* series to indicate frustration or hard labor. Is this really Astro Boy or a human boy who happens to look like Astro Boy? Is his sweat real or symbolic? Having concluded that the boy is *not* a robot but a human boy, the reader's second question may be, why does the boy look identical to Astro Boy? Is this a "coincidence" that should be ignored? Or perhaps this is an inside joke. The answer is far more complicated and unlikely to present itself on its own: in this episode of *Black Jack*, Astro Boy is making a guest appearance, playing the character of a human boy with a costume and a wig—perhaps even with a bag of stage blood.

Other, less recognizable stars appear as characters in this episode of *Black Jack*. The robber is played by Bibimba, a villainous character in *Apollo's Song* (1970). The boy's brother looks identical to Hoshi Kōichi from *W 3* (*Amazing Three*, 1965). Astro Boy's classmates Shibugaki, Tamao, and Ken'ichi also make appearances as the boy's classmates. Among them, Ken'ichi is an *akahon*-era leading boy who starred in *New Treasure Island*, *Metropolis*, and numerous others. His appearance here in this episode of *Black Jack*, therefore, has double

Figure 4.4. Astro Boy's appearance in *Black Jack*. © Tezuka Productions. Reproduced with permission.

and triple layers of quotation. Major Bega (from *Noman*, 1968) plays the chief detective, joined by the team of Sasaki Kojirō and Columbo. Sasaki Kojirō was modeled after a legendary swordsman of the Edo period, Sasaki Kojirō; he first appeared in *Benkei*, 1954. Columbo is a straightforward tribute to Detective Columbo of the American crime fiction TV series. Tezuka's Columbo plays minor roles in several works, including a schoolteacher in *Mitsume ga tōru* (*The Three-Eyed One*, 1974–1978). The list goes on. Of course, few readers are capable of immediately identifying these characters. Even so, the resemblance may strike them as vaguely familiar, the way we may recognize the "guy who always plays a terrorist in Hollywood action movies" or "the blonde girl who comes on *Law and Order* every now and then."

One of the effects of Tezuka's Star System is that it creates an implicit framing device in all of his works, that the characters are "roles" that are being "performed." Tezuka's readers are aware (if subconsciously) that the image of Tezuka's star is only "standing in" for the character. This is similar to the way that theater and film audiences know that the character we see on stage or on screen (e.g., Hamlet, Indiana Jones) is a representation. Neither Sean Connery nor Daniel Craig *is* Agent 007 James Bond, but they both *represent* the character. The image of a character in Tezuka's comics is split into two entities: character in the given narrative; performer/star who embodies the character. The relationship between the two is complex, both independent and interdependent. The physical appearance of a character is determined by the appearance of the star who is selected to play the part, since, like a character in a film or a play, a comic book character has no material existence. Because a reader is encountering the story for the first time, and because few readers would be likely to entertain the idea that the story could be cast differently, the image of the star is instantly accepted as the definitive image of the character. This is similar to how casting works in film: "In most films, [. . .] there is a fairly unproblematic fit between (the actor and the character), largely because the character, being fictional, has no existence outside of the actor's body" (DeCordova 119). Still, "casting" in comics is very different from casting in films or plays. While an actor in a film has a material body in time and space, Tezuka's stars are fictional, no more "real" than his characters. A character in a film or a play (James Bond, King Lear, Antigone) has no fixed appearance and may be portrayed by many different actors; Tezuka's star, once cast, becomes the definitive image of the character.

Tezuka often used the term *engi* (performance, acting) in his idea notebooks, a term generally reserved for embodied performance in plays and films. This not only gives us a framework through which we may perceive his comics, but it also gives us a glimpse of how Tezuka perceived acting. As absorbing as the comics may be, the stars' relationship to the audience (reader) remains detached. As Brecht described acting in theater, "The actor does not allow himself to become completely transformed on the stage into the character he is portraying. He is not Lear, Harpagon, Schweik; he *shows* them" (Brecht 137). In Astro Boy's performance in *Black Jack*, the character's recognizable features as Astro Boy never escape the readers' perception. In each panel, Astro Boy presents a double image, of himself as Astro Boy and of a character whom he embodies. In this way, even the original *Astro Boy* series rests on this double image: Astro Boy is an actor who plays himself in the series. The relationship between Astro Boy (star) and Astro Boy (role) may be similar to that of people appearing "as themselves" in fictional films or plays, such as the appearance of the film director Ken Russel as "himself" in the 2005 independent film *Brothers of the Head* or the members of the Beatles in *A Hard Day's Night*. The "acting" framework of the Star System changes, among other things, how a character's death is perceived. In Tezuka's comics, the death of a character is always "enacted." In the death scene of a character, the star does not die—even when the star is playing "himself" or "herself"—he or she simply "shows" the death. This does not mean that the Star System dilutes the emotional experience of the reader in any way, but it characterizes the experience as theatrical: it is the excellence of the actor's performance, rather than the illusion that they are witnessing an actual death, that moves them.

I have referred to Tezuka's stars as "actors" as well as "stars," but those two terms are not mutually interchangeable. As Jeremy Butler puts it, "All [. . .] stars are actors, but not all actors are stars" (11). Film theorists seem to agree that what distinguishes a star from an actor is not charisma or fame, but the interactive and intertextual nature of the performer's relationship to the role. In a definition provided by John Ellis, a star is a "performer in a particular medium whose figure enters into subsidiary forms of circulation and then feeds back into future performances" (Ellis 303). Not only their appearances, but also their previous roles, previous awards, interviews, photographs, even gossip about their private lives are intertextual with the dramatic character in the film, producing a particular stage figure. Edgar Morin defines a film star as follows: "The star is not only an actress. The characters she plays are not only characters. The characters of her films infect the star. Reciprocally, the star herself infects these characters [. . .] *from their union is born a composite creature who participates in both, envelops them both: the star*" (Morin 37–39, emphasis original).

Like film stars, Tezuka's fictional stars bring into their roles a great deal of intertextual information. Tezuka's stars have their signature habits, facial expressions, or speech patterns, as do film stars. In Tezuka's comics, such preestablished persona allow for faster and more complex character development than the pages allow. Again, this only works fully when the reader is already familiar with the stars and their appearances in other works. The Star System is in a way an exclusive system, only available to those who have had access to Tezuka's other comics. At the same time, it is also a system that encourages a strong fan culture and a sense of community.

Past roles of a particular film star enter and enhance our film consumption, shaping the star's identity and our knowledge of their relationships with the world in and outside of cinema:

If we do not see Brando's Stanley more than once, we see him again in his Terry Molloy, and even in his Fletcher Christian. Garland walks down the yellow-brick road and then back down it year after year, in Saint Louis, in the Easter Parade, and most unnervingly, in the Nuremberg courtroom. Lillian Gish and Lionel Barrymore are sweethearts in *Just Gold* (1913), a Griffith one-reeler; when they face each other thirty-four years later, in *Duel in the Sun*, the history of the movies reverberates behind them. (Affron 97)

Similarly, Tezuka's stars carry with them the history of their past roles, or Tezuka's works at large. Astro Boy brings with him the innocence and the wholesomeness of the robot boy. The image of him as an innocent robot child permeates the scene in *Black Jack*, creating multiple levels of self-referential commentaries. In the original comic book *Astro Boy*, Dr. Tenma constructs Astro Boy as a replacement for his dead son, only to abuse and abandon him upon realization that Astro Boy cannot grow like a human boy. When Astro Boy stabs himself in the episode of *Black Jack*, he bleeds human blood and feels the pain that he could not feel as a robot. The scene strikes us as doubly poignant, for we are aware of Astro Boy's previous pain of not being human, of not being able to feel human pain. On a different level, the scene makes us reflect on the shift of manga from an optimistic "child's fare" in the early 1950s into a broader medium that appeals to older generations, with more graphic, and sometimes violent or controversial content.

One of the most interesting case studies in Tezuka's Star System is Rock Home, named after Sherlock Holmes (fig. 4.5). Rock made his debut in *Shonen tantei Rock Home* (*Little Detective Rock Home*) in 1949 and soon became a regular star, playing a number of leading and supporting roles. He was slightly less wholesome than Ken'ichi, the other "leading boy" during this period: Rock was sometimes mischievous, jealous, or scheming. In *Kitaru beki sekai* (*Next World*, 1951), Rock plays a young son of a newspaper tycoon. He starts out as a sweet, innocent boy and an aspiring journalist, but his fate starts to change

Figure 4.5. Rock Home as a young boy. © Tezuka Productions. Reproduced with permission.

when he is imprisoned for a length of time. He turns bitter and violent from the emotional trauma, acting hostilely to other characters. Still, Rock, in Tezuka's words, remained "unimpressionable, rather bland and un-charismatic" during his early career. Rock finally had his big break in 1966, when Tezuka cast him as a relentlessly cold-hearted villain in *The Vampire* (Fig. 4.6). In this series, he played a character named Makube Rokurō, a pun on *Macbeth*. Rock's stage figure in this series is smart, dangerous, intelligent, cruel, smartly dressed (though he kept the same tie), and, for the first time, highly charismatic. Inspired by the prophesy of three fortunetellers, Rock domesticates half-human, half-animal creatures called vampires—though they are more like werewolves—and plans to take over the world. When vampires assume their animal shapes, they possess the fierce instinct of predatory animal combined with the intelligence of human.

Figure 4.6. Rock Home as a villain in *The Vampires*. © Tezuka Productions. Reproduced with permission.

According to Tezuka's autobiography, Tezuka received a number of passionate fan letters from young women, addressed to Rock. Some letters compared him to the French film star Alain Delon, popular among young Japanese women at the time (Tezuka, *Boku wa* 106). After *The Vampire*, Rock specialized in dark, complex roles, such as the young commander in *Hi no Tori: Mirai hen* (*Phoenix: Chapter of the Future*, 1967) and an exorcist on a mission to exterminate werewolves, who turns out to be a werewolf himself in *Wobbit* (1976). His darkest role was probably the young FBI agent in *Alabaster* (1970). Rock's character in this series is unremittingly narcissist, racist, and sadist; upon his very first appearance in the series, he describes the Japanese people—or any race other than his own (he is descried as an American of Greek decent)—as ugly and repulsive. Later, he is depicted in his hotel room adoring his own naked body in the mirror. At one point of the story, Rock rapes the series' heroine, Ami. He subsequently tortures her by covering her with oil paint. There is nothing empathetic or redeeming about Rock's character in this work. What keeps this character from being one-dimensional is the history of Rock's earlier performances. The readers' preexisting attachment to him as a Star makes his *performance*, not his *character*, perversely alluring at times.

    In the recent animation film *Metropolis* (2001) based on Tezuka's 1949 comic book, Rock appears as the adopted son of the evil Duke Red. Rock adores and respects his adopted father, though Duke Red is anything but affectionate to Rock, refusing to be called "father." Instead, Duke Red commissions a scientist to create an android girl, Tima, who resembles his lost daughter. Driven by jealousy, Rock takes on the mission of destroying Tima, persistently pursuing her throughout the multileveled city of Metropolis. In the end, Rock's scheme culminates in the complete destruction of the city. Rock's appearance in this film was a choice made not by Tezuka but by the filmmakers of the 2001 movie, since Rock does not appear in the original comic book version of *Metropolis*. Furthermore, the comic book *Metropolis* predates Rock's "villain debut" in 1966; if he had appeared in the original comic book, he would have had a very different role. Other stars that appear in this film include not only the "regulars" such as Higeoyaji and Ken'ichi, but also Pero, originally a character from an *Astro Boy* episode, "The Hot Dog Corps." Again, this character did not exist in the original, since the comic book *Metropolis* predates the character of Pero by at least twelve years. When the audiences see *Metropolis*, they associate Rock with all of his past roles, from the boyish smiles in his early appearances to his astounding performance in *The Vampires*. Rock's previous career somehow rationalizes and complicates what seems to be a poorly motivated or one-dimensional character in *Metropolis*. By Rock's appearance—as well as other Stars'—this film becomes not so much a straightforward adaptation of the original comic, but a tribute to Tezuka's entire body of work. Tezuka, who died in 1989, was not involved in the making of this film. Still, the film captures Rock's public image, repeating it with revisions and commentaries that continue to transform and enrich Rock's career as a star.

Along with the Star System, another element that creates a sense of a coherent "world" that bridges all of Tezuka's works is his frequent use of visual jokes. The jokes often puzzle new readers, perhaps much more so than the Star System. In a moment of great emotional and narrative tension, a pig-like, mushroom-like creature appears in the panel, emitting gas and/or bouncing around, with no explanation (Fig. 4.7); or, a small, one-armed man with a long nose suddenly appears and tells the character "*Omukae de gonsu* (I have come to fetch you)" (Fig. 4.8). Other characters sometimes react to the jokes; other times, they do not. Either way, in most cases, the story quickly reverts back in the next panel, as if nothing had happened. Tezuka's repertoire of recurrent jokes intersects closely with his Star System, operating under a similar mechanism.

A quick skim through any of Tezuka's work will grant at least a few variations of such jokes. Here is a typical example from one of the earlier *Black Jack* episodes called "Miyuki to Ben (Miyuki and Ben)." A delinquent teenager, Ben (played by Hyakkimaru, who debuted in *Dororo*), falls in love with a young

Figure 4.7. Hyōtantsugi. © Tezuka Productions. Reproduced with permission.

woman named Miyuki, who is in a hospital. One day, Ben asks Miyuki's doctor what her illness is. The doctor (Dr. Hanamura, one of Tezuka's regular stars) tells him, "It's cancer." Figure 4.9 is the panel immediately following the diagnosis: Ben's face turns into a bizarre pig-mushroom creature, as the caption reads: "*Gān!* (word for cancer, also a common expression of shock)."

There are two levels of jokes in this sequence, one verbal and the other visual. The verbal joke is a linguistic one, which plays on the word "cancer" (*gan*) and a colloquial exclamation, "*Gān!*" Though the precise origin of this slang is unknown, it became popular after the post–World War II period and is still commonly used to indicate shock. Considered somewhat crass, the expression is most often used in comedic routines or gag comics, or among teenagers and college students, but almost never used in "serious" situations. The visual joke is more specific to Tezuka's work. Tezuka's fans would instantly identify Ben's face in this panel as that of Hyōtantsugi, one of Tezuka's popular stars, who is known to appear at moments of great tension like this one (see fig. 4.7). It is a creature (?) that has a plump, calabash-shaped head and a piglike nose, and has patches like old clothes that have been mended. The origin of this strange star dates back to Tezuka's childhood. Tezuka, having seen a strange creature doodled on his young sister's notebook, asked her what it was. His sister then told him that it was a kind of mushroom that emits gas when disturbed; it is edible and particularly delicious in soups. Hyōtantsugi is undoubtedly Tezuka's best-known example of visual jokes as well as being one of his most popular stars. There is no shortage of Hyōtantsugi merchandise in the market, ranging from a T-shirt to a cell phone charm.

Figure 4.8. Supaidā a.k.a. Omukaedegonsu. ©
Tezuka Productions. Reproduced with permission.

Hyōtantsugi appears at least once in nearly all of Tezuka's works in some form or another. Most often, Hyōtantsugi is seen growing on the ground, sometimes in groups. A small Hyōtantsugi may grow out of a larger "parent" Hyōtantsugi. It is also common for a character's face to turn into a Hyōtantsugi at a moment of heightened emotion, as in the example of the scene with Ben. It also falls from the sky, either alone or in large quantities like hail. Hyōtantsugi sometimes inserts a commentary on a scene in the manner reminiscent of *rakugo*, a Japanese comedy form that involves a solo performer seated on a cushion on the floor. In such instances, it grows an arm to hold a paper fan (the only prop used in *rakugo* performance). Though Hyōtantsugi almost never has a role larger than a cameo, it can play an important role with the narrative. Near the end of *Buddha* (1972–1983), a man named Chunda serves supper to Budda and his followers. When Buddha asks what he is eating, Chunda tells him that it is a kind of mushroom called Hyōtantsugi, a regional specialty, adding: "You may not like it if you don't like comics" (*Buddha* Vol. 14, 200). Buddha enjoys the dish, but starts to suffer from a stomachache the next day. He eventually dies of food poisoning. Hyōtantsugi generally does not speak, except in rare occasions. Hyōtantsugi also serves as the main character in Tezuka's little-known science fiction novella, *Yōjintan* (1976).

In addition to Hyōtantsugi, Tezuka had a few other stars for the purposes of recurring visual jokes. Among them, Supaidā (Spider), or Omukaedegonsu, is nearly as popular as Hyōtantsugi. He is a small man, usually seen in profile, who appears from nowhere and says: "*Omukae de gonsu* (I've come to fetch you)" (Fig. 4.8). His appearances can sometimes be justified—he is actually coming to get someone—but it is usually entirely out of context. The joke is not in the phrase (*Omukae de gonsu*), nor his physical appearance, but in the reader's recognition. Other jokes/stars, though significantly less common,

Figure 4.9. Ben's face turns into Hyōtantsugi in *Black Jack*. © Tezuka Productions. Reproduced with permission.

include a variety of equally bizarre creatures. Bukutsugikyu is an organism that is supposedly related to Hyōtantsugi, though the only resemblance is the patches on their bodies. Bukutsugikyu has a long neck and a more mammal-like body, with short limbs underneath. It has also been described to resemble a cart of a roasted sweet potato vendor, commonly seen in Japanese cities in winter during mid-twentieth century. Butanagi is a creature that sticks to the side of the comic panel like a pupa, and emits an annoying laugh until it deflates and dies. Shimofuri mamā, a one-eyed organism with a round head and a tapered body, is an unusual example: though its appearances were rare, it later rose to a new status as a supporting character in *Nanairo Inko* (1981–1982) as the protagonist's alter ego, named Honne (honest thoughts). All of these characters, like Hyōtantsugi, are believed to be childhood inventions of Tezuka's younger sister.

Tezuka's jokes almost always occur at moments of emotional or narrative tension. The jokes take the readers abruptly out of their absorption and into a more self-conscious mode of reading, highly aware of the construction of the comics medium. This pattern of constant interruption seems incongruous to Tezuka's self-claimed goal of creating a more cinematic, dynamic, absorbing comics. Natsume Fusanosuke explains that the jokes are Tezuka's way of expressing his shyness or embarrassment for taking himself too seriously (Natsume, *Tezuka Osamu wa dokoni iru* 66). Matthew Thorn suggests that "Tezuka may have seen 'low brow' humor as an essential element of the comic medium" (Thorn 9). But are there other explanations? Can the jokes have greater function other than lowbrow humor?

One of the frameworks through which we may understand Tezuka's disruptive jokes is *theatricality*—an idea whose exact definition is up to debate, but which can at least be characterized as "not likely to be present when the performance is so absorbing that the audience forgets that it is spectating" (Davis 128). While the constant disruption of the narrative may seem foreign to the comics medium, it is not an unusual practice in live theater. A number of theater practitioners have incorporated disruption and deconstruction of the "suspension of disbelief" as their signature styles, believing it to be a more sophisticated mode of audience-performance relationship. Bertolt Brecht claimed that the effect of alienation, achieved through techniques such as placards, songs, or an aside by the actors out of character and in third person, would take the audiences out of their emotional absorption and into a more alert mental state, driven by reason not emotion. The distancing of the audience is not a phenomenon unique to a specific mode of theater such as Brecht's, but a mechanism that is common in all theatrical forms. Anne Ubersfeld characterizes theater as a paradoxical art, whose largest paradox is simultaneous absorption and distancing of the audience. The audience is constantly aware of the framework of fiction, at the same time being emotionally responsive to the events on stage.

As an avid theatergoer and an amateur actor, it is not surprising that Tezuka would have been familiar with this mode of viewing. The distance between the audience and theatrical events, mediated through the physical constraints of the theater, does not interfere with our ability to empathize, but rather, it allows us to indulge in a deeper, safer mode of identification. The following passage by Daphna Ben Chaim on theatrical spectatorship seems uncannily descriptive of the effect of visual jokes and the Star System in Tezuka's work:

Our involvement as audience members—the reason why we weep—is an involvement of a special sort. We may cry when Desdemona is smothered to death, but we do not run onstage to save her. We may be shocked when the Duchess of Malfi is presented with what she thinks are dead bodies of her husband and children, yet we perceive ironies, images and thematic implications of the scene which she, were she a real human being, probably could not. Our engagement during the theatrical experience may be intense, but it is not the kind of engagement that occurs in life experience. The difference is a function of distance. (Ben Chaim ix)

The Star System reminds the audience of the framework of fiction, reassuring them that they can safely identify with the characters and events, and the visual jokes jolt the audience out of their emotional absorption into a critical, self-conscious mode of viewing.

Another important effect achieved by Tezuka's visual jokes is intertextuality. Tezuka's jokes are similar to what Oring calls "dyadic jokes," jokes that are repeatedly performed between persons in intimate relationships. Dyadic jokes are often based on shared experiences and are generally not funny or coherent to others. A married couple may have a long running joke about a funny mishap at their wedding; a theater company's members may have jokes about past disastrous productions. Similarly, Tezuka uses jokes as a way of sharing or building intimacy on multiple levels. In the simplest sense, every appearance of Hyōtantsugi (or Supaidā) is a dyadic joke between him and the readers, a familiar image that they have shared before, and continue to share. The origin of the jokes—his sister's childhood drawings—makes this exchange even more intimate, as every reader gets a glimpse of Tezuka's childhood. Jokes also become a common language among fans and readers. By recognizing them, discussing them, quoting them, and wearing them (in the form of character merchandise), fans signal to each other that they belong to the same community, brought together by Tezuka's work.

The Star System and the visual jokes are mutually dependent, complex, obsession-inducing structures, both inclusive and exclusive. They easily allow new readers to enter its complexity (after all, the knowledge of the stars is not necessary in order to comprehend the narrative), and at the same time, they give experienced readers a sense of privilege for picking up subtle, numerous intertexts and familiar bits. The more you read, the more references you pick up. The set-up is ideal for encouraging strong fan culture and expanding readership. Jokes and stars start to take on lives of their own, living imagined lives between pages and volumes of printed comic books.

Craig Yoe's *Weird but True Toon Factoids!* repeats the bit of trivia that "the artists who drew Captain Marvel in the 1940s were forbidden to sign their work," so as not to destroy the illusion of the readers who believed that the superhero was real (116). If this is true, children believed (or so the publishers assumed) that the events in the comic books *actually* took place, as did World War II or the assassination of JFK. This is not as far-fetched as one may think, considering that all supposedly "real" historical events are also only "narrated" to us in some form of representation. That is, children may not be able to distinguish between "true" and "false" events unless they experienced the events themselves. Compared to this model, Tezuka's readers suspend a different kind of disbelief: they believe that the stars, not the *characters*, exist—but still in a world different from their own. They understand that the stories did not *actually* take place, but that they are *actually acted out*. They accept that the *characters* are not real but constructed. Through this acceptance, ironically, the *stars* become more real than ever. Tezuka's stars are just as *real* as Greta Garbo, the Beatles, or Osama bin Laden—on the one hand, their existence is as solid as our own; on the other, they live in a world completely separate from most of us. Still, through every representation, their images grow just as familiar and intimate to us as our next-door neighbor.

To close this chapter on stars and jokes, there is not a more ideal case study than TEZUKA OSAMU, a star modeled after Tezuka himself (fig. 4.10).[1] TEZUKA bares clear resemblance to the author Tezuka, both in appearance and personality: TEZUKA has a round face and a large, round nose. He wears a beret and thick glasses, without which he is practically blind. He is temperamental, impulsive, and single-minded, and at the same time a workaholic and a

---

1. Here I am using capital letters to distinguish the star TEZUKA OSAMU from the author Tezuka Osamu.

Figure 4.10. TEZUKA OSAMU, one of Tezuka's regular stars. © Tezuka Productions. Reproduced with permission.

procrastinator. It is difficult to define TEZUKA's relationship to Tezuka, since it has no equivalence in works of other cartoonists or even artists in other media. At first glance, TEZUKA's appearance seems to be an extensive version of the use of the author as character in autobiographical comics, which is common in graphic novels. We become familiar with Chris Ware and Lynda Barry as characters as well as authors; Fujiko Fujio A's *Manga michi* features two boys, Maga Michio and Saino Shigeru, who clearly represent the author and his long-time collaborator, Fujiko F. Fujio. What is different about Tezuka's use of TEZUKA is that he appears not only in autobiographies, but also in stories that clearly have nothing to do with "actual events." TEZUKA plays various roles in science fiction, mystery, and adventure. TEZUKA's appearances are sometimes compared to Alfred Hitchcock's cameo appearances in his films. Unlike Hitchcock, however, TEZUKA's appearances are not restricted to cameo, but are often leading or major supporting characters.

TEZUKA first appeared in the role of the author/cartoonist in *Kiseki no mori no monogatari (Story of the Miracle Forest* 1949), and he played a variety of roles in the following years. Most often, he appears as the author/artist, providing comic relief: in *Seinaru hiroba no monogatari (The Sacred Plaza*, 1976), "readers" abruptly appear and complain that they do not want to read a story about birds. TEZUKA, hearing this complaint, redraws all the characters. For a few pages thereafter, all the characters—previously a family of birds—are drawn as people, a family in a suburban home. Eventually, the kids go to sleep and the couple gets into a quarrel. The husband tells his wife: "Shut up and sit on your eggs!" In the next panel, the wife sits on her eggs. Readers reappear and complain that the story now makes no sense. TEZUKA reverts all the characters back into birds.

One of TEZUKA's recurring roles is Ōsamu Tetsurō, Tezuka's alter ego appearing in a number of autobiographical works, including *Kami no Toride (The Fort of Paper*, 1974), *Sukippara no blues (Hungry Blues*, 1975), and *Mako to rumi to chii (Mako, Rumi, and Chii*, 1981). By naming this character Ōsamu Tetsurō instead of Tezuka Osamu, and casting TEZUKA in the role, Tezuka keeps it ambiguous as to what extent the story is based on actual events. There is a clear distinction between Ōsamu Tetsurō (character) and TEZUKA (star): Ōsamu Tetsurō is always portrayed by TEZUKA, but TEZUKA appears in a variety of other roles in many comics. *Fort of Paper* takes place in Takarazuka city toward the end of World War II. Tetsurō, a young student, falls in love with a beautiful girl named Kyōko, who is enrolled in Takarazuka Music Academy. When Tetsuro shows his comics and talks about becoming a cartoonist, Kyōko shares her own dream of becoming an opera singer. *Hungry Blues* and *Dotsuitare* (1979) cover events during the immediate post–World War II period. *Mako, Rumi, and Chi* depicts Ōsamu Tetsuro's family life, with characters clearly modeled after Tezuka, his wife, and their three children. Sometimes, works that are less likely to have anything to do with actual events gain autobiographical frameworks through TEZUKA's performance. In *Godfather no musuko (Godfather's Son*, 1973), TEZUKA plays a middle school boy who befriends the son of a *yakuza* (Japanese mafia) family; in *Monmon yama ga naiteru yo (Mt. Monmon Is Weeping*, 1979), TEZUKA plays a grade school student named Shigeru, who befriends a mysterious man who may or may not be the spirit of a white snake disguised as human. In the *Shin ryōsai shii* series (1971), Tezuka frames each episode with a short sequence in which the author/character interviews someone about a supernatural phenomenon.

The Vampires, which earned Rock his status as a charismatic villain, was also a breakthrough for TEZUKA. He appears in the role of a cartoonist, *Tezuka Osamu*, though the story has nothing to do with actual events.[2] Unlike in earlier works, Tezuka makes it very clear that *Tezuka* is a character distinctly separate from the author. Though *Tezuka* seems uncannily similar to the public image of Tezuka, he has no power to manipulate the narrative he is in. This is quickly established in *Tezuka*'s first appearance in figure 4.10: in the scene, Toppei, a teenager from a remote village, comes to Mushi Productions and asks to become his assistant. *Tezuka*, flustered by this unexpected visitor, tells his wife to bring him some water. The wife immediately appears, carrying a glass of water on her head: she is a very large, monstrous-looking woman with hairy legs. *Tezuka* exclaims, "This is outlandish! My wife is better looking than this!" and falls down to weep. In the next panel, she is depicted as a more generic-looking, middle-aged woman. This joke works to distinguish the character *Tezuka* from the author Tezuka: instead of redrawing his wife himself, *Tezuka* has to call to some other entity (the author Tezuka) to transform his wife's appearance. *Tezuka*'s lack of power in manipulating the narrative (unlike the author in *The Sacred Plaza*) is most significant in the scene of his death. Halfway through the story, Rock kills *Tezuka* by running him off a cliff in a car. Though *Tezuka* later turns out to be alive and comes back to the story, readers (as well as other characters) are led to believe that *Tezuka* has been killed. Tezuka uses similar premises in a number of other works, casting TEZUKA as a cartoonist identical to, but separate from, Tezuka himself. In the "Tomoe no men (Mask of Tomoe, 1970)" episode in *The Crater*, TEZUKA plays a cartoonist/designer who is commissioned to design a scary mask, but who is killed by the possessed mask that the commissioner has brought as a model; in *Thunder Mask*, 1973, *Tezuka Osamu* becomes involved in a battle between two outer-space gaseous creatures, Thunder and Decandar, on his way back from the Science Fiction Convention in Osaka.

TEZUKA's acting style transforms in his recurring appearances in *Black Jack*. In this work, TEZUKA plays not a cartoonist but a doctor, a friend of Black Jack's. *Dr. Tezuka* occasionally calls Black Jack for help and advice with his patients. He could be a pediatrics physician, for most of the patient he deals with seem to be children: in "Kaizoku no ude (A Pirate's Arm)," he asks Black Jack to encourage a middle school student who lost his hand; in "Misshitsu no shonen (Boy in a Locked Room)," he asks Black Jack's help with a young patient who destroys surgical instruments with his psychokinetic ability. Unlike his earlier,

---

2. Here I am using italics to distinguish the character Tezuka Osamu from the star TEZUKA OSAMU and the author Tezuka Osamu.

slapstick performances (e.g., *The Vampires, Thunder Mask*), TEZUKA uses restrained facial expressions and subtler gestures to play *Dr. Tezuka*.

In a way, TEZUKA truly earned his status as a star in *Black Jack. Dr. Tezuka* stands alone as a character, without direct reference to cartoonist Tezuka, and with absolutely no sense of authorship. The only thing that possibly connects *Dr. Tezuka* to Tezuka, aside from their physical resemblance, is the readers' knowledge that Tezuka was also a medical doctor. Having played numerous other roles in earlier works—being chased by Rock and a herd of vampires, saving the earth from the evil hands of Decandar, and surviving fierce air raids in Osaka—readers have come to accept TEZUKA as an entity separate from (though clearly connected to) Tezuka, a familiar face they are accustomed to see in his comics.

TEZUKA's last major role was as Tezuka Ryōsen in *Hidamari no ki* (*Tree in the Sun*), Tezuka's own great-great-grandfather and the father of the protagonist, Ryōan. This is perhaps his most challenging role in his career. Ryōsen is an aging but vivacious man who pours his heart and soul into his profession, practicing progressive medical techniques; he plays a key role in starting a clinic that vaccinates people against cholera. Ryōsen is also a fun-loving womanizer, who loves to drink and spend time with *geisha*. His death is perhaps one of the most poignant scenes in the series. After an episode of stroke, Ryōsen has significantly weakened, both physically and mentally. When his family members gather around his deathbed, Ryōsen does not understand that he is dying. His last words are: "Ryōan, call in the *geisha*. Call Ponta, and Momiji Dayū. Don't let your mother know. Call Fujima Dayū too. She is a good girl. Good girl . . ." Some may contest that this character is separate from TEZUKA, because of the stylistic difference between this character's design and TEZUKA's usual appearance. However, Tezuka has often changed stars' appearances to suit the style of any given work in the past (Acetylene Lamp looks different in *Adolf* than he did in *The Lost World*, for instance). In my interpretation, Ryōsen's unmistakable likeness to the author Tezuka indicates that this character is being embodied by TEZUKA.

Tezuka did not have an entry for TEZUKA in the catalogue of stars in his idea notebook, but if he had written one at the end of his career, it may have looked like this:

TEZUKA OSAMU. Perhaps one of the most versatile talent in the studio. He debuted in *Kiseki no mori no monogatari* in 1949, and played numerous roles throughout his forty-year career. In his memorable early cameos, he provided important comic relief and introduced self-conscious humor to the narrative. His slapstick, comic acting talent is showcased in *Vampires* and *Thunder Mask*, but he is also adept at more subtle, heartfelt acting as seen in *Fort of Paper* and *Black Jack*. He is capable of performing in roles that range from age ten (Shigeru in *Mon mon Mountain Is Crying*) to seventy (Tezuka Ryōsen in *Tree in the Sun*). His performance as Ryōsen is undoubtedly worthy of an Academy Award: he shaved his head to portray this bald man, and lost at least ten kilos to play the death scene, which reduced even the most cynical audience members to tears.

Chapter 5

COMMUNITIES AND COMPETITIONS

It is well known that Fujiko Fujio, one of the most accomplished cartoonists of twentieth-century Japan, was "discovered" by Tezuka Osamu. Fujiko Fujio is a pseudonym shared between two artists, Abiko Motoo and Fujimono Hiroshi, who met in fifth grade and became best friends. They worked under one pseudonym until 1988. Their styles were so similar that most people could not distinguish one from the other; some thought they were one person. As high school students, Abiko and Fujimoto often sent fan letters to Tezuka, enclosing their comic manuscripts—originals, since Xerox machines were not invented yet. Tezuka recognized their talent and invited them for a visit at his Takarazuka home in 1951. Fujiko Fujio A (Abiko) later narrated the experience of meeting Tezuka in his autobiographical work, *Manga michi* (*The Way of Manga*, 1970–). In the scene in figure 5.1, two boys Maga Michio and Saino Shigeru arrive at Tezuka's family home in Takarazuka and are shown into the living room by Tezuka's mother. When Tezuka enters the room, the two boys jump off the couch and scream, "Wahhh, Mr. Tezuka!!" In the next panel, Tezuka is depicted as a godlike glowing figure, with the galaxy in the background. The narration reads: "This . . . this is the real Tezuka Osamu! Tezuka Osamu is now in front of us! [The two boys] froze, unable to move, as if their bodies had been struck by electricity!!" (Fujiko 236–37). Tezuka was only twenty-three years old when this event took place.

By the early 1950s, Tezuka was the most popular cartoonist in Japan, as well as one of the highest-earning artists. Tezuka's innovations and popularity inspired a large number of young people throughout Japan, making "cartoonist" a popular career dream for young children. Maruyama Akira, who served as

Figure 5.1. Tezuka Osamu appears as a character in Fujiko Fujio A's *Manga Michi*. © Fujiko Fujio. Reproduced with permission.

one of the editors of *Shonen Club*, recalls this period as a time when "one out of three people had dreamed of becoming a cartoonist at least once" (Maruyama 60). During this time, it became a common practice for aspiring cartoonists to bring their manuscripts to Tezuka. Some of them "stalked" Tezuka, showing up at his house or at hotels. Many others sent fan letters, enclosing their own comics. Tezuka sometimes approached those young artists to help him with his work. With monthly deadlines for numerous magazines, Tezuka was always in need of skilled assistants. Young artists considered it an honor to help the great master, working with little or no pay. Working for Tezuka also opened gateways for their careers. Tezuka introduced them to publishers and editors, who subsequently offered the young cartoonists their own series. This resulted in a great burst of new talents in Tokyo.

The apartment building Tokiwa-sō, where Tezuka lived during his first year in Tokyo, transformed into a commune of emerging cartoonists in the ensuing years. Terada Hiroo was the first to join Tezuka in 1953, and Fujiko Fujio moved into Tezuka's old room when Tezuka left in 1954. Ishinomori Shōtarō joined in 1956 shortly after finishing high school and moving to Tokyo, staying until 1961 after all the others had left. At one point, Tokiwa-sō served as the home for more than ten emerging cartoonists, with several other "commuters" who frequented the building. The residents (and the commuters) of Tokiwa-sō often collaborated on comics, held critique sessions, played sports together, and made home movies. The artists in the group, commonly referred to as the "Tokiwa-sō group," built on Tezuka's foundation and established long, narrative story comics—manga as we know it today—as a solid genre.

A large number of young cartoonists converging on Tokyo brought about the emergence of several other young cartoonists' communities, modeled after Tokiwa-sō. These groups include the Taiyō-kan group and the Yamagoe-kan group, centered around a hotel (Taiyō-kan) and an apartment building (Yamagoe-kan). The publishers during this period often "kidnapped" cartoonists and locked them into hotel rooms as a way to ensure that they adhere to the deadline. This common practice was called *kan-zume*, a word usually meaning "canned food," but here jokingly used to refer to "locked into a 'kan' ("house" or "residence," a common suffix for apartment and hotel buildings)." Taiyō-kan group included cartoonists who were frequently brought to Taiyō-kan for *kan-zume*. A number of cartoonists recall the experiences of *kan-zume* as intensely laborious but also invigorating, "like a school field trip": "After we finished our own work, we helped each other. When everyone was done, we would go out together, even after having stayed up all night. Our greatest pastime was going to the movies or to used bookstores" (Maki 71).

During his early years in Tokyo, Tezuka reworked some of his early *akahon* volumes. *Getsusekai shinshi* (*Gentleman from the Moon*, 1948) was revived into *Shinpen getsusekai shinshi* (*New Chapter: A Gentleman from the Moon*, 1951), and *Issennen go no sekai* (*The World One Thousand Years Later*, 1948) gained greater depth as two volumes, *Kaseki ningen* (*The Fossil Man*, February 1952) and *Kaseki ningen no gyakushū* (*The Return of the Fossil Man*, July 1952). Among them, *38 do senjō no kaibutsu* (*The Monster on the 38th Parallel*, 1953), based on *Kyūketsu madan* (*Vampire Devils*, 1947), is particularly revealing of Tezuka's increased sophistication and a shift in style. The two works have the same premise: Ken'ichi and his uncle Higeoyaji are "shrunken" into the size of viruses and sent into the body of another character; there, the uncle-and-nephew duo participate in the battle between the tuberculosis virus and white corpuscles. *The Monster on the 38th Parallel*, however, focuses more on the characters' relationships and psychological drama, rather than the adventure-battle. Inside the patient's lung, Higeoyaji and Ken'ichi meet Maude, a tuberculosis virus represented as a beautiful young woman. Ken'ichi and Maude quickly form a close friendship, tinged with innocently romantic overtones. Higeoyaji, Ken'ichi, and Maude are eventually captured by the white corpuscles, and taken to their headquarters, where they are shown documentary films about humans killed by tuberculosis. Maude argues that tuberculosis, though harmful to humans, also has the right to live. Tormented, Ken'ichi still decides to join the white corpuscles, defeating the tuberculosis in the end and returning to the human world. This sequence parodies the use of film as powerful propaganda, as in recent memory of Japan during World War II and the Allied Forces during the occupation period. This kind of depiction is characteristic of the era: the censorship by GHQ was lifted three years earlier in 1949, and the occupation of Japan officially ended in 1952. Writers and artists were now free to explore war memories without censorship. It also marks a shift in Tezuka's relationship to film, from complete absorption and glorification to more selective quotation and parody, a kind of "repetition with critical distance," which not only repeats the original but also inserts an ironic commentary (Hutcheon).

The Monster on the 38th Parallel contains one of the best-known examples of Tezuka's film quotation, taken from the famous ending of *The Third Man* (1949, Japan distribution 1952). The scene in figure 5.2 takes place just outside the white corpuscle headquarters in the patient's brain. The scene depicts Ken'ichi, after his decision to join the white corpuscle forces, noticing Maude walking toward him. Ken'ichi attempts to talk to her: "Maude-san" (panel 2), "Come back with me to the lungs" (panel 3), "You don't want to stay in a place like this either, do you?" (panel 4). Maude passes by, ignoring Ken'ichi. The scene is identical to the final scene of *The Third Man*, in which Holly Martins (Joseph Cotton) waits for Anna (Alida Valli), after the funeral of her lover Harry Lime (Orson Welles). Anna walks through the graveyard, without speaking to or even acknowledging Holly. Holly had betrayed his old friend Harry and reported him to the police, thinking that Harry's capture would prompt Anna to fall in love with him (fig. 5.3). Except for the mirroring of the image (Ken'ichi is seen on the left side of the frame while Holly is situated on the right), the two scenes are identically composed. The stern expression on Anna's face is repeated on Maude's. *The Monster on the 38th Parallel* is full of other, more obscure quotations from film. In the postscript, Tezuka lists the films he quoted, including Namiki Kyōtarō's period drama *Hirate Zōshu* (1951), Kurosawa Akira's *Ikiru* (1952), and Imai Tadashi's *Himeyuri no tō* (1953).

The Monster on the 38th Parallel, as well as other *akahon* revisions, were published in the format of *furoku* (magazine supplements). Boys' magazines during this period usually came with "supplements" which took the form of a cheaply made toy or a smaller, separate book, specifically called *bessatsu furoku*. *Bessatsu furoku* were similar to *akahon* but with no pressure to "sell," since the *furoku* automatically came with the magazines. *Furoku* allowed Tezuka to rework some of his *akahon* projects with his increased sophistication and later provided a venue for experimentation. Among them, a series of science fiction

Figure 5.2. A scene between Maude and Ken'ichi in *38 do senjō no kaibutsu* [*Monster on the 38th Parallel*]. © Tezuka Productions. Reproduced with permission.

shorts published as *Omoshiro Book*'s *bessatsu furoku* between the years 1956 and 1958 were particularly progressive. Though elements of science fiction had always been present in Tezuka's works, this series (called *Lion Books*) made use of a wider range of premises and themes that are popular in this genre even today. *Uchū kūkō* (*Space Airport*, 1957) features a horde of bizarre and whimsical space aliens, reminiscent of science fiction comedies new and old, such as the 1997 film *Men in Black*. *Kuroi uchūsen* (*The Black Space Ray*, 1956) makes a reference to Oscar Wilde's gothic horror through a character named Dorian Gray, who,

Figure 5.3. The final scene of *The Third Man*.

in this version, stays forever young through absorption of cosmic energy. *The Lion Books* series, though it never became a commercial success, won enthusiastic responses from a handful of sophisticated readers.

Following the change of venue from *akahon* to magazines, Tezuka's works diverged into many different directions. He introduced dramatic storytelling to *shojo manga* (girls' comics) in *Ribon no kishi* (*Princess Knight*, 1953), a genre previously considered trite and insignificant. He took on projects for younger children in the form of a picture book, *Awate Mimi-chan* (*Hasty Mimi-chan*, 1952) and *Boku no Songokū* (*Songoku the Monkey*, 1952), an adaptation of the Chinese epic *Journey to the West*, serialized in *Manga ō*, a magazine for young children. The force behind this was the diversification of the comics industry itself, or visual culture at large, prompted by the end of the GHQ censorship. Tōei Film Company released a number of hits during this period, marking the return of *chambara* (Japanese swordfight). Tezuka, too, undertook a few period dramas, including *Bōken kyō jidai* (*The Era of Adventure Madness*, 1951–1953), *Pisutoru o atama ni noseta hitobito* (*People with Pistols on their Heads*, 1952), and *Tange Sazen* (1954). As I mentioned earlier, the end of censorship also allowed writers to address, for the first time, the memory of World War II, or the problems of the postwar society. The opening scene of *Fukugan majin* (*Multiple-Eyed Devil*, 1957) takes place in 1945, during an air raid in Tokyo that blinds a boy's cornea. The boy, A-bō, is treated by a doctor who gives him an unusual ability to see the "truth" that others don't see. Five years later, the boy wears a mask and calls himself *Fukugan Majin* to fight the evil forces in society. The depiction of the air raid, as well as the boy's character as the physical and psychological victim of the war, is characteristic of the postcensorship Japan, and would have been censored a decade earlier.

The popular taste of the Japanese public also shifted from "modern and exotic" to "traditional and familiar" during this era. In 1952, the big hit among the magazine serials was not Tezuka's grand epic *Jungle Emperor*, but a more quotidian *Igaguri kun* by Fukui Eiichi, a story of an orphaned boy, Igaguri, who studies judo, a traditional Japanese martial art form. Using the cinematic use of perspective that he learned from Tezuka, Fukui mastered the format of magazine serials: each month, Igaguri fought against a new strong opponent, making each episode conducive to self-contained readership; in the meantime, long-term readers enjoyed Igaguri's development both as an athlete and as a young man, fostering friendship with his teammates and rivals. *Igaguri kun*'s popularity was only interrupted by Fukui's sudden death in 1954.

Though Tezuka remained one of the most successful cartoonists in Japan, keeping up with the changing trends and tastes was hard work. Competition in the comics industry became steeper by the month. New artists emerged, had a few hits, and disappeared. The most significant shift in the comics industry came in the late 1950s, when a group of artists formed a collective to launch a new form of manga that they called gekiga, literally "dramatic pictures." Harsher drawing style with broken lines and a lot of shading, as well as darker contents—most often crime narratives—characterized gekiga. Its target audience was older teenagers and young adults, the generation that had grown up with and out of *shonen* manga. In his autobiography, Tezuka described the historical background from which the trend of gekiga emerged: "The two-year period between 1955 and 1957 was a transitional time in the post-war history (of Japan) in many ways. [. . .] Unlike the unstable, unmotivated generation of the wartime and the immediate post-war period, the young people were driven to construct active new ways of living [. . .] It is only natural that manga during this period absorbed these influences" (Tezuka, *Boku wa manga ka* 163–64). Tezuka also described gekiga simply as "anti-manga-manga" (165). This new type of comics became increasingly popular, particularly through rental book-stores and numerous magazines such as *Kage* (*Shadow*). The artists who worked in this style called their work gekiga to distinguish it from manga, which had become synonymous with Tezuka-style *shonen* manga by this period. In 1958, a group of cartoonists sent out letters declaring the emergence of this new genre, gekiga, to their fellow cartoonists, publishers, and editors. The letter, titled "An Invitation to the Gekiga Factory," is cited in its entirety in Tezuka's auto-biography:

The world is in flux. Manga, which originated from Toba Sōjō, has evolved greatly. In the Shōwa era, it split into two genres, adult and children's manga. Furthermore, the adult manga genre further diverged like tree branches into subgenres with different directions, including political manga, fūzoku (porno-graphic) manga, katei (home) manga, story manga.

Likewise, children's comics diverged into many genres according to the target readers. The story manga genre, headed by Tezuka Osamu, developed quickly, raising the status of children's manga.

Recently, there has been a new trend in the world of the story manga, influenced by the advancement of media such as the film, television and radio.

This is gekiga.

The main difference between manga and gekiga is largely the target audience, though there are technical aspects as well. The reason why there has not been reading material for those who are in the transitional period between childhood and adulthood is that there has not been a venue for it. They are the target audience for gekiga. It is the *kashihon-ya* that will nurture this trend.

"Gekiga" is a new field to cultivate.

We ask for your understanding and support for Gekiga Kōbō. ("Invitation to Gekiga Kōbō," quoted in Tezuka, *Boku wa manga ka* 165)

The letter was signed by artists Saitō Takawo, Satō Masaki, Ishikawa Fumiyasu, Sakurai Masaichi, Tatsumi Yoshihiro, Yamamori Susumu, and K. Motomitsu. As the letter indicates, *kashihon-ya*, or rental bookstores, played an impor-tant role in popularizing gekiga. Rental bookstores came into existence during the Edo period and immediately became a popular venue among lower- and middle-class readers. Records indicate that there were 656 rental bookstores in and around Tokyo by the end of the eighteenth century; the number increased to more than 800 by 1944 (Kajii, *Sengo no kashihon* 98). They stayed in busi-ness during the Meiji, Taishō, and Shōwa periods, though the industry suffered during the war years from the lack of new books. Rental bookstores became popular again during the late 1940s, when they started catering mostly to children, with comics as the main attraction. Though these low-budget shops often obtained their merchandise in bulk from used bookstores, some publishers also manufactured books specifically for the rental market, printing their material on thicker, more durable paper to withstand greater circulation.

In 1959, Tezuka wrote a scathing critique of gekiga (though without naming it) in an essay called "To New Children's Manga Artists":

You have wound up writing comics for children. This is important work. Have you seriously considered just how important it is? If you have any idea [how important it is], you would not be writing anything you would not want to allow children to read. [. . .] You may say, "I am writing for older teenagers and adults!," but I must remind you that most people who use the rental bookstores are children. Those who read the detective series, like XX or OO, are mostly fourth and fifth graders. Besides, [your] drawings are not good enough to withstand adult readership anyway. (Tezuka, "Atarashii kodomo mangaka no minasan e")

Published a year later, Tezuka's *Rakuban* (*Cave-in*, 1959) is an interesting short work, not only in its theme of the unreliability of memory, but also in its self-conscious formal experimentation that alludes to the shifting trends of Japanese comics. The story revolves around a mining accident that had taken place twenty years before the story's opening. The recurring scenes of the past event are depicted through a variety of different drawing styles, in a manner that corresponds to the history of comics from the pre-Tezuka era to the emergence of gekiga.

Cave-in is told in a structure that film theorists may call "stairstep construction," consisting of alternating layers of "bound motifs" that "move the narrative forward," and "free motifs" that serve as "digressions that delay the ending" (Kristin Thompson 38). The story goes back and forth between the present event and memory sequences. At the start of the story, two men enter a cave. The older man, Maehashi, starts to tell a story of the accident that he experienced twenty years ago, when he was working as a coal miner: a cave collapsed on a group of minors, including him, killing several. A close friend, Ishii, died in the incident. After hearing the story, the younger man, Ōmura, questions the accuracy of Maehashi's memory, presenting alternate versions of the story. Ōmura points out that there are inconsistencies in Maehashi's stories. Ōmura then quotes different versions of the story, from various sources including Maehashi's interviews in the newspaper and the radio, as well as Maehashi's diary. The final version, read from the note Ishii wrote as he lay dying in the cave, reveals that the cave-in was not an accident; Maehashi had induced it to murder Ishii, to whom he had owed a large sum of money. At the same time, readers also learn that Ōmura was the son of Ishii.

The "inconsistent" drawing style of *Cave-in* makes this short story unique. The five memory scenes (free motifs) are depicted in five distinctive styles, ranging from simple, comical line drawings reminiscent of prewar children's comics to more detailed, "gekiga-like" figures. The degrees of detail in the drawing styles represent the reliability of Maehashi's story. The first version of the story Maehashi gives at the beginning of the story, a simple "cartoonish" rendition, tells a more distorted version of the story (fig. 5.4) than the later versions, told through more representational drawings that use extensive shading (fig. 5.5). In contrast, the scenes that show the "present," including the ending, are consistently rendered through Tezuka's usual drawing style.

Despite its dark narrative, *Cave-in*'s ending emphasizes compassion and forgiveness. After confronting Maehashi with his crime, Ōmura sets up a bomb and leaves the cave. Maehashi is unable to move; Ōmura had drugged his tea earlier. Ōmura walks away as Maehashi mumbles "Forgive me, Ishii, forgive me . . ." Ōmura continues walking, but soon starts to look conflicted. Ōmura stops and says to himself: "Thirty seconds." The panel shows Ōmura's face first, followed by a sequences of panels that show his feet, capturing them as they hesitate and then turn around. The final panel shows Ōmura running back into the cave to save Maehashi. The various drawing styles in this short work comment on the close relationship between certain drawing "styles" and their implied thematic "content." The gekiga-like style of drawing enables Ōmura's revenge as well as the murder ten years earlier, and Tezuka's familiar style makes it natural for Ōmura to make a compassionate choice at the end. *Cave-in* acknowledges the capacity of gekiga to depict the darker side of human nature, but at the same time it questions the value of such depiction. In the end, characters make moral choices.

With the rise of gekiga, the public started craving more graphic, more sensational contents in comics. Tezuka's name disappeared from the popularity ranking, and the former fans criticized Tezuka for his lack of experimentation. The number of fan letters decreased, and instead, letters of disappointment from previous fans inundated his studio. His choices of themes and subjects, previously celebrated as principled and persuasive, were criticized as overly didactic and moralist. In his autobiography, Tezuka describes this period as a time of severe depression, paranoia, and mood swings. The symptoms, in Tezuka's own words, "seemed to come and go in few-year cycles," and assistants and family members "suffered from (his) unreasonable anger tantrums." Tezuka started screaming and throwing objects at his assistants and editors. Tezuka's paranoia reached the first of the series of climaxes in 1958, and Tezuka

Figure 5.4. A memory scene from *Rakuban* [*Cave-in*]. © Tezuka Productions. Reproduced with permission.

Figure 5.5. A memory scene from *Cave-in.* © Tezuka Productions. Reproduced with permission.

brought himself to the mental hospital at Chiba University Medical School. The doctor who examined Tezuka suggested that he take time off and/or take a wife (Shimizu Isao 177–79; Tezuka *Boku wa manga ka* 164–66).

Tezuka took the doctor's advice and married Etsuko, a daughter of a distant relative, on October 4, 1959. Tezuka met her through an *omiai*, a common practice of "blind date" set up by parents or friends. Etsuko recounts the circumstances of the marriage as follows:

At the time, Tezuka was an extremely popular, extremely busy cartoonist, going back and forth between Tokyo and Takarazuka. I [later] heard that he was also frequenting a [psychiatric] doctor, for his schedule drove him to neurosis. His doctor recommended that he either stops working or gets married. His friends had arranged a few *omiai* for him with young actresses and pianists, but none had worked out. (Tezuka Etsuko 26)

A similar story is recounted in Tezuka's own autobiography. Both parties tell comically disastrous accounts of subsequent dates, such as Tezuka leaving in the middle of a movie to work or falling asleep at a cafe. He proposed six months later. For the formal engagement ceremony, his mother had to bring the engagement ring to Etsuko, since Tezuka's schedule did not allow him to leave Tokyo. The couple had three children, Makoto, Rumiko, and Chiiko, and stayed married until Tezuka's death in 1989. His home life as a husband and a father is comically depicted in his semiautobiographical serial, *Mako to Rumi to Chii* (Mako, Rumi, and Chi, 1979–1981).

Around the same time, Tezuka briefly returned to his medical interest. In 1958, Yasuzumi Gonpachirō, Tezuka's former mentor from Osaka University, was offered a new post as the head of the Electron Microscopy Lab at Nara Medical College. Yasuzumi immediately invited Tezuka to assist him on his research team. This prompted Tezuka to return to his interest in biology and medicine, conducting research on sperm membranes using electron microscopes. While assisting Yasuzumi's research, Tezuka also completed a doctoral dissertation, *Electron Microscope Study on Membrane Structure of Atypical Spermatozoa [sic]*. This study examines the system of sperm production of the Japanese pond snail, *cipangopaludina malleata*, a common creature that inhabits muddy rice fields all over Japan. Tezuka explains that the process of sperm production and maturation of a snail is "not much different from that of a human being. They both have nine spiral structures, which are visible when sliced vertically. It is true not only of snails but also of horses and dogs (or any animal). The structure of human sperm membranes can be very easily speculated by examining a snail specimen" (Tezuka, *Boku wa manga ka* 138). Tezuka defended the dissertation and received his doctorate on January 29, 1961.

In their 2000 essay "Ishi to shite no Tezuka Osamu: sono shirare zaru ningenzō (Tezuka Osamu as a Doctor: An Unknown Portrait)," Kojima Hideaki and Suzuki Hiroshi point out that the premises behind microscopic study of pond snails and comics, or animation films, are not entirely unrelated. "Tezuka must have noticed that, if a number of microscopic photographs taken from slightly different angles were stacked and flipped through, he could animate them" (440). Though this was clearly not the first time Tezuka played with flip-book animation, it is likely that Tezuka was interested in the electron microscope as a new fascinating toy. An electron microscope is, in Martin Kemp's words, "a technological invention that magically transcends the normal definitions of sight" (Kemp 127). Our sense of sight relies on, and is limited by, the nature of light, which consists of particles called photons. The use of electron beams—consisting of much smaller particles and more easily manipulated—instead of light in electron microscopes defies such limitations of optical microscopes, allowing for much larger magnification as well as greater clarity of the image. The resulting image is not an optical image but an electronic map of the object, which must be interpreted by a trained eye. By 1960, the instrument

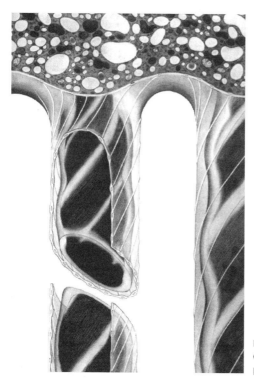

Figure 5.6. Tezuka's medical illustration. © Tezuka Productions. Reproduced with permission.

achieved the resolution 100,000 times more effective than optical microscopes. Tezuka's experiences in the microscopic lab may have been the direct inspiration for the famous sequence in *Hi no tori mirai hen* (*Phoenix: Chapter of the Future*, 1967) when the protagonist Masato goes on a journey into a cell of an animal, in which there is a universe, galaxies, planets, and animals, all of which are invisible to a human eye. Tezuka's medical illustrations, which appeared in the *Journal of Biophysical and Biochemical Cytology* between 1957 and 1960, also resemble the depictions of the miscroscopic, comic, or spiritual spaces in the *Phoenix* series. These illustrations accompanied a series of essays titled "Spermatozoa in Animals as Revealed by Electron Microscopy I–VIII," coauthored by Yasuzumi and Tezuka, along with other graduate students in Yasuzumi's lab (fig. 5.6).

In the 1960s, numerous subgenres of comics such as *kaiki manga* (horror) and *harenchi manga* (comic-erotica) became popular. These genres often featured graphic contents that made gekiga, once controversial, seem tame by comparison. *Kaiki* and *harenchi* were, by definition, undiluted explorations of gruesomeness and adolescent sexuality, while gekiga still emphasized storytelling and narration. These subgenres further diverged into smaller sub-subgenres. *Yōkai manga* (monster) and *noroi manga* (occult) became staples within *kaiki manga*; there were as many genres of sports comics as there were sports. Genre mixing had also become a common practice by this period, resulting in a number of peculiar hybrids. For example, *shojo kaiki manga* was a fusion of gruesome horror comics and flowery girls' comics, combining images of spattering blood and sparkly-eyed female characters on the same page.

Another critical development in the boys' comics in the late 1950s was the emergence of weekly (as opposed to monthly) magazines. The weekly format allowed cartoonists to experiment with more complex narrative structures, as the readers only had to wait for a week to read the next installment, with fresh memory of what has taken place. In weekly magazines, Tezuka combines his complex storytelling techniques from the late 1940s with the single-hero structure he had adopted as a magazine cartoonist. *0 Man* (1959), like Tezuka's science fiction *akahon*, is an ambitious narrative that unfolds in a cosmic scale, encompassing all of human evolution and beyond. In *0 Man*, Tezuka constantly shifts the point of view and inserts independent episodes. This work has been named as one of the two greatest achievements in postwar comics by the children's literature critic Satō Tadao in his 1964 essay.

There is a clear shift in Tezuka's subjects and thematic choices during the 1960s, perhaps as a reaction to his existing image. Tezuka's works were—and still are today—commonly characterized as "humanist" or "moralist." Tezuka often expressed his aversion to this label, wanting to be perceived as more of a challenging or even controversial artist. Just as often, however, he spoke that he wanted to continue making "good" and "moral" comics. Perhaps for this reason, some of Tezuka's works contain mixed messages, capturing the allure of the dark and the evil while also celebrating the good and the moral. This dilemma first became visible in the late 1950s in works such as *Majin Garon* (*Monster God Garon*, 1959). Garon, who was sent to the earth by the aliens, is a gigantic robot that destroys everything on earth. Garon has no moral conscience except when Pic, a little boy, is inside his chest/control booth. Garon is large, strong, monstrous looking, and often uncontrollable; Pic is small, adorable, and fragile. In a way, the pair serves as a clear metaphor for good and evil as the two coexisting, conflicting components of human nature. It is tempting to read this work as a simple tale of good versus evil, allegorizing something like "even a small seed of goodness can control the great evil in the world." Tezuka's answer, however, is not so straightforward. Throughout the series, Garon and Pic develop a close and caring relationship, and they are never complete without each other. The story's ending further complicates the metaphor: the humans put both of them on a time machine, and send them ten million years into the future. In the 1960s, Tezuka made increasingly bolder choices to unsettle his "righteous" image. Rock's memorable performance of the villain in *The Vampires* (1966) is a clear example.

As the comics industry diverged into new genres, Tezuka created his own versions of them, embellishing them with his own jokes, stars, and references. *Dororo* (1967–1968) is Tezuka's version of a *kaiki* manga, the genre that explores the supernatural and the grotesque. *Dororo* takes place in feudal Japan, featuring a thirteen-year-old boy, Hyakkimaru, whose forty-eight body parts were sold to forty-eight monsters at birth. Hyakkimaru, an abandoned baby missing fory-eight body parts, was rescued by a woodcraftsman, who gave him artificial limbs and organs made of wood. Upon the death of the woodcraftsman—his adopted father—Hyakkimaru goes on a journey to kill each of the forty-eight monsters, in order to regain his body parts and become fully human. Each episode features a duel between Hyakkimaru and a monster, interwoven with the subplot of his reckless ten-year-old sidekick, Dororo. The eerie mood and the depiction of the gory monsters in this work are clearly influenced by Mizuki Shigeru and Hino Hideshi, who are known for their exploration of the particularly "Japanese" concept of the grotesque in *kaiki* manga. *Dororo* is also conscious of the new mode of period drama that combines serene lyricism and graphic violence, commonly associated with the works of Shirato Sanpei.

Comics was also on its way to earning a higher status as art and literature. In 1964, Shirato Sanpei launched an experimental manga magazine, *Garo*. As a response to this, in 1967, Tezuka also launched *COM*—the title referred to "communication" "comics," and "community," with a tagline "a magazine for manga elites." The two magazines, *COM* and *Garo*, defined the late 1960s as the period of formal experimentation, elevating manga to an art form worthy of literary and artistic criticism. Among other accomplishments, *COM* was important in that it served as a venue for Tezuka's experimental epic *Hi no tori* (*Phoenix*) series, considered one of his most ambitious and sophisticated works. The idea for this work and the figure of a phoenix, or a firebird, had been with Tezuka for more than a decade; he had already written two separate series called *Phoenix*, in *Manga Shonen* (1954) and in *Shojo Club* (1956–1957). This new version, however, had the scope and complexity incomparable to the two previous series. It consisted of several "chapters," which were independent book-length episodes; when the chapters were read in context of one another, they formed an epic that took the readers through the history of humankind from the prehistoric time to its extinction. The phoenix character in the two previous series morphed into a more metaphoric image, a sort of "cosmic energy body" that takes the form of a bird. The story, starting simultaneously and alternately from the beginning and the end of the human civilization, was assumed to eventually "meet" in the present—but was left unfinished by the author's untimely death in 1989.

When producing works that drew on newly popular genres of comics, Tezuka always inserted his own touches to make them "original." In 1970, Tezuka published two "sex education" comics of contrasting styles, *Yakeppachi no Maria* (*Yakeppachi's Maria*) and *Aporo no uta* (*Apollo's Song*). *Yakeppachi's Maria* is framed as a light-hearted comedy: a reckless teenage delinquent, Yakeno Yanpachi, nicknamed Yakeppachi (literally "self-destructive"), gives birth to ectoplasm. The ectoplasm, named Maria, occupies the body of a blow-up doll and enters Yakeppachi's high school as a new student. Adults around Yakeppachi teach him and Maria about human sexuality and reproduction. Though Maria leaves Yakeppachi when her plastic body is destroyed, Yakeppachi soon finds a "real" human girlfriend named Mari.

The character of Maria as (literally) a sex toy can be read as a parodic commentary on *harenchi manga*, in which underdeveloped female characters serve exclusively as objects of desire for male characters as well as for young male readers. The genre of *harenchi* manga is best defined as adolescent sex jokes in a comic book format: they deal comically with adolescent sexuality, usually in a high school setting, and serve as a precursor to more explicit porn comics in later periods. The word *harenchi* denotes "indecent" or "sexual," but with juvenile and playful overtones. One of the recurring themes in *harenchi* manga is a schoolteacher fetish, featuring voluptuous female teachers who are (happily) molested by their male students. Nagai Gō (1945–) is probably the best-known cartoonist who primarily worked in this genre. *Harenchi* manga was a product of an era before sexual harassment and school violence were recognized as major social issues. Still, depictions of female nudes and adolescent sexuality in these works were severely criticized by the Parents and Teachers Association, inspiring the nationwide movement Akusho tsuihō undō (Movement Against Harmful Books), to take "harmful books" off the market. Most of the arguments against "harmful comics," however, centered around the issue of distraction from schoolwork, not around the objectification of women.

Apollo's Song explores the theme of human sexuality as does *Yakeppachi's Maria*, but in a contrastingly dark narrative. The prologue sequence shows anthropomorphized human sperm racing to meet the beautiful "queen," the egg. In his postscript to *Apollo's Song*, Tezuka describes the work as a reaction to the "dark, devastating period for Japanese youth" characterized by "radical student movements, *uchi-geba* (intra-sect conflict) among the New Left, and numerous instances of violence." The story's protagonist is an adolescent boy, Chikaishi Shōgo, who suffers from a mental disorder that makes him react violently to everything that has to do with sexual love. Shōgo is depicted stoning animals to death while they are mating, and attacking couples kissing in a park. Shōgo eventually falls in love with a beautiful psychiatrist, Hiromi, who tries to cure Shōgo by training him for a marathon. While the two live in seclusion in a mountain lodge, Hiromi also teaches Shōgo about love and human sexuality. The series is also interspersed with a number of "dream sequences" in which Shōgo appears in a different time period and place. In each dream, he falls in love with a woman, and the dream always ends with the woman's (and Shōgo's) death before their sexual union. In the series' end, Shōgo kills himself after Hiromi falls off the cliff and dies in his arms.

Apollo's Song was among Tezuka's "least favorite" works produced during his "darkest" period, between 1970 and 1973. Other works produced during this period include *Alabaster* (1970), *Dust 18* (1972, later retitled *Dust 8*), *Garasu no shiro no kiroku* (*The Record of a Glass Castle*, 1970) and *Ryōri suru onna* (*The Woman Who Cooks*, 1972). Though these works vary in styles, genres, and target audience, they are uniformly infused with a sense of desolation and hopelessness. In the postscript to *Alabaster*, Tezuka wrote: "I really dislike the darkness in this piece. I started out wanting to write something grotesque and darkly erotic, like Edogawa Ranpo's *Issun Bōshi* (*The Dwarf*) or *Injyū* (*Beast in the Shadows*),[1] but that was a big mistake. [When I attempt this,] I tend to produce works that are helplessly nihilistic. This work fell into that trap too" (222). As Tezuka grew emotionally detached from his comics, so did the readers. They strayed away, causing some of the magazine series to be discontinued. *Dust 18*, originally contracted for eighteen episodes, was interrupted after six.

In 1973, Akita Shoten, the publisher of a leading weekly boys' comic magazine *Shonen Champion*, gave Tezuka a five-week commission to write "anything he wished." Later interviews imply that the editor, who felt sorry for Tezuka for his declining popularity, offered the commission as Tezuka's "last work" before retirement. This work, *Black Jack*, turned out to be a surprise hit; it earned Tezuka not only regained popularity but also an extended commission that lasted for eight years. The protagonist of the series was Hazama Kuroo, nicknamed Black Jack, an unlicensed surgeon whose genius saves a number of lives around the world. He is unassociated with any hospital or organizations and is known for his extremely high fees—as much as one million dollars. For this reason, he is an outcast in the medical community and often gets into legal troubles. He has a distinct appearance, clad in his signature black suit and coat even in the summer. His hair is half white, and his body and face are heavily scarred (fig. 5.7).

---

1. Edogawa Ranpo (also spelled Rampo, 1894–1965) is a Japanese author known for his detective fiction, mystery, and Gothic tales. His pen name is a tribute to Edgar Allan Poe.

Figure 5.7. Black Jack. © Tezuka Productions. Reproduced with permission.

Though Black Jack first appears taciturn and amoral, readers quickly learn that he is secretly a warm and compassionate man. While he demands high fees from a wealthy patient, he often cures underprivileged patients for no charge; he also lives a humble lifestyle in a small, old house and spends his earnings to buy small islands around Japan to preserve their untouched nature. More than occasionally, his female patients fall in love with him; Black Jack, however, is still in love with the woman he loved in medical school. As the series goes on, we also get glimpses of Black Jack's background and the circumstances behind his mysterious appearance: he was in a land-mine accident at a young age, in which he lost his mother. His father abandoned his family shortly after the accident. Young Kuroo was saved by the hands of a brilliant doctor, Homma Shōtarō, and aspired to become a doctor himself. At the same time, he vowed to avenge the people who were responsible for cleaning up the land-mine site and never to forgive his father.

Each episode of *Black Jack* introduces a set of characters in complex situations, and the focus of the drama is usually not the illness but the relationships between characters. Black Jack often "cures" so much more than the patient's physical ailment. The very first episode of the series starts with a car crash, in which Akudo (a play on the word *akudoi*, meaning "evil"), a delinquent son of a local millionaire, Nikura (a play on the word *nikurashi*, meaning "hateful"), is fatally injured. When every doctor has lost hope, Black Jack is brought in to cure him for ten million dollars. When Black Jack tells them that he needs an organ donor, Nikura pressures the local police to arrest and execute an innocent boy, Debbie, so his body could be used in the operation. Two months later, Akudo recovers but immediately runs away from the hospital. Nikura is furious. Later, Akudo shows up at Debbie's mother's house; it turns out that Black Jack never performed the requested operation, but performed another—he operated on Debbie's face to make him look identical to Akudo, to trick Nikura into thinking he has killed Debbie and saved Akudo. Debbie and his mother safely escape overseas with the money Black Jack gave them.

Black Jack was among the first work in which Tezuka fully incorporated his medical background into comics. Though Tezuka had already portrayed the medical profession two years earlier in *Kirihito Sanka* (*Ode to Kirihito*), *Black Jack* thoroughly showcased his medical knowledge, featuring detailed drawings of surgical instruments, dissected organs, and tissues. Tezuka also invented a number of fictional diseases, some of which were highly convincing, while others were entirely outlandish. One of the key episodes of *Black Jack* features an eighteen-year-old woman with a large tumor, which contained body parts of her unborn twin sister. Black Jack not only removes the tumor, but also assembles the body parts in the "tumor" to construct a living human being. The character born of the tumor, Pinoko, becomes an adorable sidekick for Black Jack throughout the series.

Black Jack is often described as the "all-star" series, featuring virtually every member of his Star System. Older, minor, or once-unpopular characters reappeared in *Black Jack*, as patients, patients' family members, doctors, or nurses. Princess Sapphire from *Princess Knight* appears in numerous episodes in the roles of nurses, patients' mothers, or wives; Toppei and Chippei, the two vampire brothers in *The Vampires*, play the role of a rabid boy and his brother, among others; Hyakkimaru, the boy whose body parts were sold to demons in *Dororo*, wears a high school uniform and falls in love with a cancer patient (Dororo also appears as his sidesick in this episode) (fig. 4.9). The series attracted a new group of readers who had never heard of *New Treasure Island*, some who were encountering his work for the first time. Eguchi Hisashi, one of Japan's leading cartoonists today, was among this generation of fans:

Black Jack started when I was about nineteen, and I was immediately hooked. [. . .] I got into it not because it was by Tezuka Osamu, but simply because it was a fascinating work. That made me realize that Tezuka Osamu was an interesting cartoonist, so I went to a bookstore to buy his [older] books. [. . .] When I was in grade school, Tezuka Osamu had become a classic, not a revolutionary, sort of like the Beatles. [. . .] I was surprised to find out what his comics were really like. When I saw his drawings from the 1950s, I was utterly shocked. (Eguchi, interview, *Sight* 59–60)

Prompted by the success of *Black Jack*, Tezuka started producing a number of other hits. *Buddha*, a series that had started a year prior to *Black Jack*, gained momentum after the success of *Black Jack* and became Tezuka's longest linear narrative, lasting for ten years. It is a fictional biography of Gautama Buddha. Like the *Phoenix* series, *Buddha* tackled large and complex themes such as reincarnation, self-sacrifice, and enlightenment. The series was recently translated into English. *Mitsume ga tōru* (*The Three-Eyed One*, 1974–1978) is a contrastingly light, but nonetheless absorbing and well-crafted series. The hero, Sharaku Hōsuke, is a modern-day teenage Dr. Jekyll/Mr. Hyde who calls himself "Prince of the Evil." In his natural state, he is the last surviving descendent of the "three- eyed humans," who once ruled the earth with their extreme intelligence, supernatural powers, and wicked, cruel personalities. When his third eye is covered with a band-aid—which is most of the time—he is regressed to the level of a kindergartner, both intellectually and emotionally. This series, while being far from didactic or moralist, repeats the earlier motif of good and evil being two not-necessarily-opposing elements of the same being. Tezuka fully displays his talent as an entertainer in this work, mixing a wide range of genres from occult to high school romance, speckling it with documentary-style historical details and popular-culture jokes.

The new hits returned Tezuka to the top of the popularity ranking and to his busy schedule. During the late 1970s, Tezuka often produced more than four hundred pages of comics per month (Ban 171). This high-volume production was enabled by the assistant system, which Tezuka had invented earlier and further perfected during this period. To draw a background of grass, for instance, Tezuka created a chart that showed a dozen different ways of drawing grass; he would indicate on the manuscript how he wanted the grass to be drawn. The assistant had to look it up on the chart and faithfully copy the style of the grass onto the manuscript. The same went for fabric patterns, architectural details, trees, bushes, and leaves. The Star System also made it easy for an assistant to fill in the crowd scene or to draw supporting characters. Still, many testify that Tezuka always drew the central characters himself, even during the busiest times.

Chapter 6

SAPPHIRE AND OTHER HEROINES

In figure 6.1 we see a scene between Princess Sapphire—cross-dressed as "Prince" Sapphire—and a pirate captain, Brad, in Tezuka Osamu's 1958 girls' comics, *Ribon no kishi* (*Princess Knight*). The events leading up to the scene are as follows: Brad and his men save Prince Sapphire from drowning in the sea. After hearing about Sapphire's circumstances, Brad offers to assassinate Duralmin, the Grand Duke, whose evil conspiracy caused Sapphire to be exiled from her country, Silverland. Sapphire asks Brad what kind of reward he expects. Brad responds: "No, I don't want any of that. What I want is . . ." (Panel 1); "You" (Panel 2). Sapphire, flustered, pretends not to understand: "Ha ha ha, you want me to be a pirate on your ship?" (Panel 3). Brad corrects her "misinterpretation": "No, I want us to get married" (Panel 4). Sapphire screams: "Stop joking! I am a man!!" (Panel 5). Brad does not give up: "You can't fool me. You are dressed as a man, but I can sense that you are a woman. You are a woman fighting against something in a man's guise." Sapphire continues to protest: "Don't be ridiculous! I am a man! Not a woman!" (Panel 6). Unfortunately, her assertion seems completely ludicrous both to Brad and to the readers, in light of her delicately arched eyebrows, swanlike neck, and dainty hand clenched beside her lips.

Ribon no kishi (*Princess Knight*) is Tezuka's best-known *shojo manga* (girls' comics). The first version of *Princess Knight*, serialized in *Shojo Club* magazine from 1953 to 1956, is considered the first story comics for young girls, followed by a sequel in *Nakayoshi* from 1958 to 1959.[1] The story of *Princess Knight* is part

---

1. The page in figure 4.1 was taken from the third version, serialized also in *Nakayoshi* between 1963 and 1966.

Figure 6.1. A scene between Sapphire and Brad in *Ribon no kishi* [*Princess Knight*]. © Tezuka Productions. Reproduced with permission.

medieval folktale, part Shakespearean comedy, and part women's melodrama. By mischief of an angel named Chink, the heroine Sapphire is born with both male and female "souls" in her female body. To complicate the situation even more, Sapphire happens to be the only heir to the patrilineal kingdom of Silverland. Sapphire's parents—the king and the queen of Silverland—decide to raise her as a boy, for it would allow her to inherit the throne. Eventually, Sapphire's biological sex is revealed by the conspiracy of Duralumin the Grand Duke, who murders the king and imprisons Sapphire and her mother for having deceived the country. When Sapphire escapes from the prison, her adventures as the Ribon no Kishi—literally, "Knight with a ribbon"—begins. Sapphire eventually rescues her mother, purges the kingdom of evil forces, and marries her true love, Prince Frantz Charming.

It is not possible to discuss today's *shojo manga* without discussing *Princess Knight*, nor is it appropriate to discuss *Princess Knight* without discussing the culture of *shojo* (young women, girls), women's magazines, popular theater, and gender in Japanese postwar society at large. *Princess Knight*, like all of Tezuka's works, exists in an intimate dialogue with other cultural products, quoting and parodying discourses that surround it. *Princess Knight*, with rich references to "women's culture" outside comics, built a foundation of today's *shojo manga* as one of the major genres of comics. I have deliberately put "women's culture" in quotation marks here, to avoid a misunderstanding that it is initiated or produced by women—rather, what I am calling "women's culture" is the line of cultural products that assume female consumption, produced, most often during this period, by male artists and administrators.

The popularity of *shojo manga* often puzzles unfamiliar foreigners, for the image of young women reading "comics" seems unusual, at least in North America. Approximately 23 percent of comics in Japan are produced specifically for women (Yamada 9). This still sounds like a relatively small percentage, but there are other considerations. Many comics, particularly for young readers, are not gender specific. Also, it is generally believed that many women freely read comics that are targeted specifically at men, while few men admit that they regularly read *shojo manga;* the dynamic is similar to the stereotype of American men who would be embarrassed to see a "chick flick." Classical *shojo manga* is often characterized by romantic narrative, exotic setting, characters with large starry eyes, androgynous male characters, and emphasis on fashion and costuming, though a number of post-1970s *shojo manga* deviate from this model.

Though *shojo manga* did not fully come into existence until the 1950s, there were publications that established the culture of "female" narrative fiction and illustrations. As far as I could locate, magazines targeted at girls or young women started appearing during the Meiji period, with the earliest being *Shojokai* in 1902. A dozen other magazines followed during the Taishō period (1912–1926). Girls' magazines of this period are associated with the early development of *shojo shōsetsu* (girls' novels) and a style of illustrations called *jojōga*, colorful portraits of beautiful young women. Comics started to appear in girls' magazines in the late 1920s, though they occupied no more than a few pages. As Japan entered the second Sino-Japanese war in the 1930s, didactic articles that promote the ideal image of women, frequently referred to as *ryōsai kenbo* (good wife, wise mother), started to replace "frivolous" novels and illustrations. Most of these magazines were discontinued toward the end of World War II.

The postwar cultural reform and the absorption of American values inspired cultural producers to target women as active consumers. Between 1945 and 1950, numerous publishers launched girls' magazines, including *Shojo no Tomo, Shojo, Shojo Club, Shojo Sekai, Shojo Salon, Shojo Romance, Jogakusei no Tomo, Shojo Book, Himawari*, and *Junior Soleil*. As was the case with most other magazines during the era, they were thin A5-size brochures printed on poor-quality paper. Comics only occupied 10 percent of the total content, and most consisted of illustrated novels, articles on arts, theater, celebrities, crafts, and cooking. Prominent cartoonists in those magazines included Kurakane Shōsuke, Shimada Keizō, and Sugiura Yukio, all of whom were male. The most popular series was *Anmitsu hime* by Kurakane, featuring a charming, tomboyish princess in feudal Japan. *Anmitsu hime* inspired a number of copycat works, pirated versions, and latter-day revivals. By the mid-1950s, girls' magazines evolved into more luxurious booklets with large-format and full-color printing. The two B4-format magazines that were issued in 1955, *Ribon* and *Nakayoshi*, targeted the postwar baby-boom generation that was just reaching reading age. Comics played an increasingly important role in those magazines, as did color photographs and illustrated prose fiction.

The 1950s was also the era of "*shojo* stars," preteen celebrities who appeared in films, on radio, and in magazines. These young starlets inspired trends in young girls' fashion and hairstyles, in life as well as in comics. Matsushima Tomoko, who debuted in 1950, appeared as a character in a number of comics. The *shojo* manga characters during this period—even Anmitsu-hime—were less compelling than the unique, colorful cast of characters in *shonen* manga, who were attracting a considerable fan base. Borrowing the image and the identity of a *shojo* star gave the character instant charisma. At the same time, it provided its audience another means of star consumption. Though Tezuka never produced a work that featured existing *shojo* stars, a number of fictional stars appear in his works. The heroine of *Shiro kujaku no uta* (*The Song of a White Peacock*, 1959) is a young girl named Yuri, who performs as a pianist and singer. *Curtain wa konya mo aoi* (*The Curtain Remains Blue Tonight*, 1958) is a thriller that revolves around a teenage girl named Mejiro Chidori, who is a stage actress.

Though *Princess Knight* has become synonymous with Tezuka's *shojo manga*, it was not his first attempt at comics for young women. *Kiseki no mori no monogatari* (*Story of a Miracle Forest*, 1949) and *Kanoko no ōen danchō* (*Kanoko Is the Captain of the Cheering Party*, 1950) served as predecessors to two distinct styles of Tezuka's *shojo manga*. *Story of a Miracle Forest* is an exotic and fantastical adventure, much like *Princess Knight* and a string of later works such as *Miniyon* (1957) and *Nobara yo itsu utau* (*Wild Rose, When Will You Sing?*, 1960). Elements of costume design in this work, such as a large, feathered hat and men in white tights, are later recycled into *Princess Knight*. *Kanoko Is the Captain of the Cheering Party*, though serialized in a boys' magazine, featured many of the commonly seen components of latter-day *shojo manga*; most important, a spunky young female protagonist. The story takes place in a familiar world of contemporary Japan, with a life-size heroine with whom readers can easily identify. Kanoko, an outgoing schoolgirl, borrows her brother's clothes to play the lead role in a school play; later, in her costume, she ends up serving as the captain of the cheering squad, a role traditionally considered as the pinnacle of "macho." This style of familiar narrative in girls' comics was further developed in 1954 *Nasubi Joō* (*Queen Nasubi*), and evolved into a number of outgoing, tomboyish heroines such as Himawari in *Himawari san* (1956) and Yokko in *Yokko chan ga kitayo!* (*Here Comes Yokko!*, 1962).

Tezuka approached his first "story comics" for young women, *Princess Knight*, much the same way as he did his other magazine series, with one clear distinction: *Princess Knight* contained strong references to live theater—or more precisely, theatrical productions of Takarazuka Kagekidan, a musical theater company based in Tezuka's home town of Takarazuka—in addition to film. The story was built around a charismatic central character, a strong premise, and a sense of cinematic movement; at the same time, characters walked around in ornate costumes, constantly striking dramatic poses or stopping to break out in song. The panels showed more picturesque tableau than quick succession of images. The new printing technology also allowed Tezuka to include beautiful full-color illustrations. Tezuka explicitly quoted Takarazuka Kagekidan's sets, costumes, and musical lyrics. At first glance, this seems like an opposite move from his earlier commitment to move away from the kind of comics where the readers' view resembles "an audience viewing a stage, where the actors emerge from the wings and interact" (*Boku wa manga ka* 76–77). *Princess Knight*, however, proved that the charm of live theater and the movement of cinema could coexist in a single work.

Tezuka's quotation of Takarazuka Kagekidan's productions is not surprising, considering his relationship with the company since his childhood: Amatsu Otome and Kumono Kayoko, two sisters who both performed on the Takarazuaka stage, lived next door to Tezuka. The young actresses adored the three children (Tezuka, his sister Minako, and his brother Hiroshi), often inviting them to their house. Tezuka's mother, Fumiko, was also a Takarazuka fan who went to the theater almost weekly. Tezuka's biographies tell a number of anecdotes that reveal Tezuka's close affinities with Takarazuka Kagekidan from a young age: when two-year-old Tezuka saw an altar adorned with a curtain at the somber funeral ceremony of a relative, he loudly announced, "Curtain up and the show begins!" In middle school, he went to Takarazuka Kagekidan's costume storage to borrow costumes for a school play (Nakano 50; 58). Tezuka started contributing illustrations and short comics to two "fan magazines," *Kageki* and *Takarazuka Graph*, as early as 1946. Thoroughly familiar with Takarazuka Kagekidan's stars and production styles, Tezuka's works in these two fan publications range from caricatures of stars to parody of plays to illustrated news stories.

In the afterword to the *Complete Works* version of *Princess Knight*, Tezuka wrote: "My home town is the city of Takarazuka, famous for its Shojo Kageki. I spent my childhood and young adulthood in the sweet, extravagant ambiance of musical dramas. The characters and costumes in my works are greatly influenced by the stage. My girls' comics, in particular, contain great nostalgia for Takarazuka" (Afterword, *Ribon no Kishi* 258). Similarly, Tezuka's wife, Etsuko, recalls:

Tezuka said: "I frequented Takarazuka's shows with my mother who was a big fan. The shows introduced me to the music and costumes from around the world. They may have been pirated versions of Broadway musicals or Moulin Rouge revues, but at the time, I thought of it as great art." Later, he said that Takarazkuka Kagekidan served as the basis of the first girls' story comics, *Ribon no kishi* (*Princess Knight*). [. . .] (The character of Sapphire) reminds me of the *dansō no reijin* [beauty in male dress] of Takarazuka Kageki [. . .] I still remember Takarazuka Kagekidan's *Midsummer Night's Dream* I saw as a student. Otowa Nobuko was so adorable as Puck in her green costume. I wonder if that's where Tezuka got the idea of the angel Chink. Also, Prince Frantz [the romantic interest in *Princess Knight*] is reminiscent of top star of that period, Kasugano Yachiyo. (Afterword, *Ribon* 346)

Tezuka's affinity with Takarazuka Kagekidan was important at least in two ways: one is that it immersed young Tezuka in the "women's culture"; another is that it kindled his interest in live theater, not only as an audience member but also as an artist. At Osaka University, Tezuka was active in a student theater group, Gakuyū-za, appearing in six theatrical productions between May 1946 and November 1947. In April 1947, Tezuka starred in Chekhov's one act *The Proposal*, playing an unfortunate landowner whose attempt to ask a woman to marry him ends in disputes over landownership. His other roles in college include a cameo role in Arishima Takeo's *Domomata no shi* (*The Death of Domomata*), an old man named Sugimoto Tokuhei in Yamamoto Yūzō's *Seimei no Kanmuri* (*The Crown of Life*), Dr. Otis or "Shorty" in Sidney Kingsley's *Men in White*, and another cameo role in an adaptation of Dostoevsky's *Crime and Punishment*. It is likely that this production served as an inspiration for his 1949 manga adaptation of *Crime and Punishment*: the opening sequence is reminiscent of the set in Gakuyū-za's production, featuring multilevel scenery with staircases. Tezuka's experience in this production is one of the first anecdotes he tells in his autobiography: because of the multilevel structure of this set, the audience could only see Tezuka's feet.

Tezuka's 1946 essay titled "Manga to engeki (Comics and Theatre)" in Gakuyū-za's newsletter gives a view significantly different from the previously cited passage in *I Am a Cartoonist*. In this essay, Tezuka advocates for the use of "theatrical" techniques in comics, claiming that the transformation of the comics medium can be achieved through the approach of "writing comics as one would write a stage play." Tezuka laments the dourness that Japan and the Japanese had experienced during World War II, and critiques the state of comics and cartoons in Japan, "which is dismissed as a medium whose sole purpose is to make people laugh." Tezuka then calls for a new style of comics that "may not necessarily be funny," but which will take its readers through a wide range of emotions such as sadness, excitement, and even profound rumination. Tezuka argues that through such an approach, comics "will gain the appeal of film or theatre, and even beyond [. . .] Comics should be written as one would write a play" (Tezuka, quoted in Nakano 191–92; Ono 149–50).

Though Tezuka used the language of "wings-and-drop-approach" to critique existing comics, he did not reject theatrical references; on the contrary, many of Tezuka's comics embrace live theater. Some even contain the theatrical framework of prologues and epilogues in front of a curtain. The opening page of *The Merchant of Venice* (1955) shows Tezuka himself, wearing a wig and delivering a prologue in front of the curtain. When he wrote about his artistic processes in *Manga no kakikata* (*How to Create Comics*, 1977), Tezuka described three stages of comics writing: "Formulating Images," "Formulating Ideas," and "Formulating Comics." In the section called "How to Develop a Script" in the "Formulating Comics" chapter, Tezuka emphasized that a good script is essential to creating successful story comics, and he describes the process as if writing a play: finding a theme, conducting dramaturgical research, and developing characters (178–85). In other parts of the book, Tezuka also frequently uses references to theatrical directing such as pacing, casting, and the use of comic relief.

Princess Knight is infused not only with images and lyrics from Takarazuka Kagekidan's productions, but also with its unique mode of gender representation and sexual politics. There is not enough space in this book to adequately discuss Takarazuka Kagekidan or its impact on Japanese popular culture, but there are a number of English-language sources on this company (Brau; Robertson; Senelick, *Changing*). The company was founded by Kobayashi Ichizo in 1913 and was extremely successful by the time Tezuka was born. Its cast members—called *Takarasiennes*—are all graduates of the highly competitive Takarazuka Music Academy, where young, unmarried women between the ages of fifteen and nineteen are trained in performance skills such as dancing, singing, and acting. During their two years of training, all Takarasiennes are assigned their "stage gender," either *otoko yaku* (male role specialists) or *musume yaku* (female role specialists), which they will play for the rest of their tenure with the company, with rare exceptions. At the same time, Takarasiennes are encouraged to behave feminine and ladylike when they are offstage. Takarasiennes thus engage in complex multilayered performances of gender throughout their career, and often, beyond.

Like Takarazuka Kagekidan's *otoko yaku*, Sapphire's performance of the male gender makes no attempt at "passing," or imitating "real" men. Takarazuka Kagekidan's founder, Kobayashi Ichizo, explained Takarazuka Kagekidan's mode of male impersonation compared it to the practice of male-to-female cross-dressing in kabuki:

It is women who know the male beauty better than anyone. When a woman performs as a man, she is able to craft an image of a man who is better than a real man, from a woman's perspective. [. . .] The *onna gata* in *kabuki* represents the ideal woman through a man's perspective. She is the prototype of an ideal woman in every way, in her personality, style, in her actions. *Kabuki's onna gata* is more sensual than a real woman, a woman better than a real woman. *Kabuki* thrives on the sensuality of *onna gata* that real women cannot achieve. Takarazuka's *otoko yaku*, too, can portray men who are more attractive than real men. (Kobayashi, qtd. in Hashimoto 12)

There is a clear difference, however, between kabuki's *onna gata* and Takarazuka's *otoko yaku*. While *onna gata* are considered a prototype for real women to emulate, an *otoko yaku* does not aim to educate "real" men. *Otoko yaku*'s performance is always framed as a service to the audience rather than a subversive act of drag.

Similarly to Takarazuka's performers, Sapphire's performance of the male gender is always marked as a "duty" rather than "pleasure." The "self-sacrifice" trope in Sapphire's male guise becomes most prominent in her tormented love affair with Frantz Charming, the prince of the neighboring kingdom of Goldland. Sapphire meets him for the first time in the episode titled "Easter." Earlier in the episode, the courtesans come forward and show off their dresses. Sapphire compliments them, but later weeps alone, at not being able to wear a dress and go out herself. Having seen this, the nurse and the queen allow her to go out in a dress, giving her a flax-colored wig to conceal her identity. At the festival she meets Frantz, who immediately falls in love with the beautiful and mysterious girl with the flaxen hair. Later that night, when Frantz reencounters Sapphire, this time as a boy, he does not recognize her: "Oh, you must be the prince of this kingdom, nice to meet you. I was wondering, have you seen a flaxen-haired girl around?" The episode ends with the two of them drinking at a table. Frantz looks off, saying to himself: "Ah, I would love to meet that girl again. I wanted to have danced with her longer . . ." Sapphire also looks away, saying: "she must be thinking the same, somewhere . . ." (fig. 6.2). The reading order of comics adds another level of poignancy to this scene: Frantz, unaware that the girl and Sapphire are the same person, looks to the right, directly opposite the direction of the reading order (which is right to left). This signifies looking "to the past," reflecting on the happy memory. Sapphire, on the other hand, sorrowfully looks to the left, sensing the impending torment in their new friendship.

Sapphire performs her "duty" very well for most of the series. When Nylon, Duralmin's sidekick, tries to engage her in a conversation about "feminine" hobbies so as to expose her "true gender," Sapphire successfully comes up with tactful responses:

NYLON. Well, sir, what do you think of this? I have adorned the yoke line of my blouse with a velvet ribbon . . .
SAPPHIRE. You mean it's like curry and rice over chou a la crème.
NYLON. ?
SAPPHIRE. You told me some nonsense, so I just did the same.

The scene displays Sapphire's wit and cleverness, or her ability to convincingly embody masculinity. In the very next scene, we see Sapphire in the forest, surrounded by animals, telling them a story: "Let me continue the story I

Figure 6.2. A scene between Sapphire and Frantz, on their second meeting, in *Princess Knight*. © Tezuka Productions. Reproduced with permission.

was telling you yesterday. So, there was a princess who pretended that she was a prince . . ." Sapphire is startled when she finds the angel Chink, disguised as a human child, listening to her from behind a tree. This is their first meeting on earth. Chink speaks: "I know that story, it is about yourself." Sapphire, furious, chases Chink away: "What nonsense! What rudeness! Go away, or I will kill you!" Chink is discouraged: "'Go away, or I will kill you' . . . She really sounds like a boy. This is a disaster." Chink, desperate for proof that Sapphire is a girl, comes up with an idea: "I will imitate the Nurse's voice and speak to her. If she is really a girl, she would respond as a girl!" When Chink speaks to Sapphire in the nurse's voice from behind the bushes, she answers in the feminine language. Chink is relieved.

The Japanese language easily lends itself to gendered speech, since it employs gender-specific pronouns and sentence endings. Sapphire's use of masculine pronouns such as *boku* (I) and *kimi* (you) marks her as "male," while at the same time her small waist and shapely legs signify "female." Kobayashi was known to have banned "masculine" syntax among Takarazuka's performers to maintain the Takarasiennes' offstage identities as subservient women. A woman's appropriation of masculine speech was generally considered not so much "incorrect" but rather "inappropriate," a reflection of her crudeness, low-class status, and/or bad manners. *Otoko-yaku's* male dress and masculine speech were acceptable as long as they were confined in the theatrical space, but its use off-stage was off-limits.

In addition to the gendered speech, Sapphire also uses gestures and body language to perform her male identity, making big hand gestures and taking wide strides. This, however, is never very "convincing" to the readers. As a static medium, the comic book shows Sapphire's gestures constantly in "stop-motion," equivalent to a film still or a production photograph. Since the performance of gender through gestures depends largely on the performer's movement through space, Sapphire has an inherent disadvantage as a comic book character. Sapphire's postures do not necessarily communicate "maleness," and if anything the images call attention to the ironic incongruity between her masculine speech and her womanly figure.

In her study of the late-nineteenth-century actress Charlotte Cushman, Lisa Merrill points out the seeming contradiction between Cushman's womanly figure and her reputation as a "convincing" male impersonator in plays. Merrill locates Cushman's "manliness" in her movements in time and space, arguing that her success in playing male roles came from her use of a "series of gestures and expressions that unmistakably signified manliness to her spectators," and the still image did not fully capture her performance (124). Similarly, *otoko yaku's* masculinity is largely lost in production photographs of Takarazuka Kagekidan's production stills. The husky voice, masculine syntax, and body language that the present-day *otoko yaku* acquire in years of training cannot be preserved in a photographic reproduction. The viewers are left with puzzling images of extravagantly and incompletely cross-dressed, overly made-up, short-haired women. Performing masculinity through gestures is even more challenging for Sapphire, whose feminine body shape is accentuated, not concealed, by her costumes. Sapphire's womanly figure becomes particularly puzzling when we consider that she is only twelve years old at the beginning of the series, and that other characters in the comics seem to be oblivious to her appearance, accepting her as a boy for most of the series.

As exciting as Sapphire's adventures are, her true happiness comes from being in a traditional female role. Toward the end of the series, Sapphire prepares a meal for Frantz—who is now aware of her true identity—while hiding from the enemies. Frantz is pleasantly shocked: "You can cook, too, though you are a prince?" Sapphire answers, "Yes, I can perform women's tasks as well." While her "masculine" skills are associated with her high class, such as horse riding and fencing, her "feminine" skills are characterized by domesticity. Sapphire displays her domestic attentiveness again when she and Frantz "kidnap" Frantz's uncle, King Carne of Goldland, in order to convince him to agree to their marriage. Sapphire wins Charne's affection by performing the role of a devoted daughter, bringing water when he is thirsty, helping him shave, mending his clothes, and even scrubbing his back while he bathes in the river.

The image of Sapphire must have sent complex, if not conflicting, messages to the young female readers of the 1950s. On the one hand, *Princess Knight* liberated them through the image of a strong, intelligent, and adventurous woman in male guise; on the other, such guise was involuntary and ultimately unsuccessful. Judith Butler once pointed out that "in imitating gender, drag implicitly reveals the imitative structure of gender itself—as well as its contingency," calling attention to the "distinction between the anatomy of the performer and the gender that is being performed" (*Gender Trouble* 175). This practice, however, is only subversive so long as the performer "passes"—or at least characterizes gender as "imitative" at all. In constantly "failing" to imitate the male gender in the readers' eyes, and ultimately choosing happiness in the traditional role of a wife and a mother, Sapphire's drag reinforces, more than unsettles, the status quo.

Though it may not have subverted gender norms, *Princess Knight* transformed *shojo manga* from short gag comics to plot-driven, complex narratives, and inspired a number of other strong-willed, charismatic heroines in other artists' works. *Princess Knight* became so popular that it was followed by a sequel in *Nakayoshi* from 1958 to 1959 (later retitled *Futago no kishi* [*Twin Knights*]). *Princess Knight* had a few more reincarnations, as a TV animation series, a series drawn by an artist other than Tezuka, and numerous picture books.

Tezuka's *Nasubi joō* (*Queen Nasubi*, 1954), though somewhat forgotten today and virtually unknown outside Japan, is also an important work in the early development of *shojo manga*. Unlike *Princess Knight*, *Queen Nasubi* is infused with details of daily life not unlike its readers'. The story revolves around three friends: Nasubi is a country girl with crude manners who dreams of someday becoming a queen. Takako, an orphan living with her relatives, is a diligent student of ballet. Fujiko is the "smart one," an intelligent daughter of a police detective. This narrative structure, featuring three girls of contrasting personalities, became a staple in the genre, and was repeated in Maki Miyako's

1958 hit, *Shojo Sannin* (*Three Girls*). A more recent example includes *Warau Mikaeru* (*Smiling Archangel*, 1987) by Kawahara Izumi.

When *Queen Nasubi* started, readers preferred Takako, the beautiful aspiring ballerina, to the rougher country girl Nasubi. The story of Takako inspired a number of other heroines who are in unfortunate circumstances but who eventually find an exceptional talent and become a star. Miuchi Suzue's epic *Garasu no kamen* (*The Glass Mask*, 1976–present), a story of a poor girl named Kitajima Maya, who turns out to be a genius actress, is a quintessential example. Ballerina motifs also started to appear in the late 1950s and developed into a subgenre, producing hits such as Takahashi Makoto's *Arashi o koete* (*Beyond Storm*, 1958) and Maki Miyako's *Maki no kuchibue* (*Maki's Whistle*, 1960). Other *shojo* manga themes that span out of *Queen Nasubi* include student-teacher romance, detective mystery, magic, and mistaken identities.

The same year, Tezuka published a number of short works in girls' magazines, exploring a wide range of themes. *Tori yose shojo* (*Girl Who Calls Birds*), a fantastical fable reminiscent of European fairy tales, should probably be categorized as an illustrated story rather than comics. *Silk hat monogatari* (*A Story of a Top Hat*) is a parodic reworking of a Julien Duvivier film *Tales of Manhattan* (1942), and *Robin chan* is a somewhat bizarre mix of monster adventure and romance. *Tatsuga fuchi no otome* (*Girl by the Tetsuga Pond*) is a folklore that takes place in feudal Japan. Subject matters and settings varied, but Takarazuka references continued to be constant. A reader who is familiar with the *Phoenix* series may be disoriented to see the familiar image of phoenix singing and dancing with other characters, or acting like a sassy teenager girl, in its lesser-known 1956 *shojo* manga version. *Phoenix* was first serialized in *Manga Shonen* in 1953 as a prehistoric drama, and it was reworked in *Shojo Club* in 1956, as a sort of operatic "costume drama," encompassing ancient civilizations of Egypt, Rome, and Greece. *Niji no Toride* (*The Rainbow Fortress*, 1956) takes place in an unnamed Middle Eastern country, in a setting similar to Takarazuka's early "Orientalist" revues. *Soyokaze san* (1955) and its sequel *Himawari san* (1956), though it takes place in 1950s Japan, have "dream" and "fantasy" sequences that look distinctly like scenes in ballet or musical theater.

As I mentioned earlier, *shojo manga* was produced mostly by male artists during this period, such as Chiba Tetsuya and Akatsuka Fujio, before they transitioned to sports manga (Chiba) and gag manga (Akatsuka). This trend was quickly reversed in the late 1950s, when a group of young female artists made their debut. All of these artists, including Watanabe Masako, Maki Miyako, and Mizuno Hideko, had been avid readers of Tezuka's work. Being only slightly older than the readers, the new generation of female cartoonists dealt closely with issues and concerns of adolescent female readers, such as friendship, first love, body image, and the fear of imminent adulthood. The dominant image of the heroines shifted from the "idealized princess" to the life-size young woman with insecurities and anxieties.

Tezuka rarely produced *shojo* manga after the 1963 reworking of *Princess Knight*. However, elements from his *shojo* manga continued to appear in his comics of different genres. Yao Bikuni, the heroine of *Hi no tori Igyō Hen* (*Phoenix: Chapter of Strange Beings*, 1976) is haunted by the Sapphire-like fate of being raised as a man. The outgoing, tomboyish charm of Tezuka's early *shojo* manga characters also evolved into more fully developed characters in later years. Maria in *Yakeppachi no Maria* (*Yakeppachi's Maria*, 1970), Wato san in *Mitsume ga toru* (*The Three-Eyed One*, 1974–1978), and Senri Mariko in *Nanairo Inko* (*Seven-Colored Parrot*, 1981) are clearly direct descendents of Kanoko, Yokko, and Himawari.

After a long sabbatical from *shojo* manga, Tezuka undertook a project, *Niji no Prelude* (*The Rainbow Prelude*), in 1975. This work is full of indulgent Takarazuka references that had been infrequent since the mid-1960s. Tezuka was perhaps inspired and encouraged by the hit of *Versaille no bara* (*Roses of Versaille*, 1972–1974) by Ikeda Riyoko, which became a national sensation. While unprecedented in its dramaturgical complexity, *Roses of Versailles* was also a "revival" of classical *shojo* manga: it featured exotic settings, extravagant costumes and decor, romance, some comic relief, intertextual references and, most important, an ill-fated cross-dressed heroine. The story takes place during the years preceding the French Revolution, interspersing fictional events and characters with historical facts. Tezuka's *The Rainbow Prelude* also revolved around a historical event, the Polish revolution and the life of Fryderyk Chopin. The story opens when a young man, named Renee, stops at a used furniture shop for directions to the Warsaw Music Academy. When Renee identifies himself as an incoming student at the Academy, Yosef, a store clerk, challenges him to play the old piano in the store. As the story unfolds, Renee turns out to be a cross-dressed woman named Louise. Like Sapphire, Louise's disguise is awfully unconvincing, though no one seems to suspect. Her romantic interests, Yosef and Fryderyk, are drawn with delicately androgynous features reminiscent of Takarazuka's *otoko-yaku*, though they are clearly genetic males in the story. The title sequence in figure 6.3 features an image of a dancing ensemble in matching costumes, with androgynous men in top hats and white trousers.

While *The Rainbow Prelude* indulges in the musical-theater reference and nostalgia for early *shojo* manga, it also introduces experimentation and new vocabulary for the new era. What makes this work different from *Princess Knight*, or any other of Tekuka's existing comics, is the visual representation of mu-

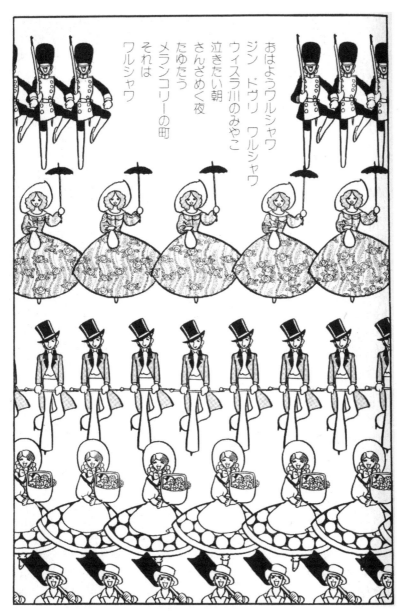

Figure 6.3. The opening scene of *Niji no prelude* [*The Rainbow Prelude*]. © Tezuka Productions. Reproduced with permission.

sic. Most of the key scenes in this work are accompanied by music, depicted through a variety of innovative symbols. In a furious, strong composition, large musical notes jump out of the piano; when Louise plays a soft, romantic tune, the page is filled with curving bars of music adorned with flowers. Some scenes suggest existing compositions, inviting the readers to imagine the music as they read. For instance, the music Yosef dares Louise to play in the first scene in the furniture shop is an etude by Chopin, who later turns out to be Louise's classmate; in another scene, Louise plays the national anthem of Poland. The story ends with Fryderyk at the piano, furiously composing his etude number twelve, "Revolution." *The Rainbow Prelude* and *Unico* (1976), a fantasy featuring an adorable baby unicorn, became Tezuka's last *shojo* manga.

The *Shojo* manga genre went through another major transformation during the early 1970s, departing further from Tezuka's style and diverging into smaller subgenres. *Shojo* manga artists during this period departed from the traditional "big-eyed" look and sweet romances, experimenting with complex narrative structures and unconventional themes. One group of such artists was called *nijū yonen gumi* (twenty-four-year group), named after the year in which most of the artists were born: Showa 24 (1959). One of the members of this group, Hagio Moto, broke the convention that *shojo* manga must have a teenage heroine. Hagio often chose preteen boys, grown women, or even men as her protagonists. The artists also experimented with new drawing styles: Yamagishi Ryōko, for instance, is known for her Art Nouveau–inspired style (Yonezawa, *Shojo manga no sekai II* 86).

One of the most important contributions of the twenty-four-year group was the establishment of *bishonen* (pretty boy) or *shonen ai* (boys' love) manga, a subgenre that Tezuka never attempted. One of Hagio's best-known series, *Thoma no shinzō* (*Thoma's Heart*, 1974), is a mysterious love story between two young boys that takes place in a German boarding school, and her *Poe no ichizoku* (*The Family of Poe*, 1972–1976) is a series that revolves around two adolescent boy vampires (named Edgar and Allan) who live eternal lives. Each episode takes place in a different time and location in European history. Other artists such as Takemiya Keiko, Aoike Yasuko, and Yamagishi Ryōko also took on projects of similar motifs: Takamiya's *Kaze to ki no uta* (*The Song of Wind and Trees*) also took place in a boarding school and is considered the greatest achievement of the *shonen ai* genre to date; Yamagishi's historical fiction *Hi izuru tokoro no tenshi* (*The Prince of the Rising Sun*) caused a controversy, for it depicted the (fictional) homosexual life of Shōtoku Taishi (574–622), a political and religious leader who introduced Buddhism to Japan.

Though the popularity of male homosexual narratives in *shojo* manga demands another book altogether to fully explore, it still seems related to the "women-dressed-as-men" character performance in earlier works. The delicately slim, androgynous bodies of the *bishonen* characters were often depicted with excessively "feminine" traits such as thick eyelashes and flowing long hair. The already-established reading protocol of *shojo* manga encouraged readers to both identify with the central characters, perceiving a boy character as a stand-in for a girl reader. A homosexual narrative between two boy characters thereby transforms into a heterosexual narrative—or even female homosexual narrative—in reception. In this way, 1970s *shonen ai* manga provides a model of communication that cannot be fixed either in homosexual or in heterosexual discourse: it allowed the readers to weave through a number of possible interpretations, functioning as a safe metaphor through which the young readers could explore and embrace their sexuality.

Shojo manga today is a large, rich genre that remains largely unexplored outside Japan. Looking at some of the *shojo* manga titles at bookstores today, one may not associate them with works of Tezuka Osamu. Tezuka's influences on the genre, however, are much more direct and deeply ingrained than may seem apparent. The reason why Tezuka did not continue to produce comics in this genre may have been that the genre, despite some critically acclaimed works in the seventies and beyond, was still regarded as somewhat inferior to *shonen* manga. *Shojo* manga, also, is a much more transient genre than *shonen* manga, except for a few highly established artists who remain popular. One former *shojo* manga artist explained to me in an interview: "In *shojo* manga, it is important that you (the artist) relate to the readers on a very basic level. You have to know what it feels like to have a crush on a boy in your homeroom class, you have to know their fashion, you have to know what kind of music they listen to. Many *shojo* manga artists are young, just out of high school. When they get older and can't relate to teenagers the same way, they disappear or transition to 'ladies comics,' comics for more mature women."

Chapter 7

TORMENTING AFFAIRS WITH ANIMATION

Tezuka Osamu often remarked: "Comics is my wife, and animation is my lover." Tezuka's relationship with animation was long and complex, characterized by a constant mix of love and hate, enchantment and disappointment, devotion and betrayal. This passionate, albeit tormenting love affair started at a young age, seeing animations on his father's film projector, or at the movie theaters. Asahi Kaikan, one of the larger movie theaters in Osaka, held an annual "New Year's Animation Festival" on January 3. Tezuka's mother took her three children to this event every year, and young Osamu grew familiar—as other Japanese children did—with Mickey Mouse, Popeye, Betty Boop, and other characters. His innocent "crush" turned into a full-fledged, all-consuming love affair when he started Mushi Productions in 1961 to make his own animation films. In 1963, Tezuka made Japan's first TV series, *Tetsuwan Atom* (*Mighty Atom*), which became a huge hit not only in Japan but also overseas.

It is a mistake, however, to assume that Japanese animation started with Tezuka. On the contrary, the history of Japanese animation goes as far back as the history of film itself. Japanese movie theaters started showing animation films as early as 1909. Émile Cohl's "Fantasmagorie" became a hit in 1910, followed by "Le Cauchemar du fantoche (The Puppet's Nightmare)" and "Un Drame chez les fantoches (A Puppet Drama)." The films featured stick-figure characters in white on black backgrounds, as if drawn with a piece of chalk on a blackboard. Following this, Shimokawa Hekoten, a cartoonist and former apprentice of cartoonist Kitazawa Rakuten, made the first Japanese animation film, *Imokawa Keizō genkanban no maki* (*Imokawa Keizō, House-sitter*), in 1916. Other early animators include Kouchi Jun'ichi and Kitayama Seitarō. Kōchi created two popular characters, Hana Heko Nai and Chamebō, and Kitayama produced a number of folktale adaptations. The Japanese government started endorsing the use of animation films as educational tools in 1923, which led to the active production of educational animation films.

Early animators experimented with their techniques, constantly evolving the form. In his efforts to make Japan's first animation film, Shimokawa Hekoten situated a camera in front of a blackboard and drew on it with white chalk; after capturing one frame, he would erase a part of the image and redraw it, then capture the next frame. Kitayama Eiga Seisakujo, a studio founded in 1921, invented a method called *kiri nuki hō* (cut-out method): it involved filming cut-out drawings of characters laid on top of a separate background drawing. Shadow puppet animation also became popular, inspired by a German shadow puppet animation *Kalif Storch*, released in 1924. In 1926, Ōfuji Shinrō (also often spelled Ofuji) invented a form called *chiyogami eiga*, a kind of puppet animation using Japanese traditional paper puppets (chiyogami ningyō). Ōfuji continued to produce chiyogami eiga until his death in 1961. His *Kujira* (*Whale*, 1950) and *Yūrei sen* (*Ghost Ship*, 1953) received awards at the Cannes Film Festival and Venice Film Festival, respectively. His achievements are commemorated through the Ōfuji Award, given annually to the most outstanding animation film at Mainichi Film Festival. Tezuka, in 1961, became the first recipient of this prestigious award. Celluloid animation, which was invented in the United States in 1913, did not become mainstream in Japan until the 1930s.

Despite Japanese animators' efforts at experimentation and originality, domestic animation struggled to compete with slicker American and European counterparts. Major movie theaters often rejected esoteric domestic animations in favor of foreign imports such as Disney's "Mickey Mouse" series. The competition became even more severe after the coming of sound film. While the audiences became increasingly more accustomed to sound animation film, most Japanese studios did not have the technology or budget to produce them. Consequently, Japanese animators found work mainly in educational films and in political PR, since the venues for these kinds of films often did not have the equipment for screening sound films. Socialist groups were particularly enthusiastic about using film as a tool for public education and outreach. The *Nihon Proletariat Eiga Dōmei* (Japan Proletariat Film Association) was founded to spread socialist messages through film, including animation. This trend continued until after the establishment of the *Chian Iji Hō* (Public Order Maintenance Act) in 1925, which prohibited socialist and communist movements.

The technological innovations and the political climate of the 1930s transformed the Japanese animation industry in many ways. Japanese manufacturers succeeded in inexpensive mass production of film stock in 1934, which allowed animators to bring the cost of production down. Meanwhile, Japan's invasion of China and participation in the Pacific War meant the restriction on foreign media; films by Japanese animators now found slots at major movie theaters. Like print comics, animation films during the war period became increasingly militaristic. By 1938, all theatrically released animation films featured war motifs, if not overt militarist propaganda. Ironically, it was during this period of censorship and propaganda that Japan produced a film that Tezuka later named as his seminal experience with animation. On April 12, 1944, Shōchiku Studio released *Momotarō umi no shinpei* (*Momotarō the Sacred Soldiers of the Sea*), a theatrical feature loosely based on Japan's attack on Palembang. In the film, the Japanese Navy is represented by the figure of Momotarō, or "Peach Boy," a hero of an ancient folktale. In the original tale, Momotarō is a boy born of a giant peach, who fights monsters and marries a princess in the end. In the film, Momotarō parachutes down on a tropical island and occupies it. The film, full of beautiful imagery despite its colonialist narrative, did not receive the critical acclaim or popularity it deserved. In the climate of Japan's impending surrender, few people were interested in seeing an animation film. Most school-age children, who would have been the target audience for the film, had been sent away to the countryside to escape the air raids long before. On May 27, a little over a month after the film's release, Shōchiku Studio burned down from a massive air raid.

Nonetheless, *Momotarō the Sacred Soldiers of the Sea* inspired Tezuka and prompted him to dream of making his own animation films. While the plot clearly serves as national propaganda, it also contained technical innovations and artistic sophistication that was previously unseen in Japanese animation. Tezuka described:

I saw this movie in a run-down movie theater in a bombed-out town. I wept, awed by what Japanese animation could do. There were adventures in this film that were so different from previous films. More importantly, it contained lyricism that wove through the entire film. The rice fields at the opening of the film. The exquisite stream in the valley. The humorous movements of the animals who work to build a military base, their movements exactly synced to the music. The chorus of three monkeys. The shadow puppet "play within the play." The last scene, Momotarō's meeting with the Monster General, featured an English-speaking monster with Japanese subtitles. (Tezuka, quoted in Yamaguchi and Watanabe, 233)

In one of the scenes on the island, Momotarō teaches a group of animals how to speak Japanese, using a song called "Aiueo no uta." Tezuka later created an homage to this scene in his 1965 animation *Jungle Emperor*. The protagonist, Leo the White Lion, teaches a similar song to other animals.

Nineteen forty-five was the year of Japan's surrender in World War II, and a year Tezuka reunited with American animation—or American films at large. He watched *Snow White* fifty times in Osaka that year. His dream of making animation films grew strong, but the reality of a Japanese animation industry was not as accessible as that of *akahon* comics. In 1946—the year Tezuka watched Disney's *Bambi* (1941) over eighty times—he visited an animation studio in Tokyo and sought employment. He was rejected since his "style was not suited for animation." When he asked if his drawings were not good enough, they explained that the process of making animation films would not be a good fit for anyone who has been successful in "lucrative" comic book industry; it is labor intensive and financially unrewarding. Though Tezuka persisted, he could not convince them (Yamaguchi and Watanabe 45).

Tezuka's first animation project finally materialized twelve years later, in 1958. Tōei Dōga, a studio that was founded as a branch of Tōei Film Company, proposed a feature film based on Tezuka's comic series *Boku no Songokū* (*Songokū the Monkey*, 1952–1959). The story is a comical retelling of a Chinese epic, *Journey to the West*: Gokū, a mischievous monkey king, accompanies a monk Sanzō Hōshi on a Journey to India to retrieve a special scripture. Tezuka participated in this project, retitled *Saiyūki* (*Journey to the West*), not only as the author of the original but also as a storyboard artist. Tezuka proposed some changes to the original story, including new characters and a new ending. While Gokū did not have a romantic interest in the comics, Tezuka gave him a girlfriend named Rin Rin in the film. At the end of the film, Gokū returns to his home village, only to find out that Rin Rin had died during his long absence. The final scene depicts Gokū, at Rin Rin's grave, promising her that he would become a great monkey. This proposed ending, typical of Tezuka's "anti-happy-ending" which had been widely accepted in the comics medium, was vetoed by the rest of the production team. In the released version of the film, Gokū happily reunites with Rin Rin in the final scene. *Journey to the West* was completed and released in 1960. The film not only did well in box offices, but also received an honorable mention at the thirteenth Venice International Children's Film Festival. It was released in the United States under the title *Alakazam the Great*.

The success of *Journey to the West*, combined with the frustration of not being the creative leader in the project, prompted Tezuka to found his own animation studio, Tezuka Dōga Gaisha (Tezuka Moving Picture Company), in June 1961. The timing coincided with Tezuka's completion of his Ph.D. and with the period during which Tezuka grew frustrated with the new trends of comics such as *gekiga*. The company changed its name to Mushi Productions in 1962 and produced its first project, *Aru machikado no monogatari* (*The Story of a Street Corner*). The thirty-nine-minute film contains no spoken text and is more of a visual poem than a narrative fiction. It takes place in a small imaginary town, and its main characters are a little girl, a family of mice, and the posters pasted on the walls. The beginning of the film depicts heartwarming incidents in the peaceful town: the poster of a violinist falls in love with that of a pianist, and the two play a duet that make other posters dance and sing. A little girl loses her stuffed bear and the family of mice carries it off. The tone of the film changes when a war breaks out and all the posters become covered with posters showing a dictator's face. Tanks enter the city, and bombs start falling, burning down buildings, trees, and posters. The violinist and the pianist, two posters in love, reunite as they are swirled up into the sky in heat and wind. The film ends with the little girl finding her stuffed bear, and young trees sprouting out of the ruin. *The Story of a Street Corner* received the inaugural Ōfuji Award at Mainichi Film Festival, as well as two other major national awards. The same year, Tezuka also produced a three-minute piece called *Osu* (*Male*). The film, about a man who has just murdered a woman, is narrated entirely through the perspective of a cat, in two round screens shaped like a cat's eyes.

Mushi Production's second major project was *Tetsuwan Atom*, based on Tezuka's comics of the same title. Apart from the three short folktale adaptations that were broadcast from NHK (Nihon Hōsō Kyōkai; Japan Broadcasting Association) in 1961, this was the first TV animation series made in Japan.[1] It started on New Year's Day in 1963 and continued weekly until December 31, 1966, with an extremely tight initial budget of approximately five thousand dollars per episode. To keep the cost low, Tezuka and his staff came up with techniques to reduce the number of drawings. It was already customary in the genre of limited animation to reduce labor and cost by isolating small moving parts from stationary parts of the drawing (such as a moving mouth superimposed over a stationary face), but Tezuka went even further. Fredrik Schodt's *Astro Boy Essays* lists eight cost- and money-saving techniques Mushi Productions invented in order to make this project happen:

1. Shooting three frames of film for every drawing instead of one or two to create the illusion of fluid movement.
2. Using only one drawing in a *tome*, or "still" shot, when shooting close-ups of a character's face.
3. Zooming in or out on face shots or physically sliding a single draw-

---

1 The short series *Instant History* was produced by Yokoyama Ryūichi, the creator of *Fuku-chan* series.

ing under the camera to create the illusion of movement with a single drawing.

4. Shooting a single short sequence of animated drawings and then repeating it again and again while sliding the background image. This was particularly useful for repetitive movements like walking or running. Six or twelve drawings could thus be used to show a movement as long as necessary.

5. When a character moved an arm or leg, animating only that portion and shooting the rest from the drawing.

6. Animating the mouth alone (rather than using full animation synchronized to the sound) and abbreviating the drawings used, showing only a fully open mouth, a shut mouth, and a partially open mouth to represent characters speaking.

7. Creating a "bank system" of images to save on the total number of drawings allowing reuse of the same drawings in different situations.

8. Using more short takes in place of single long takes that usually required more movement. (Schodt 71–72)

Among these techniques, number 7, the bank system, was particularly important. Tezuka describes the technique as follows:

As we accumulated drawings, we organized and filed them into shelves, then reused them over and over. We named this system the Bank System. It was our petty attempt to save money. It was fine as long as the viewers had forgotten about them by the time we reused them. But if we used the same sequences too many times, children would notice and complain. Then we knew that it was time to get rid of that particular sequence. [. . .] For example, for the character of Astro Boy, we stored different facial expressions like "angry," "crying," "laughing" and "surprised." We also filed "close-up," "entire body," and "far away." We started drawing isolated body parts and storing them. There were also things like rain, wind, snow, waves, smoke, volcano, avalanche, weapon, different kinds of animals, transportation, even stars that come out of their heads when characters faint. (Tezuka, *Boku wa manga ka* 191)

These techniques, invented out of necessity, strangely gave *Astro Boy* a unique, low-tech charm. *Astro Boy*'s style of movement (or the lack thereof) was often associated with *kamishibai*, or paper-play, a popular Japanese street-performance form that involves a solo storyteller and a series of cardboard placards with images printed on front, texts on the back. Viewers also associated the occasional stop-motion with *mie*, a technique used in *kabuki* theater where an actor strikes a pose to punctuate important speech or emotions. While some viewers criticized the bank system as an abomination of the animation art, others enjoyed recognizing familiar scenes and sequences in different episodes, the same way they found delight in knowing and recognizing Tezuka's stars in the Star System. In July 1964, *Astro Boy* also appeared as a theatrical feature animation. The film was based on three episodes that had already been broadcast on TV, re-edited to a single one and a half hour episode.

Following *Astro Boy*, Mushi Productions produced a number of other TV animation series. *Ginga Shonen Tai* (*Galaxy Boys Troop*, 1963), a collaboration with the puppet theater company Takeda Ningyō Za, was a unique mix of live puppets and animation. *W 3* (1965), the company's second fully animated series, started in June 1965. *Jungle Taitei* (*Jungle Emperor*, 1965), Japan's first full-color TV animation series, followed in October. Mushi Productions spent approximately fifty thousand dollars per episode on *Jungle Emperor*, ten times more than *Astro Boy*'s initial budget. *Jungle Emperor* was broadcast in the United States under the title *Kimba the White Lion*, and later served as the inspiration for Disney's *The Lion King*. During this period, Mushi Productions planned a number of other projects that ended up not being fully realized. In September 1963, the company set up plans for twenty-six independent one-hour episodes based on Tezuka's most popular comics, including *New Treasure Island*, *Princess Knight*, and *0 Man*. Scheduling difficulty and budget concerns eventually prohibited production of all but one of the episodes, *New Treasure Island*, which turned out to have nothing to do with Tezuka's hit comic book from 1947. The story was a rather straightforward adaptation of Stevenson's novel *Treasure Island*, with animals standing in for the novel's characters.

By the mid-1960s, Mushi Productions, which started with only half a dozen staff members, had grown into a large studio with 260 employees, and Tezuka often experienced frustration over losing control of his work. The demanding weekly schedule of *Astro Boy* forced the staff to come up with new stories in a "good, fast, and cheap" manner. The expedient solution was to create a new villain every week. Astro Boy fought against and destroyed new monsters and other robots one after another. Tezuka recalls his frustration during this time:

It was out of my control. Mushi Productions had grown too big for me to handle. I would throw in an idea for an episode, and the staff would ignore it in favor of another idea, a flashier and more easily executed one. It was all about profit, not quality. Critics started calling *Astro Boy* a "potboiler." Some said that they couldn't even stand to watch it. One wrote: "Tezuka has run out of all his genius ideas, there's nothing left in him." I felt destroyed. The robot boy on the

TV screen still looked like Astro Boy, but I knew that he was no longer the same Astro Boy who was my dearest son. (*Boku wa manga ka* 193)

The frustration eventually caused Tezuka to end the series by "killing" Astro Boy: in the final episode aired on December 31, 1966, Astro Boy carried a dangerous nuclear weapon into the sun, *kamikaze* pilot fashion, in order to save the earth. This ending revisits the recurring theme of self-sacrificial death in Tezuka's early works. In the same year, *Jungle Emperor* was also discontinued, for its sponsor refused to fund the series any longer. The popularity of *Jungle Emperor* had gone significantly down, partly because the beautiful color images—its main draw—were not available to most consumers who did not have color TVs. During this period, the viewers' taste had also shifted. Newly popular animation series such as *Osomatsu kun* and *Obake no Q-tarō* (*Q-tarō the Ghost*)—based on comics by Akatsuka Fujio and Fujiko Fujio, respectively—featured more nonsensical and slapstick humor rather than plot-driven narrative.

After Astro Boy's tragic death, Mushi Productions produced *Gokū no Daibōken* (*Gokū's Great Adventures*) as a kind of "replacement" series. Though it was based on the same comic book series *Songoku the Monkey*, this version was clearly different from the previous film adaptation *Journey to the West* (1958). Unlike Tōei, Mushi Productions framed it as a gag animation, emphasizing slapstick and low humor. The series marked a moderate success, as it successfully incorporated the new trends in TV animation. In the same year, a less successful *Princess Knight* also went on the air. After these two series, Mushi Productions changed its directions in 1968, departing from adaptations of Tezuka's comics and including more diverse subjects and styles. *Wampaku Tanteidan* (*Mischievous Detectives*) was an adaptation of detective novels by Edogawa Ranpo, and *Animal 1* was a wrestling narrative based on a *gekiga* by Kawasaki Noboru. Tezuka appears as an actor playing "himself" in *The Vampires*, a hybrid project combining live action and animation based on Tezuka's 1966 series. Mushi Productions continued to produce a wider range of animation series in years that followed, including *Dororo* (1969), adapted from Tezuka's period-monster drama; *Ashita no Jō* (*Tomorrow's Jō*, 1970), based on Chiba Tetsuya's hit boxing *gekiga*; *Sasurai no Taiyō* (*Wandering Sun*, 1971), a teen idol narrative, featuring, as characters, existing teen celebrities. Mushi Productions produced sixteen animation series in total, ending with *Wansa kun* in 1973.

It is dangerous to write about Tezuka's animation films as if he is the sole "author" of all of them, since it is often unclear as to what extent Tezuka held creative control over the projects. Animation is inherently collaborative, and its process requires putting together a group of people who possess different skills.

The need for large funding to make a project necessitates the presence of a corporate sponsor, which encourages commercialization and the power of the producer to determine some of the artistic choices. Tezuka himself identified this as the challenge of making animation:

What I learned from my experiences with *Journey to the West* was that, the most important thing in making animation films is not the product, but the human relations in the process. I don't know any other work that requires as much harmony between the groups of specialists involved in it. [. . .] There is no room for lone-wolf mentality or elitism. I learned in a hard way, that the more specialized skills the project requires, there is a danger of the project losing its personality. (Tezuka, *Boku wa manga ka* 181)

This balance was difficult for Tezuka throughout his life. According to his former staff, he remained a difficult collaborator. There are numerous anecdotes of Tezuka coming into the studio and insisting on someone redrawing an entire scene at the last minute. Sometimes he redrew it himself.

The experimental films were very different altogether. Unlike the TV series, these works aimed at artistic rather than commercial goals, and they assumed sophisticated adult audiences, primarily other animators and artists. Japanese visual artists were discovering experimental animation as a new form of expression in the late 1950s, and the foundation of *Animation Sannin no Kai* (*Three People Animation Group*) in 1960 further fueled the interest. The group included three prominent artists in the field: cartoonist Kuri Yōji, designer Yanagihara Ryōhei, and illustrator Manabe Hiroshi. They held annual showings, which started taking a more large-scale, open-to-the-public festival format in their fourth year, soliciting submissions from other artists. Tezuka entered two short films, *Memory* and *Ningyo* (*Mermaid*) that year, though they were not the most popular entries in the festival. Tezuka continued to participate in the festival, entering *Shizuku* (*A Drop of Water*) in 1965 and *The Story of a Streetcorner* (1962) in 1966.

Among Tezuka's early experimental films, *The Pictures at an Exhibition* (1967) received particular recognition, bringing Tezuka multiple awards, including his second Ōfuji Award. The film was made to an existing piece of music, Modest Mussorgsky's 1874 piano suite of the same title. The ten independent episodes in the film range in themes and styles: in one episode, a bee wanders into a seemingly beautiful garden in the midst of high-rise buildings, only to find that all the flowers are made of metal; in another, a plastic surgeon transforms faces of a number of people, but his face collapses when he sneezes at the end. The art styles vary from colorful, lush images to crude collages, charcoal drawings, or stick figures. Some sequences feature smooth, fluid movements while others are more jumpy. The episode of a meditating monk uses only three drawings, pushing the technique of limited animation to the extreme and elevating it to an artistic choice. The final sequence of the film shows characters in all the episodes marching toward "the gate of triumph." In the final shot, the viewers see the gate from above, as the "camera" zooms out and up, far away and into the sky. This sequence was shot in Tezuka's backyard, by physically retracting the camera from a twenty-by-twenty-eight-feet background painting.

Mushi Productions made three theatrical features for mature audiences, as an attempt to expand the target audience of animation films beyond children. Upon release of Mushi Production's first "adult" animation film, *Senya ichiya monogatari* (*One Thousand and One Nights*), Tezuka called it "animerama"—a combination of animation, cinerama, and drama. The two-hour film begins when Aladdin, a poor water merchant in Baghdad, falls in love with a beautiful female slave named Miriam. Aladdin and Miriam spend a passionate evening together, but a villain separates them and Miriam dies shortly afterward. Fifteen years later, Aladdin becomes a king and seeks revenge on the villain. The film becomes more risqué with inclusion of previously taboo themes such as incest: Aladdin, now a king, seduces a beautiful girl into his harem and discovers that the girl is his own daughter—Miriam had given birth to the child before her death. The film became a box office hit in June 1969. The company's second "adult-targeted" film, *Cleopatra* (1970), explored similar material, but with a clearly different style. Tezuka and his production team sprinkled this film with popular culture parodies. Looking at this film today, few are able to catch all the jokes. This was a part of the reason why this film, though ambitious and lavishly produced with a high budget, did not do well in box offices. Still, the two "animerama" films redefined animation film as a medium capable of eroticism and "adult" humor. This achievement, perhaps unintentionally, helped build a foundation for today's ubiquitous "adult" or pornographic *anime*—in attempting to create an animation film that is closer to live-action erotica, Mushi Production's films gave birth to the new, particular mode of eroticism that could *only* be expressed through animation.[2]

Tezuka resigned from Mushi Productions in 1971, taking responsibility for the company's financial crisis. Behind this resignation was also Tezuka's disagreement with the staff and the direction that company was taking. Although Tezuka personally absorbed the company's debts upon his resignation, Mushi

---

2. Mushi Productions produced another "adult" film, *Kanashimi no beradonna* (*Beradonna of Sadness*) in 1973, but Tezuka had already resigned from the company and had nothing to do with the production.

Productions went under two years later in 1973. After some time off from animation, Tezuka and his new company, Tezuka Productions, made Japan's first two-hour TV animation special in 1978. Tezuka maintained close control over this work, *100 man nen chikyū no tabi: Bandā Book (1,000,000 Year Trip to Earth, Bandā Book)*, writing, directing, and even drawing some of the scenes. This ninety-four-minute work was aired as a part of a special programming called "Ai wa chikyū o sukuu (Love Will Save the Earth)." Tezuka created eight more TV animation films for this programming annually between 1979 and 1986, with varying degrees of involvement. Some were based on Tezuka's existing comics (*Prime Rose*, 1983; *Mitsume ga tōru*, 1985) while others were originals. As part of the special programming, these works had strong humanitarian messages, with subject matters ranging from world peace to ethics of biotechnology. Tezuka Productions also produced a few TV animation series, including the remake of *Astro Boy* in 1980. The new series featured the same recognizable theme song, though this time with 1980s synthesizer accompaniment. Each episode was updated to suit the new generation of viewers.

Tezuka produced two of his best-known experimental animation films during the 1980s, *Jumping* (1984) and *Broken Down Film* (1985). The two films received numerous awards at international film and animation festivals. Both of these short films investigate the formal properties of animation films through self-conscious humor, the themes that permeate much of Tezuka's comics. *Jumping* is a nonverbal narrative told exclusively through a long subjective shot. The viewers see everything through the perspective of the film's protagonist, a girl skipping and jumping down a country road. As she jumps, the ground moves, an insect flies across, and a tree branch moves in and out of the screen. A car comes toward her and she jumps over it. She continues jumping, higher and farther each time, landing in the bushes, on a rooftop, or on the wing of an airplane. When she falls, she—and the viewers—find themselves in hell facing two devils. One of the devils pokes her with a giant fork, and throws her back onto the earth, on the peaceful country road where she started. *Broken Down Film* is a "faux" old film that takes place in the old West, featuring two cowboys and a female romantic interest. The scratches, noises, and misalignment in the film interact with the narrative, in a series of self-parodic visual jokes.

Despite his deep love for animation, Tezuka was not always successful at it, commercially or artistically. Some regard Tezuka's influence on Japanese animation as negative rather than positive: he is responsible for much of the money-saving (and quality-compromising) techniques in TV animations, which mark them as a "low" form of entertainment as opposed to "art." However, Tezuka and his obsession with animation clearly built a foundation for today's Japanese animation, if indirectly. One of the greatest achievements of Mushi Productions was finding and grooming young talent who later became the leaders of Japanese animation. Tomino Yoshiyuki, Dezaki Osamu, Mori Masaki, and many others who lead the Japanese animation industry today all worked under Tezuka at Mushi Productions, before creating their own internationally popular series, such as *Mobile Suit Gundam* (1981–), *Black Jack*, and *Toki no tabihito* (*Time Stranger*, 1986), respectively. "Comics is my wife, and animation is my lover"—Like an unfaithful and promiscuous lover, animation was dependent not only on Tezuka's creative impulse, but also on the work and creativity of many others. Like an overindulged lover, animation was expensive. Still, Tezuka kept going back, captivated by her charm and sometimes spending his last dime. We may say that today's Japanese animation, an overwhelming mix of profound artistic achievement and cheaply produced commercial potboilers, are all his illegitimate children.

Chapter 8

LOW HUMOR/HIGH DRAMA, THE TWO FACES OF ADULT COMICS

The morning after Tezuka's death, *Asahi Shinbun* printed a column titled "Tetsuwan Atom no message (The Message of Astro Boy)," which read as follows: "Why do the Japanese love comics so much? The sight of passengers on commuter trains all reading weekly comic magazines strikes most foreigners as strange. [. . .] Why haven't people of other countries been reading comics (like the Japanese) [. . .]? One of the answers is, that they did not have Tezuka Osamu." While this statement neatly (and movingly) sums up Tezuka's impact on twentieth-century Japanese popular culture, it also contains a bit of irony. Most likely, what the "foreigners" in the article are reacting to is the sight of *adults* reading comics on the train. While some of Tezuka's most critically acclaimed works are comics for adults, he initially caused a decline in adult-targeted comics during his early career. In the late 1940s to early 1950s, most of the young aspiring cartoonists inspired by Tezuka worked in *shonen manga*, and adult comics suffered from lack of interest and lack of new talent. Among the major comic magazines that were launched in 1946, *VAN*, *Shinsō*, and *Hope* were discontinued by 1953. *Manga*, which printed much of the wartime propaganda and later played an important part in GHQ's media and education reform, also ended its nine-year history in June 1951. Of course, the *Asahi Shinbun* passage speaks of so much more than the prevalence of comics for adults. Children who grew up reading Tezuka's comics during the immediate postwar era were conditioned for lifelong consumption of comics as entertainment. Comics for adults made a dramatic comeback in the 1960s, though not in the form that it was in the prewar years. Instead of being witty political comics, they were story comics, only with "adult" content. By "adult," I do not mean pornographic or even necessarily sexual; these were comics that appealed to adults who lived and worked as members of the Japanese postwar society, with topics ranging from politics to golf.

Tezuka Osamu started producing comics for mature readership in 1955 with two short works titled *Konchū shojo no hōrōki* (*The Travels of an Insect Girl*) and *Dai san teikoku no hōkai* (*The Fall of the Third Reich*). In *The Travels of an Insect Girl*, an insect girl attempts suicide, disillusioned by the insect world full of greed and deceit; she finds a new purpose in life after witnessing that the human world, which she had previously idealized, suffers the same. *The Fall of the Third Reich* depicts a future world reminiscent of *1984*, where the dictator constantly controls his citizens through TV monitors. Both of these works were somewhere between story comics and illustrated short story: half the time, images are laid out without comic panels; most of the texts are narrative "voiceovers" rather than speeches. Tezuka also adopted a new drawing style, with sketchier and more broken lines, different from the round, more fluid lines of his children's comics. Even the speech balloons are depicted with broken lines that do not close completely (Fig. 8.1).

In 1957, Tezuka undertook *Zōkin to hōseki* (*The Rag and the Jewel*) as the first true "story comic" for adult audiences. Unlike a *shonen* or *shojo* manga whose prerequisite was a charming protagonist, the heroine of this light-hearted romantic comedy was an unattractive, overweight office worker named Zōno Kinko. The story begins when she gets into a car accident and finds herself mysteriously transformed into a beautiful woman. She eventually discovers that she can change her appearance back and forth, into a beautiful woman and back into her old self, by being hit by a car. This popular series was followed by another successful series, *Hyōtan Komako* (1957–1958) and *Shūkan tantei tōjō* (*Here Comes Weekly Detective*, 1959). All of these stories take place in contemporary Japan, focusing more on wit and humor rather than dramatic or absorbing narrative.

As the postwar baby boomers reached their early twenties and entered the workforce in the mid-1960s, Tezuka began actively producing short, self-contained works for magazines that targeted adult audiences. These works, published in magazines such as *Manga Sunday* and *Manga Dokuhon*, were similar to *The Travels of an Insect Girl* in drawing and narrative styles. The text was handwritten without using a typeface, a practice common to adult comics. *Stardust* (1965) is a tale of capitalist greed that revolves around mounds of garbage left on the earth by space aliens; *Ware nakinurete shima to* (*An Uninhibited Island*, 1966) is a love story between a man and a small island. While the premises of these works sound reminiscent of Tezuka's imaginative science fiction, the stories develop with detached cynicism and irony, standing opposite his more "ernest" *shonen manga*—such as *Astro Boy*—with charismatic heroes

Figure 8.1. *Konchū shojo no hōrōki* [*Travels of an Insect Girl*]. © Tezuka Productions. Reproduced with permission.

and moral messages. This positioning is made particularly clear through Astro Boy's brief appearance in *Waga na wa Hyakka* (*My Name Is Hyakka*, 1964). The protagonist, Hyakka, is an android designed as an "ideal" worker created from the data collected from all the employees. He is competent not only at work, but also at seducing women, and he ends up sleeping and impregnating dozens of coworkers. The short story ends with an image of a hospital room full of his newborn children—all looking identically like Astro Boy.

In 1968, Tezuka produced *Ningen domo atsumare!* (*Rally Up Mankind!*), combining the satiric, cynical tone of his adult comics with a long continuous narrative. The protagonist, Tenka Taihei, is a Japanese man who somehow ends up in an artificial insemination experiment facility in a fictional country called Pipania. As it turns out, Taihei's sperm are double-tailed mutants that produce "sexless humans." Scientists keep Taihei in captivity, extracting his sperm and mass-producing sexless humans who are traded as slaves, soldiers, and entertainers. The sexless humans eventually revolt and take over the world, and Taihei, their father, becomes the last nonsexless human on earth. Tezuka names Karel Čapek's science fiction novel *War with the Newts* (1936) as a direct influence for this work. With the success of *Rally Up Mankind!*, Tezuka's adult comics started becoming decidedly more erotic and comical. *Nūdian rettō* (*Nude Man's Archipelago*, 1968) takes place in a future-day Japan where the government has been overtaken by a religious group called Issai Gassai Kyōdan, who bans all clothing. Now everyone must live in the nude, and those who do not comply are punished for "indecent exposure." People's idea of what is erotic has completely changed—strip dancers put on clothes on stage instead of taking them off, and porn magazines feature women with clothes on instead of off. Its theme, the alternate versions of the familiar world, is also repeated in *Hyōroku ki* (*The Record of Hyōroku*, 1968). It is a tale of a young man named Hyōroku and his father, who wander the space in a spaceship looking for a livable planet, where they could find food and women. They land on several planets that seem somewhat similar to the earth at first, but turn out to be completely bizarre. On one planet, all the females look similar to humans, but all the males are the shape and size of cockroaches.

These adult comics are perhaps the most "unlikely" of all of Tezuka's works, dealing with themes and subject matters that are uncharacteristic to him, featuring none of his usual stars or visual jokes. This genre of comics provided Tezuka with lighthearted, low-pressure challenges during the period he often described as his "darkest years," between 1968 and 1973. Having established cinematic storytelling as mainstream in comics, Tezuka also grew somewhat leery of its predominance. He wrote in 1981: "I was feeling unsatisfied with story comics and *gekiga*, where you just follow stories like a movie. I wanted to learn more about humor through adult comics. Sometimes, editors would say 'You seem more alive when you are working on adult comics.' Working with adult jokes, satire, and irony was really cathartic for me" (Tezuka, postscript, *Suppon Monogatari*).

After Tezuka came back to the forefront of *shonen manga* with the hit of *Black Jack* (1973–1983), his adult comics became few and far between. *Hitomi gokū* (*Human Sacrifice*, 1976) was his last major work in this style. Still, the defining elements of his adult comics—nonchalant nudity, nonsensical gag, and dry humor—have worked their way into Tezuka's comics of other genres, inserting a healthy dose of comical eroticism in later hits such as *The Three-Eyed One* (1974–1978) and *Don Dracula* (1979).

Contrasting to this genre of lighthearted adult comics, Tezuka also produced highly dramatic, deeply absorbing, large-scope story comics for mature readership, a genre that emerged during the late 1960s. They were called *seinen manga* (young adult comics) to distinguish themselves from *otona manga* (adult comics). *Seinen manga* became a perfect vehicle for cartoonists to explore complex themes that are too serious or too complicated for young readers, while still keeping a similar form and drawing style. *Chikyū o nomu* (*Swallowing the Earth*, 1968–1969) was Tezuka's first substantial *seinen manga* series, dealing with "grown-up" themes such as sexuality, world economy, and alcoholism. The series looks more similar to his *shonen manga* than his *otona manga*: characters look more recognizable (though none of his usual stars appear), and the panel layout is dynamic and cinematic. The story develops in an unusual structure, which Tezuka explains as a result of poor planning: "To be honest, I was hesitant when they asked me to do an epic drama. Other authors in the magazine, Shirato Sanpei and Ishimori Shōtarō,[1] all did episodic series. [. . .] My series became not only dull in the middle, but too large in scope to handle. I tried to rework the series into a collection of short episodes at one point" (Tezuka, postscript, *Swallowing the Earth*).

The themes Tezuka dealt with in *Swallowing the Earth* were not necessarily new in comics. *Gekiga* had already filled the pages with violence a decade earlier, *harenchi* already brought nudity into comics, and sexual jokes were a recurring motif in *otona manga*. The new genre of *seinen manga*, however, allowed cartoonists to explore these themes with complexity and subtlety. Here, Steven Neale's terms generic and cultural verisimilitude help characterize the difference: "generic verisimilitude allows for considerable play with fantasy inside the bounds of generic credibility, cultural verisimilitude refers us to the norms, mores, and common sense of the social world outside the fiction" (Gledhill, "Soap" 360). Whereas sex and violence established generic verisimilitude in *gekiga* and *harenchi*, it was used to establish cultural verisimilitude in *seinen manga*, as inevitable components of "real life" (Neale, "Questions" 46). In *Swallowing the Earth*, sexual frustration, as is desire, is a natural part of life: the heroine Milda is depicted tossing and turning with desire for a man named Ipponmatsu, while he drinks himself to sleep. In another scene, sex itself is de-

---

1. Cartoonist Ishinomori Shotaro (born Onodera Shotaro) used the penname Ishimori Shotaro prior to 1986. I have consistently used "Ishinomori" throughout the book, but I have used "Ishimori" here, as it is spelled in the original quote.

Figure 8.2. Milda and Ipponmatsu in *Chikyū o nomu* [*Swallowing the Earth*]. © Tezuka Productions. Reproduced with permission.

picted symbolically rather than explicitly: the scene "fades out" before Milda and Ipponmatsu make love for the first time (Fig. 8.2).

Big Comic, a magazine for *seinen manga*, became a venue for some of Tezuka's most ambitious and critically acclaimed work in years to follow. *Kirihito sanka* (*Ode to Kirihito*, 1970) is often compared to Yamazaki Toyoko's 1965 novel *Shiroi Kyotō* (*The Great White Tower*), though Tezuka denied any relations. *Ode to Kirihito*, as does Yamazaki's novel, explores issues of power and ethics within a highly hierarchical world of medicine, using Osaka University Medical School—Tezuka's alma mater—as the model. In contrast to Yamazaki's naturalistic novel, Tezuka's premise is more fantastical, involving a fictional disease called Monmō disease. When the story opens, the protagonist Osanai Kirihito and his colleagues are researching the disease, found only in a remote, mountainous village in northern Japan. This mysterious disease disfigures the patients' bodies during its advanced stages: patients grow excess body hair, their limbs shrink, their skull protrudes—in short, the disease turns them into dogs. Dr. Tatsugaura, Kirihito's superior at the hospital, believes that a virus causes the disease, though Kirihito has some doubts on Tatsugaura's theory. Kirihito becomes infected by the illness when he goes to the village for research. *Ode to Kirihito* questions our ideas of normalcy and humanity through its disturbing and often graphic scenes: Kirihito, transformed into a dog-human by the disease, is sold to a freak show in Taiwan, where he is forced to have intercourse with a female dog. There, he also meets a young circus performer Renka, who is sexually aroused by people with physical deformity. The work also reveals Tezuka's insight into the power relations within the medical community.

Stylistically, *Ode to Kirihito* contains strong references to Russian formalist film. The work uses frequent religious symbolism and juxtaposition of images, reminiscent of the montage effect in Sergei Einstein's films, most prominently *Battleship Potemkin* (1925). During the early stages of the illness, Kirihito experiences a severe headache; the scene depicts a number of abstract images to symbolize his pain (Fig. 8.3). Similarly, many scenes contain explicit religious symbolism. Figure 8.4 is the scene in which Helen Freeze, a former Catholic nun and a Monmō disease patient, is displayed in front of a large audience of medical practitioners. Helen's walk onstage is juxtaposed by an image of Christ carrying a cross; once on stage, the audience is depicted as dozens of eyes. The influence of Eisenstein's 1925 film on Tezuka's 1970 comic seems out of context, but it makes sense when we consider that *Battleship Potemkin* was first released in Japan in 1965 and was much discussed among film enthusiasts. The film was banned during the prewar and postwar occupation periods as communist propaganda.

While long *seinen manga* serials gave Tezuka a venue for exploring long narratives, some of Tezuka's "personal favorite" *seinen manga* took the format of short stories. In 1968, Tezuka started a series called *Kūki no soko* (*Under the Air*). Unlike *Swallowing the Earth*, this series did not have a continuous plot or a recurring set of characters. Each week presented a self-contained episode, ranging in subjects and genres, from Western to horror. Every episode had a clever premise, often with unexpected endings, in a manner reminiscent of Ray Bradbury or Fredric Brown. Many of the episodes introduced the theme of forbidden sexuality, including incest (*Waga tani wa michi nariki*, *Kurai mado no onna*) and bestiality (*Robanna yo*). Tezuka's intimate relationship to this series is apparent in that two of the episodes feature Tezuka himself as a character. In *Uroko ga saki* (*Cape Uroko*), cartoonist Tezuka Osamu goes to a small island to work on his comics and finds out about the deadly pollution caused by a nearby chemical factory. *Robanna yo* (*Rovanna*) depicts Tezuka's strange visit at the home of a friend named Oguri, who had been conducting experiments with a machine that transports objects through space by breaking them into particles. After he accidentally sent his wife through the machine with a

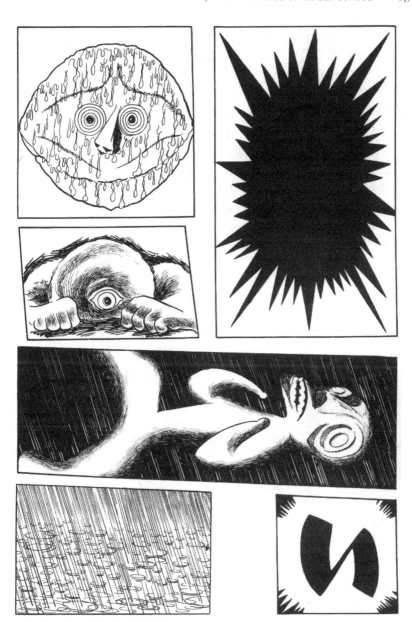

Figure 8.3. A scene of severe headache in *Kirihito Sanka* [*Ode to Kirihito*]. © Tezuka Productions. Reproduced with permission.

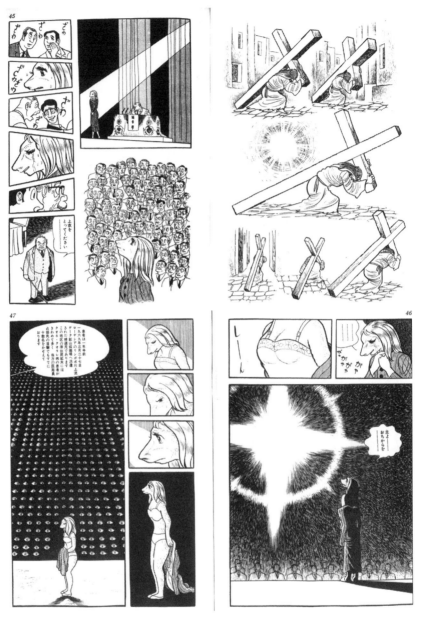

Figure 8.4. Helen Freeze walks in front of the audience in *Ode to Kirihito.* © Tezuka Productions. Reproduced with permission.

donkey, his wife goes insane. Oguri, convinced that the spirit of the wife has now transferred to the donkey, treats the donkey as the wife and the wife as the donkey.

Tezuka's *seinen manga* became increasingly dark and grotesque, as did his *shonen manga* during this period. In addition to forbidden sexuality, cannibalism started appearing as a recurrent theme. In *Tako no ashi* (*Octopus' Legs*, 1970), a president of a company visits a former employee who now lives secluded in a small village. The young man tells the president that he had caught a disease while traveling. The disease causes the man to grow extra limbs from his body, and the man has been cutting them off and eating it—he then reveals that the lunch that he served the president was made of one of his limbs. *Ryōri suru onna* (*Woman Who Cooks*, 1972) is a murder mystery that takes place in a mental hospital that houses a number of elderly patients. As it turns out, the cook—a middle-aged woman who seems and acts completely normal—has been killing patients, cooking their flesh, and feeding them to other patients. The character Urabe, who appears in *Ode to Kirihito* as Kirihito's colleague who suffers from schizophrenia, plays the part of the head doctor.

Tezuka's experimentation with the grotesque and the anti-moral culminated in *Peter Kürten no kiroku* (*The Record of Peter Kürten*, 1973), a short documentary-fiction depicting the relationship between a German serial killer Peter Kürten (1983–1931) and his wife. Peter Kürten, dubbed The Vampire of Düsseldorf, committed numerous murders, sex crimes, and assaults. The story ends with Kürten at the guillotine, uttering his last words: "I am looking forward to hearing the sound of my own blood gushing from the stump of my neck." Tezuka based his story on a 1972 book *Ie no kami* (*The God of Houses*) by Tsurumi Shunsuke. Given that Tsurumi was a manga critic as well as a philosopher and a historian, it is no surprise that Tezuka came across this material. The short story features an unusual drawing style, with extremely detailed, photographic-looking background, and occasional high-contrast images reminiscent of film noir.

In a way, Peter Kürten is the complete opposite of Tezuka's *shonen manga* heroes like Astro Boy or Ken'ichi—Peter's actions are driven not by virtue, nor for the benefit of the human race. Committing murders purely for pleasure, Peter has no remorse or guilt for his actions. He seems not only to represent the immorality as a part of human nature, but also to question the very notion of "immorality." He rejects being labeled as insane, asserting that it is not him, but the rest of society that has gone insane. Tezuka presents this killer not as a sick villain, but rather as an empathetic central figure. Readers experience Peter as a witty, charming man and a loving husband—his relationship to his wife is filled with respect and tenderness. He is clearly depicted as an attractive, identifiable character, particularly compared to the repulsive-looking police officer who captures him. Peter's character type, a man who is driven by dark desire and one who is devoid of moral consciousness, is recurrent in Tezuka's other *seinen manga* protagonists, such as Dan Takuya in *Tetsu no senritsu* (*The Iron Melody*, 1974) and Yūki Michio in *MW* (1976). In a way, these villains-heroes in *seinen manga* are descendents of Rock in *The Vampires*. Yūki Michio, in particular, has the youthful and androgynous charm of Rock.

During the final decade of his career, Tezuka's *seinen manga* became more socially and historically conscious, introducing themes such as the Holocaust (*Adolf*, 1983), Meiji Restoration (*Hidamari no ki*, 1983–1984), and biotechnology (*Neo Faust*, 1989). Tezuka inserted heavy-handed cultural verisimilitude in them by citing historical facts and figures. Though it was never meant to deceive readers into thinking that the stories were "factual," such references still lent a sense of plausibility. *Hidamari no ki* (*Tree in the Sun*) depicts Tezuka's own ancestors, though it is unclear how much fiction it contains.

Adolf is important in that it was one of the first works by Tezuka to be translated into English and that it starts to investigate the theme of national identity, conscious of the era of manga's global readership. The story revolves around three central characters, all named Adolf: Adolf Kaufmann, the son of a German diplomat father and a Japanese mother in Kobe, Japan; Adolf Kamil, a German Jew, the son of a baker; and Adolf Hitler. Adolf Kaufman and Adolf Kamil grow up as best friends in the city of Kobe, Japan. When World War II breaks out, the lives of the three Adolfs start to change in unexpected ways. Prompted by his father's death, Adolf Kaufman leaves Japan to join the Hitler Youth. Meanwhile, Adolf Kamil gets a hold of a secret document proving that Adolf Hitler was part Jewish. Friends become enemies, families are broken, and the emotional scars remain raw when the war ends. While being a historical fiction, *Adolf* is also a tale of personal identity. Half-German and half-Japanese, Adolf Kaufman despises his Japanese self; Yukie, Kaufman's mother, returns to a more "Japanese" way of life after her German husband dies; Adolf Kamil, who grew up in Japan and speaks fluent Japanese with a Kansai accent, rediscovers his Jewish heritage in the face of the Holocaust.

Japan in the global context became the theme of one of Tezuka's last—and unfinished—works, *Gringo* (1989). The hero of this story is Himoto Hitoshi, a short, stocky Japanese businessman with thick glasses. The story begins when Himoto and his family arrive in a fictional city called Canivalia in South America, where he would head the branch of a Japanese corporation called Edo Shōji. Through Himoto's life in this foreign land, Tezuka questions what it means to be "Japanese" in the era of globalization and international economy. Hélène, Himoto's French-born wife, wears kimonos and cooks traditional

Japanese food better than most Japanese women; Himoto bribes his daughter's schoolteacher in hopes that it would prevent her from facing prejudice at school; Miho, a Japanese girl and a lover of a radical political group leader, seduces Himoto because she believes he could "restore her Japaneseness." The narrative also exposes the absurdity of the Japanese corporate world as well as Japan's "inferiority complex" toward the West, at the same time affectionately portraying characters who struggle in such context. Himoto, a "stereotypical" Japanese businessman, is also a complex and unique human with pride as well as insecurities, who loves his family, makes mistakes, and bounces back. The series remains unfinished, interrupted by Tezuka's death.

Tezuka's *seinen manga* often challenged and responded to the trends and social issues of the times of their production. At the same time, they have the timeless appeal of classic cinema. They often "exoticized" what seems familiar, and familiarized what may otherwise be "exotic." Japan becomes a strange land of curiosities through the eyes of foreigners in Meiji Japan (*Tree in the Sun*), or through a glimpse into the absurdity of a traditional family (*Ayako*), or by juxtaposition of multiple national identities and cultures (*Adolf*). Readers find themselves empathizing with Kansai-dialect speaking Jews in World War II Kobe, and finding the family values in *Ayako* as utterly strange. *Gringo* continues the trend, extracting an image of Japaneseness from stereotypes and displacing it in a foreign context. Rereading *Gringo* today, I wonder how the story would have developed if Tezuka had lived to finish it. The image of Japan and the Japanese changed significantly since Himoto Hitoshi's era of international business and bubble economy. A short stocky businessman with thick glasses may still represent the image of the Japanese, but so does a bleached-blond girl in a high school uniform with a short skirt, or a spiked-haired boy in a punk outfit. As I write this, a number of Tezuka's *seinen manga* are being translated into English. I wonder how contemporary American readers are interpreting such tension between familiarity and exoticism. Then I also fantasize, now that they have gained access to some of Tezuka's finest *seinen manga*, American grown-ups will soon be reading comics on the train on their morning commute.

Chapter 9

GOD OF COMICS, MASTER OF QUOTATIONS

Throughout this book, I have discussed how various art forms, cultural products, and social and cultural discourses that surround them have entered Tezuka's works, functioning as powerful intertexts that bring with them a set of meanings and histories. The scene from *Third Man* inserts emotional gravity into *Monster on the 38th Parallel*, and the long history of comics in Japan suddenly becomes a part of the world in *Tree in the Sun* by the cameo character of Charles Wirgman. In *Intertextuality: Theories and Practices*, Michael Worton and Judith Still point out: "a text [. . .] cannot exist as a hermetic or self-sufficient whole, and so does not function as a closed system [. . .] the writer is a reader of texts [. . .] before s/he is a creator of texts, and therefore the work of art is inevitably shot through with references, quotations and influences of every kind" (1). Every author is a reader of other texts, but Tezuka was a particularly rigorous and obsessive reader, compulsively consuming texts from worlds that otherwise had little intersections with the world of comics. Tezuka's works were not "*inevitably* shot through with references," but *consciously* filled with them. As Tezuka once described his success with cinematic techniques, he "made a big impact because [he] was so conscious of it" ("Niju seiki no inshō" III). Intertextuality in Tezuka's work was not mere imitation, but a complex system of "serious truth-seeking via a plurality of voices in a specific narrative context and in an ironic mode" (Worton and Still 3). By actively quoting elements of the world outside, and calling attention to the act of quoting, Tezuka catalyzes the readers' imagination, bringing into existence a "world" so vast that it seems impossible to be contained in a comic book.

I am including a close textual analysis of Tezuka's short work *Curtain wa konya mo aoi* (*The Curtain Remains Blue Tonight*, 1958) as part of my concluding chapter. Published in a magazine targeted at female readers in their early teens, this 1958 thriller marks several shifts and transitions in the history of manga as well as Tezuka's career: the handover of the *shojo* manga industry from established male artists to young female artists; the rise of *gekiga*; Tezuka's brief return to medical science research; and the popularity of mystery and thriller narratives. My aim is to illustrate how discourses that I have discussed earlier as separate topics converge and transform each other in a single work by Tezuka.

The Plot

The heroine of *The Curtain Remains Blue Tonight* is a girl named Mejiro Tsugumi, the younger sister of the stage actress Mejiro Chidori. In the opening scene, Chidori suddenly screams and faints on stage (fig. 9.1). The curtain falls, the show is stopped, and she is rushed to a hospital. The doctors soon discover that seeing a certain shade of red causes Chidori to have a panic reaction. Tsugumi and the show's director visit Chidori at the hospital. The director informs her that her role will be covered by actress Kasa Sagie. When Chidori returns home, she tells their old nurse about the incident. The nurse seems alarmed.

The understudy, Kasa Sagie, (fig. 9.2) turns out to be not only less than adequate in the role, but also (seemingly) malicious toward Chidori and Tsugumi. When Chidori returns home and throws a dinner party, Sagie shows up wearing a red coat and holding red balloons. When Tsugumi attempts to hide the coat from her sister's sight, Sagie accuses her of trying to steal it. During the course of the evening, Tsugumi also receives a mysterious note that says, "Your sister's life will be in danger tomorrow at noon."

Later that night, Tsugumi hears a strange noise. She goes to her sister's room to find a red handkerchief left in the hallway. Chidori, having seen the handkerchief, has gone mad; she does not even seem to recognize Tsugumi. After attacking Tsugumi, Chidori faints and falls down the stairs. While Chidori is unconscious, their old nurse reveals a surprising secret to Tsugumi: Chidori is not her biological sister, but an adopted child from a foreign country where Tsugumi's father, a diplomat, had lived before she was born. A war broke out and the members of the royal family were all tortured and killed, except for the baby princess, whom the couple rescued and took with them to Japan. A red whip was used to torture the royal family, which explains Chidori's reaction to

Figure 9.1. Opening scene, *Curtain wa konya mo aoi* [*The Curtain Remains Blue Tonight*]. © Tezuka Productions. Reproduced with permission.

the color red (fig. 9.3). The nurse further warns that an assassin from Chidori's country had been trying to find and murder the princess. Tsugumi immediately goes out in the middle of the night to see Chidori's fans, asking for their help.

The next day, Tsugumi and the two fans go to the theater with Chidori. Chidori does not seem to remember anything about the incident the night before. The show begins just before noon. The two fans sneak in as ensemble members of the show (fig. 9.4), and Tsugumi watches the show from the stage left wing (fig. 9.5). During the performance, Tsugumi notices that there is a red curtain, which is not used in the show, hanging in the fly system. Tsugumi re-

Figure 9.2. Kasa Sagie in *The Curtain Remains Blue Tonight.* © Tezuka Productions. Reproduced with permission.

alizes that the assassin is going to drop the curtain in the middle of the performance, which may cause Chidori to die from shock. Tsugumi runs to the opposite wing where the fly system is operated, but it is too late. The curtain falls
onto the stage, covering Chidori. It turns out, however, that it was the blue curtain that fell. The show is stopped, but Chidori is safe.

The story quickly comes to a close: Kasa Sagie turns out to be a detective in
disguise, suspicious that the show's director is an assassin. Sagie, who foresaw
the murder plan, switched the ropes for the red and blue curtains before the
performance. Now Sagie has got the director at gunpoint. When he attempts
to run, the two fans lower a set piece of a giant temple bell, capturing him inside (fig. 9.6). The would-be killer is caught, the sisters embrace, the curtain
falls for the last time, and the epilogue is delivered by the would-be assassin, or,
more precisely, the actor who played the part (fig. 9.7).

The plot of this short comic is organized chronologically, except for the
scene of Chidori's babyhood that appears in the nurse's speech (see fig. 9.3).
The narrative structure may therefore appear less complex than the structure
of Tezuka's other works during this period, such as *Cave-in,* which alternates
present and past sequences, or *Shokei wa sanji ni owatta* (*The Execution Finished at Three*), which depicts the psychological turmoil of a man who is about

Figure 9.3. A "memory scene" from *The Curtain Remains Blue Tonight*. © Tezuka Productions. Reproduced with permission.

to be executed set in the short time between blindfolding and death. *The Curtain Remains Blue Tonight* gains the sense of suspense and surprise through what David Bordwell calls a "deceptive" narrator, initially misleading the readers into believing false information. For example, readers are led to believe that Kasa Sagie is a jealous actress who tries to sabotage Chidori's career. The "mean" impression of Sagie is accentuated by her facial expressions and body language, as well as by the placement of close-up shots in the story. The scene where the director tells Sagie that Chidori is returning to the stage the next day is followed by a silent close-up of Sagie's face, seemingly displaying the expression of resentment and disappointment (see fig. 9.2). This panel is "framed" in a manner reminiscent of a theatrical portrait. The "framing" of close-up images appear periodically in this comic, inviting the readers to dwell on the image for a moment. At the end of the story, readers may reread this image as the expression of a contemplative and analytical detective.

The Theatre

Theatre is deployed in *The Curtain Remains Blue Tonight* in two ways: as a setting where the key events of the story occur and as a narrative framework.

Figure 9.4. Two fans sneak onstage disguised as actors. *The Curtain Remains Blue Tonight.* © Tezuka Productions. Reproduced with permission.

At the same time, the comic as a whole is framed as a performance, characterizing the "performance" scenes as play(s)-within-a-play. At the end of the comic, the character of the director delivers an epilogue in front of the curtain. He then takes off his wig and costume to reveal his "true" appearance as an actor, indicating that the entire story was a "play." This ending is disorienting, deconstructing the entire plot in one panel, and capturing readers in a complex multilayered performance framework.

Though the use of an epilogue in *The Curtain Remains Blue Tonight* seems like a variation on the theatrical theme in Tezuka's earlier *shojo* manga, its function is even more complex. Tezuka's earlier works featured theatrical references early in the narrative to establish a certain mode of viewing; in *The Curtain Remains Blue Tonight*, the framework is not revealed until the end. The theatrical frame serves as an unexpected surprise rather than the basic premise. Instead of constantly reminding the readers of its staged-ness, *The Curtain Remains Blue Tonight* engages them in a more cinematic, absorptive mode of viewing, only to deconstruct it at the end.

Theater also serves as an important setting for action in two key scenes, the opening and the climactic ending. In the very first panel, the architecture of the stage is rendered in minute detail, evoking a sense of immediacy and presence. In the opening scene, the readers see the stage—where the action takes place—from a bird's eye perspective, from the left side of the auditorium. The panel frames the stage at a slight angle, implying the presence of an imaginary camera through which the readers perceive the scene (see fig. 9.1). Other scenes depict backstage details such as the dressing room and wings, giving readers ac-

Figure 9.5. Tsugumi watches her sister from the stage wing. *The Curtain Remains Blue Tonight.* ©
Tezuka Productions. Reproduced with permission.

cess to views that theater audiences do not have (see fig. 9.5). In this way, theater in this work is doubly quoted, evoking not live theater but rather films that
are set in live theater, such as Alfred Hitchcock's *Stage Fright* (1950). Tezuka also
makes frequent use of subjective shots, deep-focus shots, and close-ups, making the layout of this work more dynamic and experimental than his earlier
shojo manga. At the same time, the image in figure 9.1 shows the stage, the orchestra pit, and a part of the auditorium in equal clarity, focus, and light—an
image impossible to capture on film because the stage is lit much brighter than
the pit. This choice is characteristic of the comics medium, where the images
and events are not "recorded" from life but are symbolically represented. If the

Figure 9.6. The bell falls to capture the assassin. *The Curtain Remains Blue Tonight.* © Tezuka Productions. Reproduced with permission.

same scene is presented in a film, it may take as many as three different shots to convey all the information contained in this panel: one showing the actress on stage (in order to capture the actress in correct light, the pit and the auditorium would naturally be dark or invisible); another showing the orchestra; and another showing the auditorium, all with different levels of exposure.

The theater scenes in *The Curtain Remains Blue Tonight* clearly reference Takarazuka Kagekidan and Takarazuka Grand Theatre, though the name or location of this fictional theater is never explicitly stated. The repertoire of the company is suggestive of Takarazuka Kagekidan: throughout the story, readers see two shows: one is a musical revue, another a kabuki adaptation; the rehearsal scene in figure 9.2 shows a chorus line of dancers similar to a rehearsal photograph from Takarazuka Kagekidan (fig. 9.8).

The architecture of the theater, and its similarity to Takarazuka Grand Theatre, is already apparent in the first panel of the manga. It shows a large, Western-style orchestra, though only about a third of it is visible: there are at least three cellists, one pianist, and six violinists (or violists). Other instruments include piccolo, flute, clarinet, trombone, and trumpet. The instruments are rendered with such detail and specificity that we recognize the differences between specific instruments; for example, it is easy to tell the difference between a piccolo and a flute. Each member of the orchestra (all male) has his own music stand and scores. The pit is surrounded by an apron stage, or a walkway, decorated with light bulbs. This structure, *pont d'argent*, had been a signature feature of Takarazuka Grand Theatre since 1931, where the stars would

Figure 9.7. Epilogue. *The Curtain Remains Blue Tonight.* © Tezuka Productions. Reproduced with permission.

line up to receive the audiences' applause during the shows' extravagant finales (Hashimoto, Ichihashi, Noritake, Robertson).

Onstage, the principle performer, Chidori, sings "Sweet memories, Parisienne." The lyrics are written inside a speech balloon decorated with musical notes, indicating that the text is "sung" as opposed to "spoken." The lyrics are a clear reference to Takarazuka Kagekidan's 1927 production of *Mon Paris* or to any other revues of the late 1920s and 1930s with heavy French influence. A chorus of men in black tuxedos surrounds Chidori, two of the members kneeling down on either side of her and extending their arms toward her. There is a giant staircase upstage, on which there is a chorus of girls in dresses, with feather hats and parasols. Dancers in red tuxedos form a straight horizontal line behind them. The back wall, barely visible behind the enormous staircase, has arabesque details and rows of light bulbs against a black background. Just downstage of the back wall is a portal, with red roses painted or attached to it. In front of it is another portal, in a more elaborate shape, with soft curved lines forming an arch. Furthest downstage is the first portal, which consists of a white lattice pattern, also decorated with red roses. The set does not have any details to set the play in any particular geographical location or historical moment. In contrast to the level of precision with which Tezuka rendered his orchestra, the set appears surprisingly unspecific.

At first glance, it may almost seem that all Tezuka intended to do with the set was to present the general ambiance of a "theater," and therefore he did not need to pay much attention to the details of the show being performed. However, there is another element in this image that keeps us from dismissing the absence of style as lack of care or intention. Tezuka has indicated, in expert precision, the presence of functional scenery on this stage: borders and legs. Behind the portals that I have already discussed, Tezuka has drawn black velour masking. They are hung in all the appropriate places, with vertical lines indi-

Figure 9.8. A rehearsal photograph from Takarazuka Kagekidan.

cating their fullness, implying Tezuka's familiarity with the theater space. Seen in this light, the lack of dramaturgical information in the set is less likely a product of carelessness than a depiction of the style characterized by *the lack of* style, which consists of pastiche of various existing styles and cultural references.

What gives away this stage picture as a Takarazuka production is that all performers onstage are depicted with clear markers of femininity: the one kneeling on Chidori's right side has recognizably long eyelashes, and the line of men upstage on the staircase wear tights rather than trousers, displaying their shapely legs. The performers' "feminine" features become particularly notable when contrasted with the male musicians in the orchestra pit, with bald heads and facial hair. In a later scene where the two fans disguise themselves as performers (see fig. 9.4), readers also see that they look comically out-of-place among dainty female performers.

The second show performed in this theater is a kabuki adaptation, *Dōjōji*. The show was in the repertoire of Takarazuka Kagekidan since its first tour to Europe. I will discuss the scene in detail later in this chapter.

Character: Mejiro Chidori

The character Mejiro Chidori presents an image somewhere between a 1950s *shojo* star and a Takarazuka *musume-yaku*. *Shojo* stars, very young performers most of whom had no formal training or exceptional talent, appeared primarily in films, radio, and most of all, in magazine photography. While the theater in this manga clearly insinuates Takarazuka Kagekidan, Chidori's status as an autonomous star without the opposite *otoko-yaku* seems closer to that of a *shojo* star rather than a member of the Takarazuka ensemble. Her name, Mejiro Chidori (literally "Silvereyed Plover"), is a direct reference to the singer Misora

Hibari (literally, "Beautiful sky, Skylark") who started out as a *shojo* star during the late 1940s and who remained one of the top singers of Japanese popular music until her death in 1988.

Chidori, however, displays remarkable professionalism and commitment to her art that is not associated with the young, innocent *shojo* stars (with the exception of stars that continued their career, such as Misora Hibari). On her hospital bed after the initial collapse, Chidori tells her sister: "I am like a stage fairy . . . I will die if I am not performing." The line also implies that Chidori performs primarily as a stage actress rather than in other media such as film, which is atypical of a *shojo* star.

Chidori is also reminiscent of the Takarazuka star Amatsu Otome, who lived next door to Tezuka when he was growing up in the city of Takarazuka. This association is most strongly captured in the last scene of the manga, where Chidori performs in a production of *Musume Dōjōji* (also spelled *Musume Doujouji* or *Musume Dojoji*), a kabuki adaptation. Amatsu was a master of Japanese dance who performed this repertoire on the Takarazuka stage a number of times and served as the instructor of dance at the Takarazuka Music Academy later in her career. Chidori's upbringing as the (adopted) daughter of a diplomat fits perfectly into the profile of a student at the Takarazuka Music Academy, for according to its admission policy the students must be from "good families."

Chidori presents an image of a teen idol somewhere between a *shojo* star and a Takarazuka performer, who possesses the autonomous star status of a *shojo* star, but with exceptional talent, training, professionalism, and discipline of a Takarazuka performer.

Character: Mejiro Tsugumi

The heroine of the story, Mejiro Tsugumi, is Chidori's younger sister. Despite her sister's fame and popularity, Tsugumi does not seem to be interested in the world of show business herself. She seems content to be her sister's caretaker, managing the household while their parents are away. Tsugumi's character is surprisingly bland as a heroine of the story: compared to Tezuka's earlier heroines such as Princess Sapphire and Himawari san, Tsugumi's personality is not nearly as unique nor charismatic. While Tsugumi is clearly the focal character of the story, her sister, Chidori, remains—literally and figuratively—in the spotlight.

Though the "future *ryōsai kenbo*" (good wife, wise mother), much like Takarazuka Kagekidan performers, had always been presented as feminine

Figure 9.9. Tsugumi visits her sister at the hospital. *The Curtain Remains Blue Tonight.* © Tezuka Productions. Reproduced with permission.

ideal in Tezuka's earlier *shojo* manga, the heroines did not always start out as the demure, proper, and insightful wives-to-be. Rather, Tezuka's narratives often involve heroines with unconventional personalities transforming themselves into more conventional female roles. The cross-dressed Princess (Sapphire) marries Prince Charming and gives birth to twins; the short-tempered tomboy Himawari falls in love with a boy and learns to be more ladylike. For Tsugumi, however, this transformation does not occur. She starts out as a *ryōsai kenbo* and ends as one: though she is very young (probably in her early teens), she is already assigned the role of the family's caretaker, for her parents are away and her sister is busy with her stage career. In her very first appearance, she is seen with a small child (fig. 9.9). It is never explained in the narrative who the child is, though it is likely that he or she is their younger sibling. The image of Tsugumi with a child creates an impression of motherliness and maturity, though Tsugumi is the younger of the two sisters. It is also significant that the child never appears again or is never mentioned after this scene; he/she is not an integral part of the narrative, but merely a "prop" that helps establish Tsugumi's character upon her first entrance.

Tsugumi's endeavor as an amateur detective is motivated by her love for her sister, not by yearning for adventure. Tsugumi, like Princess Sapphire, did not choose an adventurous and dramatic life, but was thrown into it by an outside force. Sapphire's actions were hence characterized as selfless or even self-sacrificing, and her passion for adventure is easily transferable to other tasks, like serving as a wife and a mother. In Tsugumi's case, the line between adventure and domesticity is further blurred; the fate she must face is not her own, but someone else's.

Character: Old Nurse

The old nurse is depicted as an old-fashioned, nagging, and authoritative figure. In the scene of her first appearance, she complains that it is shameful that Chidori, a daughter of a diplomat, has chosen a career in show business. Her complaint reflects the view of acting as an unsuitable occupation for women, a view that was already perceived as old-fashioned by the 1950s. Her prejudice against women performers is also apparent in the scene of the dinner party. When Chidori announces that dinner is served, her guests immediately jump to the table and start consuming the food, making noises and uttering in casual language "Wow, this tastes great!" The nurse, carrying a platter, mumbles, "How vulgar!"

The nurse's character becomes suddenly more complex when she reveals the secret of Chidori's background. This event not only solves the mystery of Chidori's illness, but also explains the nurse's seeming coldness toward Chidori. In light of this new information, readers are prompted to reevaluate the character of the nurse: her resistance to accept Chidori's performance career, and her fixation on the "class difference" between Chidori and her friends, may be based on something more complex than the prejudice against women performers. The nurse, who has been the primary caretaker of the two sisters from babyhood, has succeeded in raising Chidori as a completely passable young Japanese woman, hiding her royal heritage. Assuming that Chidori's life is constantly in danger from foreign assassins, it is natural that the nurse is concerned about Chidori having such a high-profile career.

Character: Tezuka Osamu

Tezuka created TEZUKA OSAMU as one of his stars, casting him in a variety of comics, often in the role of himself—cartoonist Tezuka Osamu—though not always in an autobiographical context. TEZUKA's most prominent roles

Figure 9.10. TEZUKA OSAMU appears as a doctor. *The Curtain Remains Blue Tonight.* © Tezuka Productions. Reproduced with permission.

include the manga artist Tezuka Osamu in *The Vampires*, who is murdered by the villain Makube Rokuro (played by Rock), and the late Edo-peroid Tezuka Ryōsen (Tezuka's own great-great-grandfather) in *A Tree in the Sun.*

In *The Curtain Remains Blue Tonight*, TEZUKA makes a cameo appearance as a doctor in the scene of the hospital where Chidori is recovering from the first collapse. In the scene, two fans question why Chidori collapsed after seeing red confetti, though she had seen the color red so many times before; TEZUKA, in his white labcoat, explains, "It only happens with a certain shade of red" (fig. 9.10). Tezuka returned to his medical interests a year prior to the publication of this manga, conducting research at the electron microscope lab at Nara Medical College. The casting of himself as a doctor foreshadows his later, recurring appearances as a physician in *Black Jack* and in *A Tree in the Sun,* as well as a line of early 1970s work that draws directly on his medical training.

As an additional note, the two fans who provide comic relief throughout the story and contribute to the capturing of the assassin at the end are played by Tezuka's stars based on his fellow cartoonists, Baba Noboru and Fukui Eiichi. The two speak with *Kansai-ben*, the dialect from the Kansai-Osaka area. The dialect functions as an indication of geographic location (though other characters speak standard Tokyo Japanese) as well as comic relief: Tezuka himself spoke with the same accent, for the city of Takarazuka is located in the Kansai area. *Kansai-ben* is often associated with improvisational and stand-up comedy.

Osaka is considered the comedy center of Japan, and many comedians learn to speak the dialect as an integral part of their performance. The employment of *Kansai-ben* instantly gives a comical flair to the two characters.

Kasa Sagie and the Rehearsal Scene

During the first half of the narrative, Kasa Sagie functions as a representation of hierarchical and competitive life in Takarazuka Kagekidan. During her rehearsal as Chidori's replacement, she is scolded by the director, "No, no, no, Kasa, how do you think you could replace Mejiro Chidori with a performance like that?!" (see fig. 9.8). Sagie's acts of "meanness"—wearing a red coat to Chidori's house, calling Tsugumi a thief—are reminiscent of common anecdotes of conflicts among students at the Takarazuka Music Academy (Tōgō).

Kagie, however, turns out to be a detective in disguise, which excuses her not only for her seemingly "mean" actions, but also for her lack of performance skills.

Character: The Director

The role of the director is played by one of Tezuka's classic stars, Mason, modeled and named after the film actor James Mason (fig. 9.11). Though Tezuka often created stars based on existing personalities such as fellow cartoonists, friends, editors, and cartoon characters by other artists, Mason is an unusual star in Tezuka's Star System in that he explicitly refers to an existing film star. Tezuka's star Mason debuted in *Nasubi Joō* (*Queen Nasubi*) in 1955. In this series, Mason's role was inspired by James Mason's role of General Rommel in the 1951 film *The Desert Fox*. Mason continued to appear in Tezuka's works, wearing military uniforms most of the time. In the episode called "Anaphylaxis" in *Black Jack*, he co-stars with Sapphire, playing the part of an army general. Mason commissions Black Jack to save the life of his son who was wounded in battle, for the sole purpose of returning him to the battlefield so that he may die an honorable death. The son, after recovering from the surgery, commits suicide.

The casting of Mason in the role of a theater director seems atypical, but is also strangely appropriate given the strict, military-like training regimen of the Takarazuka Music Academy. His strict, authoritative interaction with Kasa Sagie in the rehearsal scene is typical of the roles Mason tends to play and at the same time reminiscent of Takarazuka Kagekidan directors.

Japan and the Orient

Ethnic identities of manga characters are often ambiguously represented. Though Chidori is a princess from a foreign country, she is completely passable as Japanese and as a biological sister of Tsugumi. This premise alone is not entirely unconvincing, particularly considering that there are many Chinese and Korean immigrants in Japan who pass as Japanese. It is the image of this unspecified "foreign country" that presents a larger puzzle (see fig. 9.3). The costumes seem to indicate that the "foreign country" here is located in the Middle East, a place earlier represented by Tezuka in other works such as *Niji no toride* (*The Rainbow Fortress*).

This premise raises a strange question regarding Chidori's ethnic identity. Why has Chidori, a Middle Eastern princess, been able to "pass" as ethnically Japanese all her life? This becomes particularly puzzling given that the other characters in the "memory scene" sport "exotic" features. Here, the image of Chidori suggests that race and ethnicity, like gender, is performative: "it has no ontological status apart from the various acts which constitutes its reality" (Butler, *Gender* 173). Chidori, who grew up in Japan, who has no knowledge of her true heritage, is depicted as a "Japanese girl" without any indication of ethnically specific appearance.

Perhaps more simply, it has to do with the ways in which the idea of racial differences is radically simplified in comics—as "people that are like us" and "people that are not like us." This is somewhat parallel to the Japanese understanding of race and ethnicity, in which people are divided into two large categories: *nihonjin* (Japanese) and *gaijin* (non-Japanese, literally "outside people"). There are categories such as *hakujin* (literally "white people") and *kokujin* ("black people") within the *gaijin* category, and there are certainly stereotypes associated with certain races and ethnicities, but for most Japanese, who have little chances of direct contact with people of "other" races, *gaijin* simply remains "people that are not like us"—people to whom they cannot truly relate. Tezuka's principal characters who would otherwise fall into the *gaijin* category, such as Rock Home, are often depicted identically to other (Japanese) characters; meanwhile, foreigner characters that are not relatable are often depicted with clear markers of their differences. For example, African people in *Jungle Emperor* are depicted as stereotypical "natives," causing a controversy (Covert).

While another work, *The Rainbow Fortress*, depicts the ancient Middle East (the city of Baghdad) as a place filled with mythical monsters, magic, and miracles, the contemporary Middle East is depicted here as a place characterized by conflict, violence, and brutality. Meanwhile, the Japanese (Tsugumi's father) is portrayed as a strong, courageous man who saves the baby princess from the evil torturers. The premise is reminiscent of Takarazuka Kagekidan's first revue production, *Mon Paris* (1927), in which a Japanese protagonist rescues a young Chinese girl from evil bandits. The unique mode of Orientalist discourse that permeates the Takarazuka Kagekidan's early revues, which contrasts the strong, masculine, righteous Japan with the rest of the "Orient" that is primitive, feminine, and uncivilized, is repeated in this manga of the late 1950s (Tokutomi).

Dōjōji

Though the citation of Takarazuka's eclectic exoticism is ubiquitous in Tezuka's *shojo* manga, what makes this short story unusual is its parody of Takarazuka's *kabuki* adaptation. The last scene of the story takes place in the same theater as the first scene. The announcement is heard: "The show, *Haru no odori* (*The Dance of Spring*), is about to begin . . ." The title of the show, *The Dance of Spring*, had been in the Takarazuka Kagekidan's repertoire since 1927. The show was a visually stunning "Japanese revue" based on *kabuki*, *nō (no, noh)*, and *miyako odori* numbers, which was presented in a number of reworked versions. After the director-choreographer Umemoto Rikuhei resigned from Takarazuka Kagekidan and joined Takarazuka's rival company Shōchiku Shojo Kageki, the series was produced by Shōchiku.[1] In the next panel, the orchestra starts playing and the show begins. Then, the readers see Tsugumi and the stage from the right wing. On the stage there is a giant temple bell, foliage drop, and borders of flowers, which seem to be a typical set for *Kyō Kanoko Musume Dōjōji* (often shortened and called *Musume Dōjōji*), one of the most popular plays in the *kabuki* repertoire, adapted from a *nō* play, *Dōjōji*. Chidori performs the lead *Shirabyōshi*, the serpent-woman. This is clearly a depiction of Takarazuka adaptation of *Musume Dōjōji*, performed by female performers and accompanied by an orchestra.

Musume Dōjōji was one of Takarazuka's favorite *kabuki/nō* adaptations, and it was in their repertoire on their first tour to Europe in 1938. The *kabuki* version of the play is also a visual feast in stage décor, featuring intricate costumes (a serpent in the disguise of a dancer) and a functional set that involves a giant bell (fig. 9. 11). *Musume Dōjōji* had been performed by Takarazuka Kagekidan a number of times as a part of their yearly *Haru no odori* (*Dance of Spring*) program, including their 1957 version.

---

1. Umemoto and *Haru no odori* eventually returned to Takarazuka Kagekidan.

Figure 9.11. A kabuki production of *Musume Dōjōji*.

Dōjōji is often regarded as a play that deals closely with female sexuality. More prominently in the original *nō* version than in the *kabuki* adaptation, *Dōjōji* "presents us with a dramatically compelling vision of stark conflict: the masculine forces of noble and pure spirituality (the priest of Dōjōji temple) battling the feminine forces of profane and bestial sexuality (a woman transformed by passion into a fire-breathing serpent who seeks revenge on the temple bell)" (Klein 291). The two key features of the *nō* version are the *ranbyōshi* (literally "crazy rhythm") dance of the serpent-woman and *kaneiri*, or the bell-entering-scene, where the performer jumps into the temple bell. Both of these routines are considered to be among the most challenging techniques for a *nō* performer (Kawatake, Klein). In *The Curtain Remains Blue Tonight*, Chidori performs in the role of the serpent-woman, disguised as a beautiful young dancer, moving slowly with a small shoulder drum. The play's themes of possession and disguise are layered upon Chidori's innocent figure, functioning as an unsettling symbolism for her dark, mysterious fate. The image also evokes aural sensation, inviting readers to imaginatively "hear" the irregular, intense rhythm of *ranbyōshi*, serving as the background music in the story's climax.

In the *nō* version, this dance goes on for a long time. Long silences, high-pitched vocalization, and the piercing sound of a flute build up almost unbearable tension toward the climax of the play, the *kaneiri* scene, in which the bell suddenly comes crashing to the floor as the woman leaps into it. In *The Curtain Remains Blue Tonight*, the *kaneiri* scene happens twice: first, the curtain—not the bell—falls on stage, enveloping Chidori. After it is revealed that it was the blue curtain that fell, readers see Sagie pointing a gun at the director. Sagie speaks: "Ha ha, I switched the ropes. What's wrong?" Tsugumi is shocked. "The director was the assassin?!" When he attempts to run away, the bell falls, capturing him in it (see fig. 9.6).

In Place of Conclusion

Intertexts that I have introduced in this analysis are by no means exhaustive. I am certain that I have overlooked, or chose to ignore, a number of references that may or may not be inserted by the author. I also know that another reader would pick up a completely different set of quotations. My hope, however, is that this analysis gives a sense of the breadth and depth of Tezuka's use of quotations, parodies, and allusions. The "God of Comics" crafted his text by combining vocabularies and techniques from multiple forms of art and other discourses. In doing so, he constantly made commentaries on the histories, traditions, and social meanings of the forms he borrowed—as well as on his own act of borrowing. Investigating the intertextual references in Tezuka's works reveals the intersections of various art forms and cultural practices that may otherwise seem disparate. The comics do not merely "reflect," but question and critique the discourses that they repeat, by means of recontextualization and parody.

Last and perhaps more important, I must emphasize that Tezuka's work—and comics in general—transformed not only itself but also other art forms in this intertextual dialogue. Most scholars would agree that manga has been an important part of Japanese popular culture, but few have the understanding that manga has influenced, and continues to influence, many aspects of Japanese art and culture since the beginning of the twentieth century. In recent scholarship, manga's position in Japanese culture has been compared to "air" (Gravett; Kinsella) due to its naturalized existence and abundance; it is only natural that the artists and cultural producers who breathe this "air" have produced works that are heavily informed by manga and its thematic and stylistic trends. Tezuka's approach of "borrowing"—combining art forms, cultures, and frameworks in intricately inter-referenced parody filled with ironic references—has inspired, and continues to inspire, processes of numerous artists working in Japan's postwar era.

EPILOGUE

The train sped through the countryside and my bag was heavy on my lap. As we were pulling away from Nagoya station, a middle-aged man asked me if I needed help putting it up on the shelf. I said I would rather hold onto it, it was important. The bag was full of comic manuscripts that my brother and I had slaved over for the last year or so. There was also a plastic container full of sugar cookies that I spent two days baking in my little toaster oven, carefully cut and elaborately iced in the shapes of Tezuka's popular comic book characters. It was March 1986, and I had just finished elementary school. I had been a member of the Tezuka Osamu Fan Club for about a year. The fan club magazine had advertised that the studio was open for fan visitation on Mondays, and this was what I asked for as a graduation present.

I had encountered Tezuka's work for the first time in second grade, when my parents brought home four volumes of *Umi no Toriton* (*Toriton of the Sea*, 1968). This tale of a human-mermaid, Toriton, made a strong impact on me, resonating with my former knowledge of Greek mythology (characters were named after Greek gods), fairy tales, science, and ancient civilizations. I then went on to read everything Tezuka had published; this took a long time, given that Tezuka had already had a forty-year career as a cartoonist before I encountered his work for the first time. Most of the works I was reading had been published before I was born. During the mid-1980s, Tezuka's works were considered "classics," not particularly hip or radical—but they appealed not only to me but also to my younger brother. We sought out copies of his books at used bookstores, slowly building our collection. We soon started writing and drawing our own comics, as did the characters in Fujiko Fujio's *Manga michi*. While other kids played "cops and thieves," we played "cartoonists and editors," taking turns assuming the roles of the cartoonist, the assistant, and the editor. Our collaborative "magazine," *Gekkan Onoda* (*Monthly Onoda*), was drawn on typing paper, and bound together with pieces of scotch tape. More than any other comics of the contemporary era, Tezuka's works encouraged and empowered us to create our own. Now, looking back, it was perhaps the rather uncomplicated drawing styles of the previous era that made us feel like "we can do this," or it may have been that, recognizing the snippets of films, folktales, mythologies, and other familiar images in Tezuka' works, we felt that we were entitled to make manga out of what surrounded us, using even Tezuka's works as our intertexts.

The studio occupied two floors of a surprisingly small building in Shinjuku district. I was not expecting to see Tezuka on this trip—I knew from fan magazines that he had a separate studio, an apartment room where he worked alone. Only assistants worked at the main studio. At the time of my visit, Tezuka was working on his latest *Phoenix* chapter, the *Chapter of the Sun*. Assistants were busy drawing elaborate backgrounds and pasting in the texts, with research images spread out on their desks. There was another group of visitors, older boys from one of Tokyo's suburbs.

My memory of meeting Tezuka, unfortunately, is hazy and perhaps unreliable. It may have been my uncle who pointed him out to me in the hallway, as we were getting off the elevator. He was in his late fifties at the time, a tall, solidly built man, in his signature beret, a turtleneck, and a sport coat. I remember watching him as he gave instructions to his assistants in a slightly nasal voice. I was too shy to speak to him at first; I was afraid that I would get in his way. I finally got up the courage after I saw the older boys asking for his autograph. I said, in a voice that must have been only barely audible, "Will you look at my comics?" This was the moment in which I became a part of the long history of young aspiring cartoonists bringing their works to their masters, an old-fashioned practice no longer common in the 1980s. I slipped into the scene of *Manga michi* where the characters Michio and Shigeru bring their comics to Tezuka, or another scene in Tezuka's *Dotsutare* where TEZUKA showed his works to Yokoi Fukujiro. Or, more precisely, these scenes slipped into my life as intertexts, carrying with them the histories of all aspiring cartoonists who had approached Tezuka in the same way since the 1950s.

Tezuka smiled, said, "Sure," and looked through our manuscripts. He then said something to the effect of: "You are really good. Wait three years. In three years, if you have improved greatly, then you should become cartoonists." I shook his hands, overwhelmed, not knowing quite what to feel or what to say. Afterward, Tezuka made a brief small talk with my uncle. "I am so jet-lagged," he said, having flown in from an overseas festival. "I got these at duty-free, but not everyone smokes here. Would you like one?" Tezuka handed a pack of cigarettes to my uncle, who chuckled and accepted them. He left shortly after. I stayed a while longer, watching the assistants work, dreaming of occupying one of the desks and painting *beta* or drawing backgrounds. I promised myself that—though Tezuka did not necessarily invite me to—I was going to come back in three years. On my way out, I gave the Tupperware container full of sugar cookies to one of his assistants. "You should have given them to Mr. Tezuka!" the assistant exclaimed. "He loves sweets." But I was too shy.

My promise was not kept. Tezuka died in February 1989, two years and eleven months after I met him at Tezuka Productions. This sounds like a tragic anecdote of a dream unfulfilled, but, in reality, it is not as dramatic. By the time I finished ninth grade, my interests had already diverged from comics into other areas. My brother and I no longer played together but spent time with our own separate groups of friends. *Gekkan Onoda* had long been discontinued, with no plans for new issues. Still, Tezuka's death left me with a sense of loss and clearly marked the end of my short career as an "aspiring cartoonist."

Almost twenty years later, I somehow found myself in Chicago, writing not comics but a dissertation on comics, and running a theater company. A few years after that, I directed a theatrical production based on Tezuka's short works, at Georgetown University in Washington, D.C. One evening, sitting in a rehearsal room with a group of students, I told them the story of meeting Tezuka. Before I could finish, I started weeping. "This is how I am keeping my promise," I told them, "and I think the show would have made Tezuka happy." My students sat there, perplexed—but also inspired, they later told me—by this sudden and uncharacteristic burst of sentimentalism. Most of my students have never heard of Tezuka, but have all heard of manga. My courses are not about comics but about theater and performance. Still, Tezuka's work found its way into my scholarly and creative work, not only as the subject of study but also as intertexts, as frameworks, or as methodological models of interdisciplinary "borrowing." As Tezuka parodied, quoted, re-contextualized, and re-performed arts and discourses of his own era, I re-contextualize and re-perform Tezuka's work, hoping that this will inspire and encourage other artists and scholars in my own cultural and historical moment.

BIBLIOGRAPHY

Works by Tezuka Osamu

Note: This is not a complete list of works created by Tezuka Osamu, but a list of his works cited in this book. In most cases, there are several versions of the same work. I have listed the versions that I examined in writing this book, which, in some cases, may not be the most accessible or popularly circulated.

Tezuka Osamu. *o Man.* 1959–1960. Tezuka Osamu manga zenshū. Vol. 21–24. Tokyo: Kōdansha, 1978.

"38 do senjō no kaibutsu [Monster on the 38th Parallel]." 1953. *38 do senjō no kaibutsu.* Tezuka Osamu manga zenshū. Vol. 43. Tokyo: Kōdansha, 1981. 5–75.

Adorufu ni tsugu [Adolf]. 1983–1985. 4 vols. Tokyo: Bungei Shunjū, 1985.

Arabasutā [Alabaster]. 1970–1971. 3 vols. Tokyo: Akita Shoten, 1981.

Aporo no uta [Apollo's Song]. 1970. Tezuka Osamu manga zenshū. Vol. 35–37. Tokyo: Kōdansha, 1977.

"A-ko chan B-ko chan tankenki [The Adventures of A-ko chan and B-ko chan]." 1946. *Mā-chan no nikkichō.* Tezuka Osamu manga zenshū. Vol. 129. Tokyo: Kōdansha, 1982. 37–66.

"Atarashii kodomo mangaka no minasan e [To New Children's Manga Artists]." *Honoo* October 1959. 35.

Ayako. 1971–1973. Tezuka Osamu manga zenshū. Vol. 197–99. Tokyo: Kōdansha, 1981.

Banpaiya [The Vampires]. 1966–1967. Tezuka Osamu manga zenshū. Vol. 142–44. Tokyo: Kōdansha, 1979.

Banpaiya [The Vampires]. 1968–1969. Tezuka Osamu manga zenshū. Vol. 320. Tokyo: Kōdansha, 1993.

Bōken kyō jidai [The Era of Adventure Madness]. Tezuka Osamu manga zenshū. Vol. 40. Tokyo: Kōdansha, 1978.

Boku no manga jinsei [My Life in Manga]. Tokyo: Iwanami, 1997.

Boku no songokū [Songokū the Monkey]. 1952–1959. Tezuka Osamu manga zenshū. Vol. 12–19. Tokyo: Kōdansha, 1977–80.

Boku wa manga ka [I Am a Cartoonist]. Tokyo: Kōdansha, 1984.

Budda [*Buddha*]. 1972–1983. Tezuka Osamu manga zenshū. Vol. 287–300. Tokyo: Kōdansha, 1983–84.

Burakku Jakku [*Black Jack*]. 1973–1983. 25 vols. Tokyo: Akita Shoten, 1974–1995.

Burunga issei [*Burunga the First*]. 1968–1969. Tezuka Osamu manga zenshū. Vol. 169–70. Tokyo: Kōdansha, 1983.

Chikyū o nomu [*Swallowing the Earth*]. 1968–1969. Tezuka Osamu manga zenshū. Vol. 259–60. Tokyo: Kōdansha, 1982.

"Chinnen to Kyō-chan." 1946. *Mā-chan no nikkicho*. Tezuka Osamu manga zenshū. Vol. 129. Tokyo: Kōdansha, 1982. 25–35.

Chitei koku no kaijin [*The Mysterious Underground Man*]. 1948. Tezuka Osamu manga zenshū. Vol. 253. Tokyo: Kōdansha, 1982.

"Dai san teikoku no hōkai [The Fall of the Third Reich]." 1955. *Zōkin to hōseki*. Tezuka Osamu manga zenshū. Vol. 258. Tokyo: Kōdansha, 1982. 89–99.

Dasto 8 [*Dust 8*]. 1972. Tezuka Osamu manga zenshū. Vol. 91–92. Tokyo: Kōdansha, 1979.

"Dōberuman [Doberman]." 1970. *SF fanshī furī* [*SF Fancy Free*]. Tezuka Osamu manga zenshū. Vol. 88. Tokyo: Kōdansha, 1979. 69–100.

Don Dorakyura [*Don Dracula*]. 1979. Tezuka Osamu manga zenshū. Vol. 248–50. Tokyo: Kōdansha, 1982.

Dororo. 1967–1968. Tezuka Osamu manga zenshū. Vol. 147–50. Tokyo: Kōdansha, 1981.

Dotsuitare. 1980. Tezuka Osamu manga zenshū. Vol. 312. Tokyo: Kōdansha, 1993.

Enzeru no oka [*Angel's Hill*]. 1960–1961. Tezuka Osamu manga zenshū. Vol. 75–76. Tokyo: Kōdansha, 1978.

"Fausuto [Faust]." 1950. *Fausuto*. Tezuka Osamu manga zenshū. Vol. 60. Tokyo: Kōdansha, 1979. 7–128.

"Fukugan majin [Multiple-Eyed Devil]." 1957. *Raion bukkusu* [*Lion Books*]. Vol. 7. Tezuka Osamu manga zenshū. Vol. 276. Tokyo: Kōdansha, 1983. 129–219.

Fūsuke. 1969–1972. Tezuka Osamu manga zenshū. Vol. 83. Tokyo: Kōdansha, 1979.

"Gachaboi ichidaiki [Gachaboi's Record of One Generation]." 1970. *Kami no toride* [*Fort of Paper*]. Tezuka Osamu manga zenshū. Vol. 274. Tokyo: Kōdansha, 1983. 7–49.

Garasu no shiro no kiroku [*The Record of the Glass Castle*]. 1970–1972. Tokyo: Akita Shoten, 1994.

"Goddo fāzā no musuko [Godfather's Son]." 1973. *Goddo fāzā no musuko*. Tezuka Osamu manga zenshū. Vol. 179. Tokyo: Kōdansha, 1982. 5–35.

Guringo [*Gringo*]. 1987–1989. 3 vols. Tokyo: Shōgakukan, 1988–89.

Hidamari no ki [*A Tree in the Sun*]. 11 vols. 1981–1986. Tokyo: Shōgakukan, 1983–87.

"Himawari san." 1956. *Tezuka Osamu shojo manga kessakusen* [*The Masterworks of Shojo Manga by Tezuka Osamu*]. Tokyo: Kōbunsha, 1997. 45–131.

Hi no tori: Fukkatsu hen [*Phoenix: Chapter of Resurrection*]. 1970. Gekkan Manga Shonen Bessatsu. Vol. 5. Tokyo: Asahi Sonorama, 1976.

Hi no tori: Igyō hen [*Phoenix: Chapter of Strange Beings*]. Gekkan Manga Shonen Bessatsu. Tokyo: Asahi Sonorama, 1981.

Hi no tori: Mirai hen [*Phoenix: Chapter of Future*]. 1967–1968. Gekkan Manga Shonen Bessatsu. Vol. 2. Tokyo: Asahi Sonorama, 1976.

Hi no tori: Ransei hen [*Phoenix Chapter of Turbulent Era*]. 1978–1980. 2 vols. Gekkan Manga Shonen Bessatsu. Vol. 7–8. Tokyo: Asahi Sonorama, 1980.

Hi no tori: Reimei hen [*Phoenix: Chapter of Dawn*]. 1967. Gekkan Manga Shonen Bessatsu. Vol. 1. Tokyo: Asahi Sonorama, 1976.

Hi no tori shojo crabu ban [*Phoenix Shojo Club Version*]. 1956–1957. Tezuka Osamu manga zenshū. Vol. 200. Tokyo: Kōdansha, 1980.

"Hyōroku ki [The Record of Hyōroku]." 1968. *Shōto arabesuku* [*Short Arabesque*]. Tezuka Osamu manga zenshū. Vol. 239. Tokyo: Kōdansha, 1982. 97–126.

"Hyōtan Komako." 1957–1958. *Hyōtan Komako.* Tezuka Osamu manga zenshū. Vol. 84. Tokyo: Kōdansha, 1980. 7–74.

Janguru taitei [*Jungle Emperor*]. 1950–1954. Tezuka Osamu manga zenshū. Vol. 1–3. Tokyo: Kōdansha, 1977.

"Kami no toride [Fort of Paper]." 1973. *Kami no toride.* Tezuka Osamu manga zenshū. Vol. 274. Tokyo: Kōdansha, 1983. 51–90.

"Kanoko no ōen danchō [Kanoko is the Captain of the Cheering Party]." 1950. *Shonen tantei Rokku Hōmu* [*Rock Home, Boy Detective*]. Tezuka Osamu manga zenshū. Vol. 381. Tokyo: Kōdansha, 1997. 117–25.

"Kasei Hakase [Dr. Mars]." *Kasei Hakase.* 1947. Tezuka Osamu manga zenshū. Vol. 339. Tokyo: Kōdansha, 1994. 3–113.

"Kasei kara kita otoko [The Man from Mars]." *38 do senjō no kaibutsu.* Tezuka Osamu manga zenshū. Vol. 43. Tokyo: Kōdansha, 1981. 77–123.

"Kaseki ningen [The Fossil Man]." 1952. *38 do senjō no kaibutsu.* Tezuka Osamu manga zenshū. Vol. 43. Tokyo: Kōdansha, 1981. 125–67.

"Kaseki ningen no gyakushū [The Fossil Man Strikes Back]." 1952. *38 do senjō no kaibutsu.* Tezuka Osamu manga zenshū. Vol. 43. Tokyo: Kōdansha, 1981. 169–220.

"Kaseki tō [Fossil Island]." 1951. *Kaseki tō.* Tezuka Osamu manga zenshū. Vol. 73. Tokyo: Kōdansha, 1979. 7–140.

"Kāten wa konya mo aoi [The Curtain Remains Blue Tonight]." 1958. *Tezuka Osamu shojo manga kessakusen* [*The Masterworks of Shojo Manga by Tezuka Osamu*]. Tokyo: Kōbunsha, 1997. 143–55.

"Kenjū tenshi [Gun Angel]." 1949. *Kenjū tenshi.* Tezuka Osamu manga zenshū. Vol. 324. Tokyo: Kōdansha, 1993. 5–99.

"Kiseki no mori no monogatari [The Story of the Miracle Forest]." 1949. *Mori no yonkenshi.* Tezuka Osamu manga zenshū. Vol. 323. Tokyo: Kōdansha, 1993. 121–216.

Kingu Kongu [*King Kong*]. 1947. Osaka: Fuji Shobo, 1947.

Kirihito sanka [*Ode to Kirihito*]. 1970–1971. Tezuka Osamu manga zenshū. Vol. 31–14. Tokyo: Kōdansha, 1977.

Kitaru beki sekai [*Next World*]. 1951. Tezuka Osamu manga zenshū. Vol. 45–46. Tokyo: Kōdansha, 1977.

"Konchū shojo no hōrōki [The Travels of an Insect Girl]." 1955. *Zōkin to hōseki.* Tezuka Osamu manga zenshū. Vol. 258. Tokyo: Kōdansha, 1982. 101–9.

Kūki no soko [*Under the Air*]. 1968–1970. Tezuka Osamu manga zenshū. Vol. 264. Tokyo: Kōdansha, 1982.

"Kuroi ushūsen [The Black Space Ray]." 1957. *Raion bukkusu* [*Lion Books*]. Vol. 7. Tezuka Osamu manga zenshū. Vol. 276. Tokyo: Kōdansha, 1983. 59–91.

Kyaputen Ken [*Captain Ken*]. 1960–1961. Tezuka Osamu manga zenshū. Vol. 25–26. Tokyo: Kōdansha, 1978.

Kyūketsu Madan [*Vampire Devils*]. 1948. Tokyo: Serindo, 1976.

"Mā-chan no nikkichō [The Diary of Mā-chan]." 1946. *Mā-chan no nikkichō.* Tezuka Osamu manga zenshū. Vol. 129. Tokyo: Kōdansha, 1982. 5–23.

Mahō yashiki [*Magic House*]. 1948. Tezuka Osamu manga zenshū. Vol. 217. Tokyo: Kōdansha, 1982.

Majin Garon [*Monster God Garon*]. Tezuka Osamu manga zenshū. Vol. 266–67, 377–79. Tokyo: Kōdansha, 1982, 1996.

"Mako to Rumi to Chī [Mako, Rumi and Chī]." 1981. *Mako to Rumi to Chī*. Tezuka Osamu manga zenshū. Vol. 273. Tokyo: Kōdansha, 1983. 7–180.

Manga Daigaku [*Manga University*]. 1950. Tezuka Osamu manga zenshū. Vol. 39. Tokyo: Kōdansha, 1977.

Manga no kakikata [*How to Write Comics*]. Tokyo: Kōbunsha, 1977.

Manga no shūgi [*The Secret of Manga*]. Tezuka Osamu manga zenshū. Vol. 391. Tokyo: Kōdansha, 1997.

"*Manon Resukō* [*Manon Lescaut*]." *Kageki*, April 1947, 47.

Metoroporisu [*Metropolis*]. 1949. Tezuka Osamu manga zenshū. Vol. 44. Tokyo: Kōdansha, 1979.

Middo naito [*Midnight*]. 1986–1987. 6 vols. Tokyo: Akita Shoten, 1986–1988.

"Miniyon." 1957. *Tezuka Osamu shojo manga kessakusen* [*The Best of Shojo Manga by Tezuka Osamu*]. Tokyo: Kōbunsha, 1997. 133–41.

Mitari tottari utsushitari [*Seeing, Filming and Projecting*]. Tokyo: Shōgakukan, 1980.

Mitsume ga tōru [*The Three-Eyed One*]. 1974–1978. Tezuka Osamu manga zenshū. Vol. 101–13. Tokyo: Kōdansha, 1977–1981.

"Monmon yama ga naiteru yo [Mt. Monmon is Weeping]." *Taigā bokkusu* [*Tiger Books*]. Vol. 4. Tezuka Osamu manga zenshū. Vol. 124. Tokyo: Kōdansha, 1978. 7–31.

"Mori no yonkenshi [Four Swordsmen in the Forest]." 1948. *Mori no yonkenshi*. Tezuka Osamu manga zenshū. Vol. 323. Tokyo: Kōdansha, 1993. 5–120.

MW. 1976–1978. 3 vols. Tokyo: Shōgakukan, 1978.

Nanairo inko [*Seven-colored Parrot*]. 1981–1982. 7 vols. Tokyo: Akita Shoten, 1981–1892.

Nasubi Joō. 1954–1955. Tezuka Osamu manga zenshū. Vol. 214. Tokyo: Kōdansha, 1983.

Neo Fausuto [*Neo Faust*]. 1988. Tokyo: Akahi, 1992.

"Niji no pureryudo [The Rainbow Prelude]." 1975. *Niji no pureryūdo*. Tezuka Osamu manga zenshū. Vol. 87. Tokyo: Kōdansha, 1977. 7–92.

"Niji no toride [The Rainbow Fortress]." 1956–1957. *Niji no toride*. Tezuka Osamu manga zenshū. Vol. 30. Tokyo: Kōdansha, 1980. 7–80.

"Nijusseiki no inshō: Tezuka manga no hōhō ishiki [The Impression of the Twentieth Century: Methods of Tezuka's Manga]." Interview with Iwatani Kokushi. *Eureka* 15, 2 (1982): 96–127.

Ningen domo atsumare! [*Rally Up, Mankind!*]. Tezuka Osamu manga zenshū. Vol. 81–82. Tokyo: Kōdansha, 1978.

"Norakuro modoki [Pseudo Norakuro]." *Maru* February 1984.

"Nūdian rettō [Nude Man's Archipelago]." 1968. *Suppon Monogatari*. Tezuka Osamu manga zenshū. Vol. 67. Tokyo: Kōdansha, 1981. 117–81.

"Omae ga hannin da! [You Are the Murderer!]." *Tetsuwan Atomu Bekkan.* Vol. 1. Tezuka Osamu manga zenshū. Vol. 251. Tokyo: Kōdansha, 1982. 125–42.

"Petā Kyuruten no kiroku [The Record of Peter Kürten]." 1973. *Hi no yama* [*The Mountain of Fire*]. Tezuka Osamu manga zenshū. Vol. 265. Tokyo: Kōdansha, 1983. 7–58.

"Pisutoru o atama ni noseta hitobito [People with Guns on Their Heads]." 1952. *Tange Sazen*. Tezuka Osamu manga zenshū. Vol. 68. Tokyo: Kōdansha, 1981. 109–55.

Puraimu rōzu [*Prime Rose*]. 1982–1983. Tezuka Osamu manga zenshū. Vol. 347–50. Tokyo: Kōdansha, 1995.

"Rakuban [Cave-in]." 1959. *Rakuban*. Tezuka Osamu manga zenshū. Vol. 319. Tokyo: Kōdansha, 1998. 3–24.

Ribon no Kishi [*Princess Knight*]. 1963–66. Tokyo: Kōdansha, 1977. Tezuka Osamu manga zenshū. Vol. 4–6. 1977.

Futago no kishi [*Twin Knights*]. 1958–1959. Tezuka Osamu manga zenshū. Vol. 54. Tokyo: Kōdansha, 1978.

Ribon no kishi Shojo Kurabu ban [*Princess Knight Shojo Club Version*]. 1953–1956. Tokyo: Kōdansha, 1999.

"Robin chan." 1954. *Kaseki tō*. Tezuka Osamu manga zenshū. Vol. 73. Tokyo: Kōdansha, 1979. 141–57.

Rokku bōkenki [*The Adventures of Rock*]. 1952–54. Tezuka Osamu manga zenshū. Vol. 7–8. Tokyo: Kōdansha, 1977.

Rosuto wārudo [*The Lost World*]. 1948. Tezuka Osamu manga zenshū. Vol. 130. Tokyo: Kōdansha, 1982.

Rosuto wārudo shike ban [*The Lost World Private Version*]. 193?. Tezuka Osamu manga zenshū. Vol. 360–61. Tokyo: Kōdansha, 1994.

"Ryōri suru onna [Woman Who Cooks]." 1972. *Sasupishon* [*Suspicion*]. Tezuka Osamu manga zenshū. Vol. 284. Tokyo: Kōdansha, 1984. 217–47.

Saboten kun [*Cactus Boy*]. 1951–1953. Tezuka Osamu manga zenshū. Vol. 69. Tokyo: Kōdansha, 1980.

Sandā masku [*Thunder Mask*]. 1972. Tezuka Osamu manga zenshū. Vol. 270. Tokyo: Kōdansha, 1983.

"Seinaru hiroba no monogatari [The Sacred Plaza]." 1977. *Metamorufōze* [Metamorphosis]. Tezuka Osamu manga zenshū. Vol. 88. Tokyo: Kōdansha, 1977. 175–204.

Shin Takarajima [*New Treasure Island*]. Tezuka Osamu manga zenshū. Vol. 281. Tokyo: Kōdansha, 1984.

Shin Takarajima [*New Treasure Island*]. 1947. Rpt. in *Jun Manga*. Ed. Nishigami Haruo. Osaka: Bunshindo, 1968.

"Shin Ryōsai shii: Jorōgumo [New Ryosai's Weird Tales: Spider]." 1971. *Taigā bokkusu*. Vol. 4. Tezuka Osamu manga zenshū. Vol. 124. Tokyo: Kōdansha, 1978. 141–91.

"Shin Ryōsai shii: Otsune [New Ryosai's Weird Tales: Otsune]." 1971. *Taigā bokkusu*. Vol. 4. Tezuka Osamu manga zenshū. Vol. 124. Tokyo: Kōdansha, 1978. 193–243.

"Shinpen getsusekai shinshi [Gentleman from the Moon, New Version]." 1951. *Heigen Taiheiki*. Tezuka Osamu manga zenshū. Vol. 38. Tokyo: Kōdansha, 1977. 133–212.

"Shin Sekai Rurū [The New World Rurū]." 1951–1952. *Shin Sekai Rurū*. Tezuka Osamu manga zenshū. Vol. 42. Tokyo: Kōdansha, 1977. 7–131.

"Shiruku hatto monogatari [The Story of a Top Hat]." 1954. *Tonkara dani monogatari* [*The Story of Tonkara Valley*]. Tezuka Osamu manga zenshū. Vol. 382. Tokyo: Kōdansha, 1997.

"Shiro kujaku no uta [The Song of a White Peacock]." 1959. *Niji no pureryūdo* [*The Rainbow Prelude*]. Tezuka Osamu manga zenshū. Vol. 87. Tokyo: Kōdansha, 1983. 7–24.

"Shokei wa sanji ni owatta [The Execution Ended at Three]." 1968. *Tokei jikake no ringo* [*The Clockwork Orange*]. Tezuka Osamu manga zenshū. Vol. 261. Tokyo: Kōdansha, 1982.

"Shonen tantei Rokku Hōmu [Rock Home, Boy Detective.]" *Shonen tantei Rokku Hōmu*. Tezuka Osamu manga zenshū. Vol. 381. Tokyo: Kōdansha, 1997. 3–52.

"Shūkan tantei tōjō [Here Comes the Weekly Detective]." 1959. *Hyōtan Komako.* Tezuka Osamu manga zenshū. Vol. 84. Tokyo: Kōdansha, 1980. 77–201.

"Sukippara no burūsu [Hungry Blues]." *Kami no toride [Fort of Paper].* Tezuka Osamu manga zenshū. Vol. 274. Tokyo: Kōdansha, 1983. 91–122.

"Sutā dasuto [Stardust]." 1965. *Zōkin to hōseki.* Tezuka Osamu manga zenshū. Vol. 258. Tokyo: Kōdansha, 1982. 111–19.

"Taigā hakase [Dr. Tiger]." 1950. *Majin Garon [Monster God Garon].* Vol. 2. Tezuka Osamu manga zenshū. Vol. 267. Tokyo: Kōdansha, 1982. 131–225.

"Tako no ashi [Octopus' Legs]." 1970. *Shōto arabesuku [Short Arabesque].* Tezuka Osamu manga zenshū. Vol. 239. Tokyo: Kōdansha, 1982. 127–34.

"Tange Sazen." 1954. *Tange Sazen.* Tezuka Osamu manga zenshū. Vol. 68. Tokyo: Kōdansha, 1981. 5–108.

"Tatsuga fuchi no otome [Girl by the Tatsuga Pond]." 1954–1955. *Kaseki tō.* Tezuka Osamu manga zenshū. Vol. 73. Tokyo: Kōdansha, 1979. 159–78.

"Tetsu no senritsu [The Iron Melody]." 1974. *Tetsu no senritsu.* Tezuka Osamu manga zenshū. Vol. 96. Tokyo: Kōdansha, 1980. 7–143.

Tetsuwan Atomu [Astro Boy]. 1952–1968. Tezuka Osamu manga zenshū. Vol. 221–38. Tokyo: Kōdansha, 1979–1981.

Tezuka Osamu shojo manga kessakusen [The Masterworks of Shojo Manga by Tezuka Osamu]. Tokyo: Kōbunsha, 1997.

Tezuka Osamu rando [Tezuka Osamu Land]. Tokyo: Yamato Shobō, 1977.

Tezuka Osamu rando II. Tokyo: Yamato Shobō, 1978.

Tezuka Osamu manga zenshū [The Complete Works of Tezuka Osamu]. 400 vols. Tokyo: Kōdansha, 1977–1997.

Tsumi to batsu [Crime and Punishment]. 1953. Tezuka Osamu manga zenshū. Vol. 10. Tokyo: Kōdansha, 1977.

"Uchū Kūkō [Space Airport]." *Raion bukkusu [Lion Books].* Vol. 6. Tezuka Osamu manga zenshū. Vol. 275. Tokyo: Kōdansha, 1983. 169–285.

Umi no Toriton [Toriton of the Sea]. 1969–1971. Tezuka Osamu manga zenshū. Vol. 189–92. Tokyo: Kōdansha, 1979.

Unico. See *Yuniko.*

W3. 1965–1966. Tezuka Osamu manga zenshū. Vol. 139–41. Tokyo: Kōdansha, 1980.

"Waga na wa Hyakka [My Name is Hyakka]." 1964. *Tetsuwan Atomu Bekkan.* Vol. 1. Tezuka Osamu manga zenshū. Vol. 251. Tokyo: Kōdansha, 1982. 115–23.

"Ware nakinurete shima to [An Uninhibited Island]." 1966. *Zōkin to hōseki.* Tezuka Osamu manga zenshū. Vol. 258. Tokyo: Kōdansha, 1982. 151–67.

"Wobitto [Wobbit]." 1977. *Metamorufōze.* Tezuka Osamu manga zenshū. Vol. 88. Tokyo: Kōdansha, 1977. 127–74.

Yakeppachi no Maria. 1970. Tezuka Osamu manga zenshū. Vol. 268–69. Tokyo: Kōdansha, 1983.

"Yōjintan." 1986. *Tezuka Osamu shōsetsu shū [Tezuka Osamu Novel Anthology].* Tezuka Osamu manga zenshū. Vol. 384. Tokyo: Kōdansha, 1996. 191–204.

"Yūbijin [Man with Tail]." 1949. Tezuka Osamu manga zenshū. Vol. 254. Tokyo: Kōdansha, 1982. 5–130.

"Yumemonogatari [The Story of a Dream]." *Kageki,* August 1947, 35.

Yuniko [Unico]. Tezuka Osamu manga zenshū. 1976–1979. Tezuka Osamu manga zenshū. Vol. 285–86. Tokyo: Kōdansha, 1983.

Za Krētā [*The Crater*]. 1969–1970. 2 vols. Tokyo: Akita Shoten, 1970.
"Zōkin to hōseki [Rags and Jewels]." 1958. *Zokin to hoseki.* Tezuka Osamu manga zenshū. Vol. 258. Tokyo: Kōdansha, 1982. 7–88.

English-Language Sources

Adams, Kenneth. "Protest and Rebellion: Fantasy Themes in Japanese Comics." *Journal of Popular Culture* 25, 1 (1991): 99–127.

Addiss, Stephen. *Zenga and Nanga: Paintings by Japanese Monks and Scholars.* New Orleans: New Orleans Museum of Art, 1976.

Affron, Charles. "Generous Stars." *Star Texts: Image and Performance in Film and Television.* Ed. Jeremy Butler. Detroit: Wayne State University Press, 1991. 90–101.

Allison, Anne. *Permitted and Prohibited Desires: Mothers, Comics, and Censorship in Japan.* Boulder: Westview Press, 1996.

Altmann, Rick. *Film/Genre.* London: British Film Institute, 1999.

Anderson, Joseph L., and Donald Richie. *The Japanese Film: Art and Industry.* Expanded ed. Princeton: Princeton University Press, 1982.

Bazin, André. "The Evolution of the Language of Cinema." *Film Theory and Criticism: Introductory Readings.* Ed. Leo Baudy and Marshall Cohen. 5th ed. Oxford: Oxford University Press, 1999. 43–56.

Ben Chaim, Daphna. *Distance in the Theatre: The Aesthetics of Audience Response.* Ann Arbor: UMI Research Press, 1984.

Berndt, Caroline. "Popular Culture as Political Protest: Writing the Reality of Sexual Slavery." *Journal of Popular Culture* 31, 2 (1997): 177–87.

Blyth, Reginald. *Japanese Humor.* Tokyo: Hokuseido Press, 1957.

Bordwell, David. *Narration in the Fiction Film.* Madison: University of Wisconsin Press, 1985.

Bordwell, David, and Kristin Thompson, eds. *Film History: An Introduction.* New York: McGaw-Hill, 1994.

Bordwell, David, Janet Steiger, and Kristin Thompson, eds. *The Classical Hollywood Cinema: Film Style and Mode of Production to 1960.* New York: Columbia University Press, 1985.

Bornoff, Nicholas. *Pink Samurai: Love, Marriage & Sex in Contemporary Japan.* New York: Pocket Books, 1991.

Brau, Lorie. "The Women's Theatre of Takarazuka." *TDR* 34, 4 (1990): 79–96.

Braw, Monica. *The Atomic Bomb Suppressed: American Censorship in Occupied Japan.* Armonk: M. E. Sharpe, Inc., 1991.

Brecht, Bertold. *Brecht on Theatre: The Development of an Aesthetic.* Ed. and trans. John Willett. London: Mehuen, 1964.

Brooke, James. "Heart of Japanese Animation Beats in a Robot Boy." *New York Times,* April 7, 2003, natl. ed.: A4.

Brophy, Philip, ed. *Tezuka: The Marvel of Manga.* Victoria: National Gallery of Victoria, 2006.

Burch, Nöel. *To the Distant Observer: Form and Meaning in the Japanese Cinema.* Berkeley and Los Angeles: University of California Press, 1979.

Butler, Jeremy G., ed. *Star Texts: Image and Performance Film and Television.* Detroit: Wayne State University Press, 1991.

Butler, Judith. *Gender Trouble*. New York: Routledge, 1990.

Canetti, Elias. *Crowds and Power*. Trans. Carol Stewart. New York: Viking Press, 1960.

Covert, Brian. "Manga, Racism & Tezuka." *Japan Times Weekly*, April 18, 1992: 1–4.

Crafton, Donald. *Emile Cohl, Caricature, and Film*. Princeton: Princeton University Press, 1990.

Crockett, Lucy Herndon. *Popcorn on the Ginza: An Informal Portrait of Postwar Japan*. New York: W. Sloane Associates, 1949.

Crofts, Stephen. "Authorship and Hollywood." *Wide Angle*, May 3, 1983, 16–22.

Davis, Tracy. "Theatricality and Civil Society." *Theatricality*. Ed. Tracy C. Davis and Thomas Postlewait. Cambridge: Cambridge University Press, 2003. 127–55.

DeCordova, Richard. "The Emergence of the Star System in America." *Stardom: Industry of Desire*. Ed. Christine Gledhill. New York: Routledge, 1991. 17–29.

———. *Picture Personalities: The Emergence of the Star System in America*. Urbana: University of Illinois Press, 1990.

Dolan, Jill. "Gender Impersonation Onstage: Destroying or Maintaining the Mirror of Gender Roles?" *Gender in Performance: The Presentation of Difference in the Performing Arts*. Ed. Laurence Senelick. Hanover: University Press of New England, 1992. 3–13.

Donahue, Ray T., ed. *Exploring Japaneseness: On Japanese Enactments of Culture and Consciousness*. Westport: Ablex Publishing, 2002.

Dower, John. *Japan in War and Peace*. New York: New Press, 1993.

Dyer, Richard. *Stars*. London: Educational Advisory Service, British Film Institute, 1979.

"Eclectic: Japanese Manga." *The Economist*, December 16, 1995, 82–84.

Eisner, Will. *Comics and Sequential Art*. Tamarac: Poorhouse Press, 1985.

———. *Graphic Storytelling*. Tamarac: Poorhouse Press, 1996.

Ellis, John. "Stars as a Cinematic Phenomenon." *Star Texts: Image and Performance in Film and Television*. Ed. Jeremy Butler. Detroit: Wayne State University Press, 1991. 300–315.

Fearey, Robert A. *The Occupation of Japan, Second Phase: 1948–50*. New York: Macmillan, 1950.

Fejes, Fred, and Sean Ledden. "Female Gender Role Patterns in Japanese Comic Magazines." *Journal of Popular Culture* 21, 1 (1987): 155–76.

Fell, John L. *Film and the Narrative Tradition*. Norman: University of Oklahoma Press, 1974.

Gans, Herbert J. *Popular Culture and High Culture: An Analysis and Evaluation of Taste*. New York: Basic Books, 1975.

Garber, Marjorie. *Vested Interests: Cross-Dressing and Cultural Anxiety*. New York: Harper, 1992.

Gledhill, Christine. "Genre and Gender: The Case of Soap Opera." *Representation: Cultural Representations and Signifying Practices*. Ed. Stuart Hall. London: Sage, 1997. 337–86.

———, ed. *Stardom: Industry of Desire*. New York: Routledge, 1991.

———, ed. *Star Signs: Papers from a Weekend Workshop*. London: British Film Institute, 1982.

Gordon, Andrew, ed. *Postwar Japan as History*. Berkeley and Los Angeles: University of California Press, 1993.

Gravett, Paul. *Manga: 60 Years of Japanese Comics*. London: Harper Design International, 2004.

Halford, Aubrey, and Giovanna Halford, eds. *The Kabuki Handbook*. Tokyo: Tuttle, 1956.

Harvey, Robert C. "The Aesthetics of the Comic Strip." *Journal of Popular Culture* 12 (1979): 640–52.

Hirano, Kyoko. *Mr. Smith Goes to Tokyo: The Japanese Cinema under the American Occupation, 1945–1952.* Washington, D.C.: Smithsonian Institute, 1992.

Hoffer, Bates L. "The Impact of English on the Japanese Language." *Exploring Japaneseness: On Japanese Enactments of Culture and Consciousness.* Ed. Ray T. Donahue. Westport: Ablex Publishing, 2002. 263–76.

Horn, Maurice. *Women in the Comics.* New York: Chelsea House Publishers, 1977.

Hutcheon, Linda. *Irony's Edge: The Theory and Politics of Irony.* London: Routledge, 1994.

——. *A Theory of Parody: The Teachings of Twentieth-Century Art Forms.* London: Methuen, 1985.

Inge, M. Thomas. *Comics as Culture.* Jackson: University Press of Mississippi, 1990.

Ito, Kinko. "Images of Women in Japanese Comic Magazines in Japan." *Journal of Popular Culture* 27, 4 (1994): 81–95.

Jones, Gerald. "The Big and the Small." Introduction. *Adolf: 1945 and All That Remains.* By Tezuka Osamu. Trans. Oniki Yōji. San Francisco: Cadence Books, 1996. 7–11.

Keene, Donald. "Onnagata and Kabuki." *Japan Quarterly* 30, 3 (1983): 293–96.

King, Tappan W. "The Image in Motion." *Journal of Popular Culture* 8 (1975): 11–18.

Kinsella, Sharon. *Adult Manga: Culture and Power in Contemporary Japanese Society.* Honolulu: University of Hawaii Press, 2000.

——. "Japanese Subculture in the 1990's: Otaku and the Amateur Manga Movement." *Journal of Japanese Studies* 24, 2 (1998): 289–316.

Kiyama, Henry. *The Four Immigrants Manga: A Japanese Experience in San Francisco, 1904–1924.* Berkeley: Stone Bridge, 1999.

Klein, Susan Blakeley. "When the Moon Strikes the Bell: Desire and Enlightenment in the Noh Play Dojoji." *Journal of Japanese Studies* 17, 2 (1991): 291–322.

Kondo, Dorinne. *About Face: Performing Race in Fashion and Theatre.* New York: Routledge, 1997.

——. *Crafting Selves: Power, Gender, and Discourses of Identity in a Japanese Workplace.* Chicago: University of Chicago Press, 1990.

Kunzle, David. *The Early Comic Strip: Narrative Strips and Picture Stories in the European Broadsheet from c. 1450 to 1825.* Berkeley and Los Angeles: University of California Press, 1973.

——. *The History of the Comic Strip: The Nineteenth Century.* Berkeley and Los Angeles: University of California Press, 1990.

Kurosawa Akira. *Something Like an Autobiography.* Trans. Audie E. Beck. New York: Vintage Books, 1983.

Kuwahara, Yasue. "Japanese Culture and Popular Consciousness: Disney's *The Lion King* vs. Tezuka's *Jungle Emperor*." *Journal of Popular Culture* 31, 1 (1997): 37–48.

Lacassin, Francis. "The Comic Strip and Film Language." *Film Quarterly* 25, 4 (1972): 11–23.

Lane, Richard. *Images from the Floating World: The Japanese Print.* New York: G. P. Putnam's Sons, 1978.

Lent, John, ed. *The Asian Film Industry.* Austin: University of Texas Press, 1990.

——, ed. *Animation in Asia and the Pacific.* Bloomington: Indiana University Press, 2001.

——, ed. *Themes and Issues in Asian Cartooning: Cute, Cheap, Mad, and Sexy.* Bowling Green: Bowling Green State University Popular Press, 1999.

Levi, Antonia. *Samurai from Outer Space: Understanding Japanese Animation.* Chicago: Open Court, 1996.

Liddle, Joanna, and Sachiko Nakajima. *Rising Suns, Rising Daughters: Gender, Class, and Power in Japan.* London: Zed Books, 2000.

Marschall, Richard. *America's Great Comic-Strip Artists: From the Yellow Kid to Peanuts.* New York: Stawart, Tabori & Chang, 1989.

McCloud, Scott. *Reinventing Comics: How Imagination and Technology Are Revolutionizing an Art Form.* New York: HarperCollins, 2000.

———. *Understanding Comics: The Invisible Art.* Northhampton: Kitchen Sink Press, 1993.

Melrose, Susan. *A Semiotics of the Dramatic Text.* New York: Macmillan, 1994.Merrill, Lisa. *When Romeo Was a Woman: Charlotte Cushman and Her Circle of Female Spectators.* Ann Arbor: University of Michigan Press, 1999.

Michener, James. *The Hokusai Sketchbooks: Selections from the Manga.* Tokyo: Tuttle, 1958.

Minear, Richard H. *Dr. Seuss Goes to War: The World War II Editorial Cartoons of Theodor Seuss Geisel.* New York: New Press, 1999.

Morean, Brian, and Lise Skov, eds. *Women, Media and Consumption in Japan.* Richmond: Curzon Press, 1995.

Morin, Edgar. *The Stars.* Trans. Richard Howard. New York: Grove Press, 1960.

Napier, Susan. *ANIME from Akira to Princess Mononoke: Experiencing Contemporary Japanese Animation.* New York: Palgrave, 2000.

Neale, Steve. *Genre.* London: BFI, 1981.

———. *Genre and Hollywood.* London: Routledge, 2000.

———. "Questions of Genre." *Screen* 31,1 (1990): 45–66.

Okudaira Hideo. *Chōjū Giga: Scrolls of Animal Caricatures.* Trans. Kaneko Shigetaka. Honolulu: East-West Center Press, 1969.

Otsuka Eiji. "Comic-Book Formula for Success." *Japan Quarterly* 35, 3 (1988): 287–91.

Parker, Ginny. "Learning Japanese, Once About Resumes, Is Now About Cool; Business Majors of '80s Yield To Kids Smitten by Anime; Up at 4 a.m. for Cartoons." *Wall Street Journal* (Eastern edition). New York: August 5, 2004, A.1.

Quinn, Michael. "Celebrity and the Semiotics of Acting." *New Theatre Quarterly* 6, 22 (1990): 154–61.

Richie, Donald. *A Hundred Years of Japanese Film.* New York: Kodansha America, 2001.

Robertson, Jennifer. "Gender-Bending in Paradise: Doing 'Female' and 'Male' in Japan." *Genders* 5 (1989): 188–207.

———. *Takarazuka: Sexual Politics and Popular Culture in Modern Japan.* Berkeley and Los Angeles: University of California Press, 1998.

———. "Theatrical Resistance, Theatres of Restraint: The Takarazuka Revue and the State Theatre Movement in Japan." *Anthropological Quarterly* 64, 4 (1991): 165–78.

Roman, Annette. "Editing the Unspeakable." Introduction. *Adolf: Days of Infamy.* By Tezuka Osamu. Trans. Oniki Yōji. San Francisco: Cadence Books, 1996. 4–6.

Rosenstone, Robert. *Revisioning History: Film and the Construction of a New Past.* Princeton: Princeton University Press, 1995.

Sabin, Roger. *Adult Comics: An Introduction.* London: Routledge, 1993.

———. *Comics, Comix & Graphic Novels.* London: Phaidon, 1996.

Said, Edward. *Orientalism.* New York: Vintage Books, 1979.

Sato, Barbara. *The New Japanese Women: Modernity, Media, and Women in Interwar Japan.* Durham and London: Duke University Press, 2003.

Schodt, Fredrik. *The Astro Boy Essays: Osamu Tezuka, Mighty Atom, Manga/Anime Revolution*. Berkeley: Stone Bridge, 2007.

———. *Dreamland Japan: Writings on Modern Manga*. Tokyo: Kodansha International, 1994.

———. *Manga! Manga!: The World of Japanese Comics*. Tokyo: Kodansha International, 1983.

Scott, James C. *Domination and the Arts of Resistance: Hidden Transcripts*. New Haven: Yale University Press, 1990.

Senelick, Laurence. *The Changing Room: Sex, Drag and Theatre*. New York: Routledge, 2000.

———, ed. *Gender in Performance : The Presentation of Difference in the Performing Arts*. Hanover: University Press of New England, 1992.

Slide, Anthony. *Great Pretenders: A History of Female and Male Impersonation in the Performing Arts*. Lombard: Wallace-Homestead Book Co., 1986.

Tezuka, Osamu, Gompachiro Yasuzumi, and H. Tanaka. "Spermatogenesis in Animals as Revealed by Electron Microscopy VIII: Relation between the Nutritive Cells and the Developing Spermatids in a Pond Snail, Cipangopaludina Malleata Reeve." *Journal of Biophysical and Biochemical Cytology* 7 (1960): 499–504.

Thompson, Kristin. *Exporting Entertainment*. London: British Film Institute, 1985.

Thorn, Matt. "Tezuka's Modernism." Introduction. *Adolf: The Half-Aryan*. By Tezuka Osamu. Trans. Oniki Yōji. San Francisco: Cadence Books, 1996. 7–11.

Toba Sojo. *The Animal Frolic*. New York: G. P. Putnam's Sons, 1954.

Treat, John Whittier. *Contemporary Japan and Popular Culture*. Honolulu: University of Hawaii Press, 1996.

———. *Writing Ground Zero: Japanese Literature and the Atomic Bomb*. Chicago: University of Chicago Press, 1995.

Ubersfeld, Anne. *Reading Theatre*. Toronto: University of Toronto Press, 1999.

Ueda, Atsushi, ed. *The Electric Geisha: Exploring Japan's Popular Culture*. Trans. Miriam Eguchi. Tokyo: Kodansha International, 1994.

West, Shearer. *The Image of the Actor: Verbal and Visual Representation in the Age of Garrick and Kemble*. London: St. Martin's Press, 1991.

Whittier John. *Contemporary Japan and Popular Culture*. Honolulu: University of Hawaii Press, 1996.

Worton, Michael, and Judith Still, eds. *Intertextuality: Theories and Practices*. Manchester: Manchester University Press, 1990.

Yoe, Craig. *Weird but True Cartoon Factoids!* New York: Gramercy, 1999.

Japanese-Language Sources

Aki Saburō. "Zassō o tabete [Eating Weeds]." *Shonen Club*, June 1942, 33–34.

Akita Takahiro. "Internet ni okeru manga no tenbō [View of Manga on Internet]." *Ritsumeikan Gengo Bunka Kenkyū* 13,1 (2001): 119–29.

Akiyama Masami, ed. *Maboroshi no sensō manga no sekai [The World of Wartime Comics]*. Tokyo: Natsume Shobō, 1998.

———, ed. *Meisaku komikku shū: Kodomo no shōwa shi [Masterpieces of Comics: Children's History of Shōwa]*. Tokyo: Heibon, 1984.

Ariyama Teruo. *Senryō ki media shi kenkyū: jiyū to tōsei, 1945 nen [Japanese Media during the Occupation: Freedom and Regulation, 1945]*. Tokyo: Kashiwa Shobō, 1996.

Ban Toshio and Tezuka Productions. *Tezuka Osamu*. 2 vols. Tokyo: Asahi, 1994.

Berndt Jaquiline. "Jobun: Manga kenkyū o meguru uchi to soto [Introduction: Manga Studies—Internal and External Perspectives]." *Ritsumeikan Gengo Bunka Kenkyū* 13,1 (2001): 77–82.

Comic Box. Tezuka Osamu Memorial Issue. May 1989.

"Dōkisei Zadankai [Same-year Student Roundtable]." *Kageki*, February 1947, 50–55.

Fujiko Fujio A. *Manga michi [The Way of Manga].* Vol. 1. Tokyo: Chuko Bunko, 1996.

Fujimoto Yukari. "Shojo manga wa nihon no shojo ga motomeru janru ka: Shojo manga no tokusei to shite no jūsōteki na sekaikan [Girls' Manga: A Form Seeking 'Japanese Girls'?: The Stratified Worldview Characteristic Shojo Manga]." *Ritsumeikan Gengo Bunka Kenkyū* 13, 1 (2001): 131–36.

Hakamata Yūko. "Rebyū no henkan: Kishida Tatsuya kara Shiraishi Kanezō e [The Transformations of the Revue: From Kishida Tatsuya to Shiraishi Tetsuzō]." *Eureka* 33, 5 (2001): 182–94.

Hanafusa Mari. Interview. *Takarazuka '97.* Ed. Otoda Chieko. Tokyo: Heibon, 1997. 88–89.

Hasegawa Tsutomu. *Tezuka Osamu shi ni kansuru yattu no gokai [Eight Common Misunderstandings about Mr. Tezuka Osamu].* Tokyo: Kashiwa, 1990.

Hashimoto Masao. *Ca C'est Takarazuka.* Tokyo: Yomiuri Shinbunsha, 1988.

———. *Takarazuka Kageki no 70 nen [The 70-Year History of Takarazuka Kageki].* Takarazuka: Takarazuka Kagekidan, 1984.

———. *Yume o egaite, hanayaka ni: Takarazuka Kageki 80 nenshi [Create a Dream, with a Panache: The 80-Year History of Takarazuka Kageki].* Takarazuka: Takarazuka Kagekidan, 1994.

Hirano Kyōko. *Tennō to seppun [The Emperor and a Kiss].* Tokyo: Kōshisha, 1998.

"Hisshō no bakudan o tsukuru [Making the Bomb of Victory]." *Shonen Club,* June 1942, 32.

Ichihashi Kōji, ed. *Takarazuka Kageki no 50 nen shi [The 50-Year History of Takarazuka Kageki].* 2 vols. Takarazuka: Takarazuka Kagekidan, 1962, 1964.

Ichioku nin no Tezuka Osamu [One Hundred Million People's Tezuka Osamu]. Tokyo: JICC, 1989.

Ide Magoroku. *Neji kugi no gotoku: Yanase Masamu no kiseki [Like a Twisted Nail: The Life of Yanase Masamu].* Tokyo: Iwanami, 1996.

Ii Sadamu. *Jidai de yomu nichibei eigashi [A History of Japanese and American Film].* Tokyo: Takagi Shobō, 1999.

Ijima Tadashi. "Shōwa 21 nendo no gaikoku eiga [Foreign Films of the Year 1946]." *The Filmcrit,* May 1947, 17–21.

———. "Eiga haiyū ni tsuite [On Film Actors]." *The Filmcrit,* June 1947, 18–22.

Inomata Katsuhiko. *Sekai eiga meisaku zenshi [Masterpieces of Foreign Films].* 2 vols. Tokyo: Gendai, 1974.

Ishigami Mitsutoshi. "Hitasura Tezuka manga bakari o otte [Following Tezuka's Manga]." Yamamoto 65–82.

———. *Tezuka Osamu no jidai [The Age of Osamu Tezuka].* Tokyo: Tairiku Shobō, 1989.

———. "Tezuka Shonen to maboroshi no senzen eiga [The Young Tezuka and Prewar Films]." Shimotsuki, 131–52.

Ishiko Jun. "Atom koso katsugeki to roman no shōchō: Tezuka Osamu manga no omoshirosa no himitsu [Astro Boy Is the Ultimate Action and Romance: What Makes Osamu Tezuka's Manga Interesting]. *Nihon Jidō Bungaku* 29, 12 (1983): 40–47.

———. *Kodomo no manga o dōsuru: papa, mama, majime ni kagae te [What to Do with Children's Comics?: Papa, Mama, Think Seriously Please].* Tokyo: Shinzansha, 1976.

———. *Nihon manga shi [History of Japanese Comics].* Tokyo: Shakai Shisosha, 1988.

———. *Nihon no shinryaku chūgoku no teikō: manga ni miru nicchū sensō jidai [Japanese Invasion, Chinese Resistance: Seeing the China-Japan War through Comics]*. Tokyo: Otsuki Shoten, 1995.

———. *Shin manga gaku [New Manga Scholarship]*. Tokyo: Mainichi Shinbunsha, 1978.

Ishiko Junzō. *Gendai manga no shisō [Critical Thoughts in Contemporary Manga]*. Tokyo: Taihei Shuppansha, 1970.

———. *Komikku ron [A Theory of Comics]*. *Ishiko Junzō Anthology*. Vol. 3. Tokyo: Kitahuyu Shobō, 1988.

———. *Manga geijutsu ron: gendai nihonjin no sensu to yūmoa [Theory of Manga as Art]*. Tokyo: Fuji Shoin, 1967.

———. *Sengo manga shi nōto [Notes on Postwar Comics]*. Tokyo: Kinokuniya, 1973.

Ito Ippei. "Tezuka Osamu no ningen sei [Tezuka Osamu's Humanism]." *Yamamoto*, 109–28.

Iwasaki Akira. *Eiga ni miru sengo sesō shi [History of Postwar Era through Films]*. Tokyo: Shin Nihon Shuppansha, 1973.

———. *Senryō sareta sukurīn [The Occupied Screen]*. Tokyo: Shin Nihon Shuppansha, 1975.

Iwatani Kokushi. "Tezuka Osamu no dokuji sei [The Uniqueness of Tezuka Osamu]." *Yamamoto*, 10–30.

Jinbo Michiomi. "Butai kōsen to okeshō ni tsuite [Stage Lighting and Make-up]." *Kageki*, August 1929, 30–31.

Junna Risa. Interview. *Takarazuka '97*. Ed. Otoda Chieko. Tokyo: Heibon, 1997.

Kajii Jun. *Sengo no kashihon bunka [Rental Book Culture of the Post–World War II Period]*. Tokyo: Tokosha, 1979.

———. *Tore, yōchō no jū to pen: senjika manga nōto [Take Your Gun and Pen: Notes on Wartime Comics]*. Tokyo: Waizu Shuppan, 1999.

Kashima Shigeru. "'Taishū o tsukanda jitsugyō ka [The Tycoon Who Captured the 'Masses']." *Tokyojin*, May 1998, 34–40.

Kawasaki Kenko. *Takarazuka: shōhi shakai no spekutakuru [Takarazuka: Spectacle in the Consumer Society]*. Tokyo: Kōdansha, 1999.

———. "Takarazuka Kagekidan 2001 nen e no hishō [Takarazuka Kagekidan's Flight into the Year 2001]." *Tokyojin*, May 1998, 80–85.

Kawatake Toshio. *Kabuki*. Tokyo: University of Tokyo Press, 2001.

Kazahana Mai. Interview. "Okyakusama ga miryokuteki dato omotte kureru butai ga tsukuretara [I Wish to Create the Stage That the Audiences Will Find Alluring]." *Takarazuka '97*. Ed. Otoda Chieko. Tokyo: Heibon, 1997. 84–85.

Kishida Tatsuya. "*Haremu no kyūden* o jōen suru ni tuite [On premiering *The Palace of Harem*]." *Kageki*, August 1928, 78–85.

———. "Mon Pari saijōen ni tsuite [On re-performance of *Mon Paris*]." *Kageki*, October 1927, 22–25.

———. "Ōbei no gekijō o nozoite aruku [Peeking into Western Theatres]." *Kageki*, July 1927, 6–11.

———. "Pari yori rondon yori [From Paris, from London]." *Kageki*, April 1927, 28–29.

———. "*Waga pari yo* o jōen suru ni tsuite [On staging *Waga Pari yo*]." *Kageki*, September 1927, 2–8.

Kobayashi Ichizō. "Atarashi imi deno butai kantoku [The New Definition of the Director]." *Kageki*, April 1923, 2–4.

———. "Daigekijō no zōka to butai souchi yori umaruru geki [Theatre of Large-Capacity Auditoriums and Stage Set]." *Kageki*, February 1925, 2–5.

———. "Dansō no reijin towa [What Is danso no reijin?]." *Kageki*, April 1935, 10–12.

———. "Gaikoku muki no kageki towa? [What Is kageki for Foreign Audiences?]" *Kageki*, October 1926): 8.

———. *Itsuō Jishaden*. [Autobiography.] Tokyo: Nihon Tosho Center, 1997.

———. "Jigyō to shite no geki [Theatre as an Enterprise]." *Kageki*, January 1925, 2–5.

———. "*Mon pari yo [Mon Paris]*." *Kageki*, October 1927, 2–3.

———. "Takarazuka shojo kagekidan tobei no hanashi [Takarazuka Shojo Kagekidan's US Tour]." *Kageki*, June 1927, 2–3.

———. *Watashi no Ikikata [My Way of Life]*. 1935. Osaka: Hankyu Dentetsu, 2000.

Kojima Hideaki. "Tezuka Osamu: Igakusha to shite no ningenzō [Osamu Tezuka: A Portrait as a Medical Scholar]." *Rekishi to Tabi*, April 2001, 98–103.

———, and Hiroshi Suzuki. "Ishi to shite no Tezuka Osamu: Sono shirarezaru ningenzō [Osamu Tezuka as a Medical Doctor: An Unknown Portrait]." *Igaku no ayumi [History of Medicine]* 195, 6 (2000): 437–42.

Kondō Hidezō, Yukio Sugiura, and Nakamura Atsuku. *Mohan sangyō senshi hōmon ki [Reports on Model Civilians]*. Tokyo Sangyō Hōkoku Kai, ed. Tokyo: Tokyo Sangyō Hōkoku Kai, 1943.

———, ed. *Waga seishun no zange roku [Confessions of Our Youths]*. Tokyo: Sekkasha, 1958.

Kondō Kumi. "Shirai Tetsuzō to chanson." *Takarazuka beru epokku II*. Ed. Tsuganezawa Toshihiro and Natori Chisato. Tokyo: Kōbe Shinbun Sōgō Shuppan Center, 2001. 55–66.

———. "Seiyō ongaku no madoguchi to shiteno Takarazuka Kageki: Takarazuka kokyōgaku kyōkai no eikō to shōchō [Takarazuka as a Window to the Western Music: The Glory and Disappearance of Takarazuka Symphonic Association]." *Takarazuka beru epokku*. Ed. Tsuganezawa Tōshihirō and Natori Chisato. Tokyo: Kōbe Shinbun Sōgō Shuppan Center, 1997. 152–68.

Kunie Mamoru. "Samazama na shiten [A Variety of Perspectives]." *Osamu Tezuka*. Tokyo: The National Museum of Modern Art, 1990. 84–87.

Kure Tomohusa. "Tezuka Osamu no imi: aru sengo seishin no igyō [The Meaning of Tezuka Osamu: The Great Accomplishment of a Postwar Soul]." *Bungakukai* 43, 4 (1989): 234–40.

Maki Miyako. "Anokoro . . ." Yonezawa Yoshiharu. *Shojo Manga no Sekai*. Vol 1. 70–71.

Makino Mamoru, ed. *Kindai eiga, engeki, ongaku shōshi [Bibliography of Modern Cinema, Theatre and Music]*. Tokyo: Yumani Shobō, 1992.

Miki Heisuke. *Takarazuka kara sekai ga mieru [Seeing the World through Takarazuka]*. Tokyo: Shichiken, 1994.

Minejima Masayuki. *Gendai manga no 50 nen: manga ka puraiba-shi [50 Years of Contemporary Manga: A Private History of a Cartoonist]*. Tokyo: Aoya Shoten, 1971.

Mishima Akimichi. "Waga nanyō dojin no buyō [The Dance of the South Sea Natives]." *Kageki*, August 1930, 16–18.

Miyamoto Hirohito. "Shōwa 50 nen dai no manga hihyō, sono shigoto to basho [The Work and the Place of MANGA Critiques, 1975–1984]." *Ritsumeikan Gengo Bunka Kenkyū* 13, 1 (2001): 83–94.

Nakahara Etsuko. "Metamorphosis." *Tezuka Fan Magazine*, January 1984.

Nakano Gorō. "Aoge kibō no aozora [Look up at the Blue Sky of Hope]." *Shonen Club*, November 1945, 38–41.

Nakano Haruyuki. *Tezuka Osamu no Takarazuka*. Tokyo: Chikuma Shobō, 1994.

Natsume Fusanosuke. "Manga hyōgen ron no 'genkai' o megutte [Concerning the 'Limits' of Manga Expression]." *Ritsumeikan Gengo Bunka Kenkyū* 13, 1 (2001): 95–104.

———. *Natsume Fusanosuke no manga gaku* [*Theory of Manga by Fusanosuke Natsume*]. Tokyo: Yamato, 1988.

———. *Sensō to manga* [*War and Manga*]. Tokyo: Kōdansha, 1997.

———. *Tezuka Osamu no bōken* [*Adventures of Tezuka Osamu*]. Tokyo: Shōgakukan, 1998.

———. *Tezuka Osamu wa Dokoni Iru* [*Where Is Tezuka Osamu?*] Tokyo: Chikuma, 1992.

Nihon Manga Kai, ed. *Manga kōza* [*Manga Seminar*]. Tokyo: Nihon Manga Kai, 1934.

Niizeki Seika. *Tokkan Suihei.* Tokyo: Nakamura Shoten, 1934. Rpt. in *Maboroshi no sensō manga no sekai* [*The World of Wartime Comics*]. Ed. Akiyama Masami. Tokyo: Natsume Shobō, 1998. 57–87.

Nimiya Kazuko. *Takarazuka no kōki: Osukaru kara posto feminizumu e* [*The Scent of Takarazuka: From Oscar to Postfeminism*]. Tokyo: Kōsaido, 1995.

———. *Tezuka manga no kokochi yosa: zuka-fan ryū Tezuka ron* [*The Comfort of Tezuka's Comics: A Perspective from a Takarazuka Fan*]. Tokyo: Kōei, 1996.

Nishigami Haruo, ed. *Jun Manga.* Osaka: Bunshindō, 1961.

Noritake Kamesaburo. "Takarazuka Monogatari [Takarazuka Story]." *Takarazuka Kageki no 50 nen shi* [*The 50-Year History of Takarazuka Kageki*]. Takarazuka: Takarazuka Kagekidan, 1962. 87–198.

Okamoto Ippei. *Atarashii manga no kakikata* [*New Ways of Drawing Manga*]. Tokyo: Senshinsha, 1930.

———. *Ippei Manga Kōza* [*Ippei's Manga Lecture*]. Tokyo: Sōkisha, 1981.

Ono Kōsei. "Nihon to America ni okeru chōhen monogatari manga no hatten [On the Development of Narrative Comics in Japan and North America]." *Ritsumeikan Gengo Bunka Kenkyū* 13, 1 (2001): 105–17.

———. *Tezuka Osamu manga no uchū e tabidatsu* [*Tezuka Osamu Departs for the Universe of Manga*]. Tokyo: Bronzu Shinsha, 1989.

Osamu Tezuka. Tokyo: The National Museum of Modern Art, 1990.

Ōshima Nagisa. *Taiken teki sengo eiga ron* [*Experiential History of Postwar Films*]. Tokyo: Asahi Sensho, 1975.

Ōshiro Noboru. *Kasei Tanken* [*The Adventure on Mars*]. 1940. Tokyo: Shōgakukan, 2005.

———. *Tocchin Butai* [*Tocchin Unit*]. Tokyo: Nakamura Shoten, 1938. Rpt. in *Maboroshi no sensō manga no sekai* [*The World of Wartime Comics*]. Ed. Akiyama Masami. Tokyo: Natsume Shobō, 1998. 218—47.

Ōshita Eiji, *Tezuka Osamu: Roman Daiuchū* [*Tezuka Osamu, the Romantic Universe*] Tokyo: Kōdansha, 2002.

Ō Takarazuka 60 nen: Domburako kara Berubara made [*Oh Takarazuka, 60 Years: From Domburako to Berubara*]. Tokyo: Asahi Shinbun, 1976.

Otoda Chieko, ed. *Takarazuka '97.* Tokyo: Heibon, 1997.

Ozaki Hideki. *Gendai manga no genten: warai gengo e no atakku* [*The Origins of Contemporary Manga: Investigating the Language of Humor*]. Tokyo: Kōdansha, 1972.

Sahō Kazuo. "Gairai gaijutsu sūhai ni taishite [On Western Art Worship]." *Kageki*, June 1923, 53–55.

Sakakibara Satoru. *Nihon kaiga no asobi* [*The Sense of Play in Japanese Paintings*]. Tokyo: Iwanami, 1998.

Sakamoto Gajō. *Tanku Tankurō.* 1935. Tokyo: Kōdansha, 1970.

Sakurai Tetsuo. *Tezuka Osamu: Jidai to kirimusubu kyogensha* [*Tezuka Osamu: An Artist Who Confronted His Times*]. Tokyo: Kōdansha, 1990.

Sakuramono Tomio. *Sensō to manga* [*War and Comics*]. Tokyo: Sōdōsha, 2000.

Satō Tadao. *Nihon no manga* [*Japanese Comics*]. Tokyo: Hyōron, 1973.

Seida Shigeru. "Kanashimi no warutsu o odoru Ashihara Kuniko [Ashihara Kuniko, Dancing the Waltz of Sorrow]." *Kageki*, August 1937, 75–78.

Shimada Keizō. *Bōken Dankichi [Dankichi's Adventures]. Shonen Club.* 1933–1939. Rpt. in *Bōken Dankichi zenshu [The Complete Bōken Dankichi]*. Tokyo: Kodansha, 1967.

———. *Nekoshichi Sensei [Mr. Nekoshichi]. Tokyo Nichinichi Shinbum.* January 1939–August 1940. Rpt. in *Meisaku komikku shū.* Ed. Akiyama Masami. Tokyo: Heibon, 1989: 71–77.

Shimizu Akira. *Sensō to eiga: senjichū to senryōka no nihon eigashi [War and Cinema: The History of Japanese Cinema during the War and Occupation].* Tokyo: Shakai Shisōsha, 1994.

———. "Nihon eigakai to stā [Japanese Film Industry and the Stars]." *The Filmcrit,* June 1947: 27–30.

Shimizu Isao. "Kindai katūn no tanjō [The Birth of Modern Cartoon]." *Ritsumeikan Gengo Bunka Kenkyū* 13.1 (2001): 171–76.

———. *Koramu manga kan [House of Manga].* Tokyo: Shinshindō. 1984.

———. *Manga no rekishi [History of Manga].* Tokyo: Iwanami, 1991.

———. "Manga no rekishi to Tezuka Osamu: Ponchi kara Tezuka manga e no michinori [Tezuka Osamu and the History of Manga: From Ponchi to Tezuka Manga]." *Yamamoto,* 31–64.

———. *Manga shonen to akahon manga: sengo manga no tanjō ["Manga shonen" and Red-book Manga: The Birth of Postwar Comics].* Tokyo: Z_ION, 1989.

———. *Nihon kindai manga no tanjō [The Birth of Modern Japanese Comics].* Tokyo: Yamakawa, 2001.

———. *"Nihon" manga no jiten [Dictionary of "Japanese" Comics].* Tokyo: Sanseidō, 1985.

———. *Taiheiyō sensō matsuki no manga [Comics at the End of the Pacific War].* Tokyo: Bijutsu Dōjinnsha, 1971.

———. *Taiheiyō sensō ki no manga [Comics during the Pacific War].* Tokyo: Bijutsu Dōjinsha, 1971.

———. *Tezuka Osamu manga no miryoku [The Appeal of Tezuka Osamu's Manga].* Tokyo: Seizan, 1979.

———. *Zusetsu manga no rekishi [Pictorial History of Manga].* Tokyo: Kawade, 1999.

——— and Yumoto Goichi. *Gaikoku manga ni kakareta nihon [Japan Depicted in Foreign Comics].* Tokyo: Maruzen Books, 1994.

Shimotsuki Takanaka, ed. *Tanjō! Tezuka Osamu: manga no kamisama o sodateta bakku guraundo [Tezuka Osamu Is Born!: The Background That Nurtured the God of Manga].* Tokyo: Asahi Sonorama, 1998.

Shirai Tetsuzō. "Foriberuzēru no rebyū [The Revues at Folies-Bergère]." *Kageki,* August 1930, 6–11.

———. "Fura fura dansu ni shippo [Disappointed by the Hula Dance]." *Kageki,* December 1928, 18–19.

———. "Parasu to konserumaiyōku no yoru [Nights at the Palace and the Concert Mayol]." *Kageki,* September 1930, 2–5.

———. "Pari no rebyū [Paris Revue]." *Kageki,* April 1929, 12–13.

———. "Pari tanshin: Kigutsu o haita musume [A Short Note from Paris: A Girl in Wooden Clogs]." *Kageki,* December 1929, 14–16.

———. "Rebyū parisetto [Revue Parisette]." *Kageki,* August 1930, 102–7.

———. "Rondon dayori [A Note from London]." *Kageki,* March 1929, 8–11.

Shirai Tetsuzō, Anna Jun, Matsu Akira, Misato Kei, and Uehara Mari. Roundtable.

"Ryūgujo, tsukihi no tatsu no mo yume no uchi [The Palace under the Sea, Days and Months Pass Like a Dream]." *Ō Takarazuka 60 nen: Domburako kara Berubara made* [*Oh Takarazuka, 60 Years: From Domburako to Berubara*]. Tokyo: Asahi Shinbun, 1976. 128–34.

Shiraki Ayaka. Interview. "Nido to modorenai sekai, shiawase o kamishimete sugoshi tai [The World I Will Never Return, I Want to Live in Happiness]." *Takarazuka '97.* Ed. Otoda Chieko. Tokyo: Heibon, 1997. 92–93.

Shishido Sakō. *Spīdo Tarō* [*Speed Tarō*]. 1935. Tokyo: San'ichi Shobō, 1988.

Shonen Club. June 1942.

Shoshida Yoshishige, Yamaguchi Masao, and Kinoshita Naoyuki, eds. *Eiga denrai: Cinematograph and meiji no nihon* [*Cinema Imported: Cinematograph and the Meiji Japan.*] Tokyo: Iwanami, 1995.

Spies, Alwyn. "Kokoro o iyasu shojo manga to josei no byōuri ka [Shojo Manga and the Pathologization of the Feminine]." *Ritsumeikan Gengo Bunka Kenkyū* 13, 1 (2001): 137–48.

Suntory Museum of Art, ed. *Emaki shōuchū: E no naka ni ikiru hitobito* [*Micro Universe in the Scrolls: People Who Live in the Pictures*]. Tokyo: Suntory Museum of Art, 2001.

Tagawa Suihō. *Norakuro Shōtaicho.* Tokyo: Kōdansha, 1936.

Takahashi Mizuki. "Manga kenkyū ni kansuru ikkousatsu [Considerations about Manga Study]." *Ritsumeikan Gengo Bunka Kenkyū* 13, 1 (2001): 149–54.

Takarazuka Kagekidan, ed. *Viva Takarazuka!* Tokyo: PHP, 1991.

Takenaka Iku, Hiraga Yoshito, Kishida Tatsuo, Shirai Tetsuzō, Hori Masaki, Inoue Masao, Nojima Ichirō, Maruo Chōkei, and Noritake Kamezaburō. "Parijian no mita *parisetto* zadankai [*Parisette* through the Eyes of Parisians]." Interview. *Kageki,* September 1930, 20–25.

Takeuchi Osamu. *Sengo manga no 50 nenshi* [*The 50-Year History of Postwar Comics*]. Tokyo: Chikuma Bunko, 1995.

———. *Tezuka Osamu ron* [*A Theory of Tezuka Osamu*]. Tokyo: Heibon, 1992.

Tanaka Yachio. "Tezuka Jichū sanka [Praise for Tezuka Jichū]." *Yamamoto.* 129–53.

Tanaka Yuko. "Kibyoshi to Manga [Kibyoshi and Manga]." *Nihon no Bigaku* [*The Aesthetics of Japan*] 30 (2000): 30–41.

"Tetsuwan Atom no messēji" *Asahi Shinbum,* February 10, 1989.

Tezuka Etsuko. Afterword. *Ribon no kishi shojo kurabu ban* [*Princess Knight Shojo Club Version*]. Tokyo: Kōdansha, 1999. 344–48.

———. *Otto Tezuka Osamu to tomo ni: Komore bi ni ikiru* [*With My Husband Tezuka Osamu*]. Tokyo: Kōdansha, 1995.

Tezukanian Hakubutsukan, ed. *Tezuka Osamu no shinjitsu to nazo to himitsu to rirekisho* [*The Truth, Myths and Secrets of Tezuka Osamu*]. Tokyo: Sangasha, 1993.

Tezuka Osamu Manga Museum. *The Tezuka Osamu Manga Museum.* Tokyo: Tezuka Productions, 1994.

Todo Akiho, Matsumoro Akira, Takeda Akira, and Kanō Yoshimitsu, eds. *Kanjirin.* Revised ed. Tokyo: Gakken, 2001.

Tōgō Haruko. "Jōkyūsei wa kowakatta [I Was Scared of the Senior Students]." *Ō Takarazuka 60 nen: Domburako kara Berubara made* [*Oh Takarazuka, 60 Years: From Domburako to Berubara*]. Tokyo: Asahi Shinbun, 1976. 111.

Tokunaga Etsutarō and Kita Kōji. "Rakkasanbutai parenban senki [Parachute Force Palembang Battle Stories]." *Shonen Club,* June 1942, 58–67.

Tokutomi Natsuko. "Rebyū ni miru orientarisumu [Orientalism in the Revue]." *Takarazuka beru epokku II*. Ed. Tsuganezawa Toshihiro and Natori Chisato. Tokyo: Kōbe Shinbun Sōgō Shuppan Center, 2001. 68–77.

Tokuyama Takako. "Mūran rūju no hane ōgi: Takarazuka butai ishō no genten o saguru [Feathered Fan of Moulin Rouge: Analyzing the Origins of Takarazuka Costumes]." *Takarazuka beru epokku*. Ed. Tsuganezawa Toshihiro and Natori Chisato. Tokyo: Kōbe Shinbun Sōgō Shuppan Center, 1997. 142–51.

———. "Shōwa shoki no butai isyō—Kinoshita Makoto kara no kikigaki o chushin ni [Stage Costumes of the Early Shōwa Era—Based on Interviews with Kinoshita Makoto]." *Takarazuka beru epokku II*. Ed. Tsuganezawa Toshihiro and Natori Chisato. Tokyo: Kōbe Shinbun Sōgō Shuppan Center, 2001. 130–36.

Tsuganezawa Toshihiro and Natori Chisato, eds. *Takarazuka beru epokku*. Tokyo: Kōbe Shinbun Sōgō Shuppan Center, 1997.

———. *Takarazuka beru epokku II*. Tokyo: Kōbe Shinbun Sōgō Shuppan Center, 2001.

Tsurumi Shunsuke. *Ie no Kami* [*House of God*]. Tokyo: Tankosha, 1972.

———. *Manga no sengo shisō* [*Postwar Thought in Manga*]. Tokyo: Bungei Shunjū, 1973.

———. Etō Fumio and Yamamoto Akira, eds. *Taishū bunka no sōzō* [*The Creation of Mass Culture*]. Tokyo: Kenkyūsha Shuppan, 1973.

Ukai Masaki, Nagai Yoshikazu, and Fujimoto Ken'ichi, eds. *Sengo nippon no taishū bunka* [*Mass Culture in Postwar Japan*]. Tokyo: Shōwado, 2000.

"Wareware no shōgai no saikō no toshi gohyō [The Best Years of Our Lives Review]." *CINE-AMERICA* July 1948, 20–25, 29.

Waseda University. *Senryō ka no kodomo bunka: 1945–1949* [*Children's Culture under Occupation: 1945–1949*]. Tokyo: Nichimai, 2001.

Watanabe Yasushi. "Animēshon ni miserare ta manga no kamisama [The God of Manga Who loved animation]." Shimotsuki Takanaka. 100–130.

———. and Yamaguchi Katsunori, eds. *Nihon animēshon eiga shi* [*The History of Japanese Animation*]. Tokyo: Yubun, 1977.

Yamada Kazuo. *Itsuwari no eizō: sensō o kaku me* [*Deceptive Images: Perceptions of War*]. Tokyo: Shin Nihon Shuppan, 1984.

Yamamoto Noboru, ed. *Tezuka Osamu*. Vol. 1 of Gendai manga siatā [*Contemporary Manga Theatre*]. Tokyo: Seizansha, 1979.

Yokoyama Ryūichi. *Edokko Ken-chan*. 1936. Tokyo: Chūō Kōronsha, 1992.

———. *Fuku-chan butai kessakushu* [*The Best of Fuku-chan Butai*]. Tokyo: Asahi Shinbun, 1940.

———. *Fuku-chan zuihitsu* [*Fuku-chan Essays*]. Tokyo: Kōdansha, 1967.

Yokozawa Hideo. "Takarazuka Kageki, sono enshutsu no myōmi o saguru [Exploring the Unique Directing Techniques of Takarazuka Kageki]." Tsuganezawa and Natori. 45–54.

Yomiuri Shinbun Bunka Bu, ed. *Eiga hyaku nen: eiga wa kōushite hajimatta* [*One Hundred Years of Cinema: This Is How the Cinema Began*]. Tokyo: Kinema Jumpō, 1997.

Yomota Inuhiko. *Nihon eigashi 100 nen* [*100 Years of Japanese Film*]. Tokyo: Shieisha, 2000.

Yonezawa Yoshihiro, ed. *Shojo manga no sekai* [*The World of Girls' Comics*]. 2 vols. Tokyo: Heibon, 1991.

———. *Shonen manga no sekai* [*The World of Boys' Comics*]. 2 vols. Tokyo: Heibon, 1996.

———. *Tezuka Osamu manga taizen* [*Tezuka Osamu Manga Catalogue*. Tokyo: Heibon, 1997.

Yoshimura Kazuma. "Toi o jizoku suru tameni [In Order to Continue the Critique: In Place of a Postscript]." *Ritsumeikan Gengo Bunka Kenkyū* 13, 1 (2001): 177–82.

Yoshitomi Yasuo. "Tezuka Osamu to boku [Tezuka Osamu and Me]." Yamamoto. 83–108.

Films and TV Programs

Akumatō no purinsu: mitsume ga tōru [*The Prince of the Devil Island: The Three-Eyed One*]. Tōei Dōga. Nihon Television. August 25, 1985.

All the King's Men. Dir. Robert Rossen. Tristar/Columbia, 1949.

Aru machikado no monogatari [*Tales of a Street Corner*]. Dir. Tezuka Osamu. Mushi Productions, 1962.

Astro Boy. Dir. Konaka Kazunari. Tezuka Productions. Fuji. April 7, 2003.

Bambi. Dir. David Hand. Walt Disney Productions, 1942.

Banpaiya [*The Vampire*]. Prod. Imai Yoshiaki. Mushi Productions. Fuji. 1968–1969.

The Best Years of Our Lives. Dir. Willian Wyler. Goldwyn, 1946.

Broken Down Film. Dir. Tezuka Osamu. Tezuka Productions, 1985.

Citizen Kane. Dir. Orson Welles. RKO, 1941.

Cleopatra. Prod. Tezuka Osamu. Mushi Productions, 1970.

Crossfire. Dir. Edward Dmytryk. Paramount, 1947.

The Desert Fox. Dir. Henry Hathaway. With James Mason. 20th Century Fox, 1951.

Dororo. Mushi Productions. April 6–September 28, 1969.

Fantasia. Dir. Samuel Armstrong, James Algar, Bill Roberts, Paul Satterfield, Hamilton Luske, Jim Handley, Ford Beebe, T. Hee, Norm Ferguson, and Wilfred Jackson. Walt Disney Productions, 1946.

Ginga shonentai [*Galaxy Boys*]. Mushi Productions and Takeda Ningyō Za. NHK. April 7, 1963–April 1, 1965.

Gokū no daibōken [*Gokū's Adventures*]. Mushi Productions, 1967.

The Grapes of Wrath. Dir. John Ford. 20th Century Fox, 1940.

A Hard Day's Night. Dir. Richard Lester. United Artists, 1964.

Himeyuri no tō. Dir. Imai Tadashi. Tōei, 1953.

Hirate Zōshu. Dir. Namiki Kyotaro. Shin Tōhō, 1951.

His Butler's Sister. Dir. Richard Wallace. Universal Studios, 1943.

Ikiru [*To Live*]. Dir. Akira Kurosawa. Tōhō, 1952.

Janguru Taitei [*Kimba the White Lion*]. Dir. Hayashi Shigeyuki. Mushi Productions. Fuji, Tokyo. October 6, 1965–September 28, 1966.

Jumping. Dir. Tezuka Osamu. Tezuka Productions, 1984.

Kureopatora [*Cleopatra*]. Prod. Tezuka Osamu. Mushi Productions, 1970.

Madame Curie. Dir. Mervyn Leroy. Warner Bros., 1943.

Mata au himade [*Till We Meet Again*]. Dir. Imai Tadashi. Toho, 1950.

Memory. Dir. Tezuka Osamu. Mushi Productions, 1964.

Metropolis. Dir. Fritz Lang. Madacy Entertainment, 1927.

Metropolis. Dir. Rintaro. Tezuka Productions, 2002.

Momotarō umi no shimpei [*Momotarō's Sacred Marines*]. Dir. Seo Mitsuse. Shochiku, 1944.

Ningyo [*Mermaid*]. Prod. Tezuka Osamu. Mushi Productions, 1964.

1,000,000 nen uchū no tabi: Bandā Bukku [*Space Travel 1,000,000 Years: Bander Book*]. Dir. Tezuka Osamu. Tezuka Productions. Nihon Television. August 27, 1978.

Osu. Dir. Tezuka Osamu. Mushi Productions, 1962.

Pictures at an Exhibition. Dir. Tezuka Osamu. Tezuka Productions, 1966.

Rapas en Famille. 1897. Dir. Constant Girel.

Ribon no kishi [*Princess Knight*]. Prod. Tezuka Osamu. Mushi Productions. FNS, Tokyo. April 2, 1967–April 3, 1968.

Saiyūki. Dir. Okawa Hiroshi. Toei Productions, 1958.

Senya ichiya monogatari [*One Thousand and One Night Stories*]. Prod. Tezuka Osamu. Mushi Productions, 1969.

Shin Takarajima [*New Treasure Island*]. Dir. Tezuka Osamu. Mushi Productions. Fuji, Tokyo. January 3, 1965.

Shizuku. Mushi Productions, 1966.

Snow White and the Seven Dwarfs. Walt Disney Productions, 1937.

Taimu surippu 10,000 nen: puraimu rōzu [*10,000 Year Time Slip: Prime Rose*]. Tezuka Productions. Nihon Television. August 27, 1983.

The Tales of Hoffman. Dir. Emeric Pressburger and Michael Powell. Lopert, 1951.

Tetsuwan Atom [*Astro Boy*]. Prod. Tezuka Osamu. Mushi Productions. Fuji, Tokyo. January 1, 1963–December 31, 1966.

Tezuka Osamu sōsaku no himitsu [*Tezuka Osamu, the Secret of Creation*]. NHK, Tokyo. January 10, 1986.

The Third Man. Dir. Carol Reed. Lion International Films, 1949.

Urutora Q [*Ultra Q*]. Dir. Tsuburaya Eiji. Tsuburaya Productions. TBS, Tokyo. January 2–July 3, 1966.

W 3. Dir. Tezuka Osamu. 1966.

Wansa kun. Mushi Productions. Kansai Television. April 2– September 24, 1973.

Yasashii raion [*The Kind Lion*]. Prod. Tezuka Osamu. Screenplay and art. Yanase Takashi. Mushi Productions, 1970.

INDEX

Shizuku (*A Drop of Water*), 136
Shojo Club, 27, 104, 111, 114, 123
Shojo sannin (*Three Girls*), 123
Shojo stars, 18, 114–15, 161–62
Shokei wa sanji ni owatta (*The Execution Finished at Three*), 155
Shonen ai, 126–27
Shonen Club, 27, 29, 34–35, 63, 64, 90
Shonen tantei Rock Home (*Little Detective Rock Home*), 74
Shūkan tantei tojō (*Here Comes the Weekly Detective*), 141
Silk hat monogatari (*The Story of a Top Hat*), 123
Snow White and the Seven Dwarfs, 131
Soyokaze san, 123
Speed Tarō. See Shishido Sakō
Stage Fright, 158
Star System, 18, 66–88, 109, 110, 164–65, 166
Steinberg, Saul, 34
Still, Judith, 18, 152
Sugiura Yukio, 48, 52, 114
Sukippara no blues (*Hungry Blues*), 36, 85
Supaidā, 77, 79
Suppon monogatari (*The Story of a Snapping Turtle*), 143
Suzuki Hiroshi, 101

Tagawa Suihō, 27, 29, 33
Taguchi Beisaku, 25
Taiyō-kan, 91
Takahashi Makoto, 123
Takahashi Nobuharu, 49
Takamizawa Junko, 29
Takarajima (*Treasure Island*), 45
Takarazuka (city), 27–28, 85, 89, 100, 115, 162, 165–66
Takarazuka Kagekidan, 115–27, 152–70; fan magazines, 39, 116; music academy, 85, 162, 166; musume-yaku (female-role players), 118, 161; otoko-yaku (male-role players), 118–21, 124, 161
Takemiya Keiko, 15, 126
Takeuchi Osamu, 13
Tako no ashi (*Octopus' Legs*), 149
Tales of Manhattan, 123

Tanaka Yachiyo, 40
Tatsuga fuchi no otome (*Girl by the Tatsuga Pond*), 123
Tatsumi Yoshihiro, 96
Terada Hiroo, 90
Tetsu no senritsu (*The Iron Melody*), 150
Tetsuwan Atom. See *Astro Boy*
Tezuka Dōga Gaisha, 131
Tezuka Etsuko, 12, 100–1, 116; as fictional character, 84, 85, 86. See also Tezuka Osamu: family and marriage
Tezuka Osamu: as actor, 117; appearances in his own comics, 83–88, 146, 149, 164–66; autobiography, 12, 34, 42, 43, 76, 95, 96, 100, 101, 115, 117, 133, 134–35, 136; childhood, 27–28, 50, 82, 116; family and marriage, 12, 85, 100–1; on his own work, 16–17, 34, 42, 43, 76, 95, 96, 100, 101, 115, 116, 133, 134–35, 136, 143, 144; as manga no kamisama (God of Comics), 3, 12, 13, 18, 170; medical background, 4, 37, 61–62, 65, 101–2, 117, 145; mental illness, 98–100; on other cartoonists' work, 27, 32, 33, 34, 42, 55, 95, 97, 130
Tezuka Osamu Manga Zenshū (*Complete Works of Tezuka Osamu*), xii, 15, 43, 116
Tezuka Productions, 138–39, 171–72
Theater, 117, 153–70. See also Takarazuka Kagekidan; Tezuka Osamu: as actor
Theatricality, 81
Third Man, The, 92, 94, 152
38 do senjō no kaibutsu (*The Monster on the 38th Parallel*), 91–94, 152
Thoma no shinzo (*Thoma's Heart*), 126
Thompson, Kristin, 49, 97
Thunder Mask, 86, 87
Tiger Hakase no chin ryoko (*Dr. Tiger's Strange Trip*), 62
Toba Sōjō (Kakuyū), 19–23, 25, 96
Tôbaé, 25
Toba-e, 25
Tōei Film Company, 94, 131; Tōei Dōga (animation branch), 131, 135
Toki no tabihito (*Time Stranger*), 139
Tokiwa-sō, 90–91
Tokkan Suihei, 30
Toland, Greg, 56, 60